THE ENGLISH PAST

Books by A. L. Rowse

History

THE ENGLAND OF ELIZABETH
THE SPIRIT OF ENGLISH HISTORY
SIR RICHARD GRENVILLE OF THE *REVENGE*
TUDOR CORNWALL
THE USE OF HISTORY

Essays

THE ENGLISH SPIRIT
ON HISTORY
THE END OF AN EPOCH

Poetry

POEMS OF A DECADE, 1931–1941
POEMS CHIEFLY CORNISH
POEMS OF DELIVERANCE

Autobiography

A CORNISH CHILDHOOD

Stories

WEST COUNTRY STORIES

THE ENGLISH PAST

*Evocations of Persons
and Places*

BY

A. L. ROWSE

LONDON
MACMILLAN & CO. LTD
1951

PRINTED IN GREAT BRITAIN

PREFACE

Now that the great days of England are perhaps over — it is extraordinary to think that we have lived through the very greatest of them in our own lifetime — it is somehow consoling to pursue and evoke the past, recent as well as remote, to weave together in the mind some design from the fragments that remain, in places that hold these echoes for us still. It is strangely fascinating too — the more one pursues these themes, the more one realises the inexhaustible riches of an old and civilised country, the memories of the soil, the depth of mould.

The purpose of this book is to bring together a number of evocations of persons and places. My aim is to see the people through the places where they lived or which their lives touched, and the places through them and their eyes. My object is not literary criticism — there is far too much criticism in contemporary writing : a fungoid growth smothering and devitalising the creative. I prefer the juices of life. My interest is in life, my desire to depict and reveal it, even in those long dead, in the places that once knew them and retain some imprint of them still. Here in a Berkshire garden is a tree under which Swift wrote ; there the dress which Charlotte Brontë wore on her wedding tour, the teacups the girls drank out of, the view they looked out on from their bedroom at Haworth ; the mining village that was the scene of D. H. Lawrence's early life, the dwellings where he lived, that witnessed the growth of genius and the anguish of that symptomatic spirit ; the tombs of the Hobys at Bisham and the story they reveal ; the pastoral background of Milton's family on the threshold of Oxford.

This book is, in a sense, a sequel to — though different in character from — an earlier book of essays, *The English Spirit*. Both books may be taken as illustrating themes from my little book, *The Spirit of English History*.

As on many occasions now, I have the pleasure of acknowledging what I owe to my friends, companions of these walks and studies : in especial to Jack Simmons, Norman Scarfe, David Treffry, L. J. (Don) King of Michigan. I am indebted, as for many other kindnesses, to my friend Arthur Bryant for my first introduction to Hillesden and Claydon, and to Mr. Ralph Verney for allowing me to see his portrait of Dr. Denton ; to Lady Tweedsmuir for her kind permission to reprint the essay on John Buchan from her book, *John Buchan : By his Wife and Friends* ; to Bruce McFarlane for lending me the original inventory of the Powells' house at Forest Hill.

The essay on All Souls College came into being as the result of an invitation from Mr. Leonard Russell to deal with the subject as a characteristic, if unique, English institution for his *Saturday Book, 1945.* Otherwise I do not think it would have occurred to me to write it ; but perhaps it may be useful, since, though there are histories of the college, there is no other description of its nature and character. The essay on Hillesden also appeared first in the same annual ; that on Alun Lewis as a Foreword to his posthumous *Letters.*

All the rest of the studies — the great bulk of the book — are new and appear here for the first time.

A. L. ROWSE

OXFORD,
All Souls' Day, 1950

CONTENTS

ALL SOULS (1945)

ALL SOULS COLLEGE is one of those characteristic English institutions that are so hard to explain to the stranger. And not to the stranger only. I confess that when I was an undergraduate at Oxford I had only the vaguest idea of what sort of college it was. I knew that it had no undergraduates; I believed that it was inhabited, if at all, by a few old gentlemen with beards. Though I read for hours in its Library — the Codrington, most congenial and satisfying of college libraries — and occasionally attended lectures in the Hall, it was not until I stood, or rather sat, for the Fellowship examination that I entered those mysterious, enticing penetralia.

It was an alarming experience, as all those who have been through the ordeal will agree. Few, very few, are chosen. But once received into the companionship of that society, I can say — like so many others before me — that it has been the greatest thing in my life.

The difficulty people have in grasping the nature of the college lies in the absence of undergraduates. (Though until quite recently it had four Bible Clerks: a rare kind of bird now dying out; one of the last of them being the Head of a Cambridge college.) But if there are no undergraduates, what does the college do and whom does it teach? Why is it so different from all other colleges in the country? These are the questions that are frequently asked of Fellows who unwarily let themselves in for showing the punctual tourist around the college — questions more regular than that of the American lady who, peering into a coalhole, was heard to ask, " Are these old ruins inhabited ? "

In fact, Americans and Canadians begin to understand something of what All Souls is when you explain to them that it is a graduate college. But that is only the beginning. The truth is that the college is unique. There is no other institution quite like it. And I have heard it said by Cambridge men — who have no All Souls, nor any equivalent — that they could very well do with one. I think they could, for I am a great believer in the institution and in the idea of which it is an embodiment.

The essence of the idea is that of a college which, at the same time as it plays a full part in the activities of the University in research and teaching, is also making a contribution to the public life of the nation through others of its Fellows who are engaged upon work in the outer world.

There are two elements in All Souls: the strictly University element and those whose work lies mainly outside. And yet they are not two colleges, but one college. The division is less rigid than you might suppose — as with everything that is truly English; for the most academic of its members are imbued with ideas of public duty and are not averse to playing some part in public affairs, while the most eminent of its Fellows in the outside world, whether Archbishop or Lord Chancellor, Viceroy of India or editor of *The Times*, takes a responsible interest in the affairs of the University and would resent being regarded as not an academic person in the fullest sense.

The advantage, not only to the college, but to the University and the nation, of this twin character of All Souls is immeasurable. It is, in fact, what gives it its distinction and makes it unique.

With all respect to academic standards — and I share them — we may admit that the disadvantage of a purely collegiate life is that people are apt to get out of touch with the outside world, to become narrow and confined in their outlook, to become pedants or pedagogues. One notices it in the conversation of small common-rooms, that can become a trifle in-bred. Things have the defects of their qualities. On the other hand, too, is it not a good thing — especially in the decline of cultural standards in the contemporary world — that as many as possible of the leaders of our national life should exemplify good academic standards? (The exact converse of that principle was to be seen in Nazi

Germany.) All Souls provides, of its very nature, a valuable junction, a meeting ground where both can converse to mutual profit. Speaking for myself, I know what an education it has been to me to enjoy the conversation over years of men eminent in public affairs and responsibility. If I could think that we academics had as much to offer them in return I should be well content.

In the reforming days of the Victorian Age there were people whose idea of University Reform was to reform All Souls out of existence. That somewhat bogus figure, Max Müller (cf. Mommsen on him : " Haf you no hombogs of your own that you must import hombogs from Jairmany ? "), had the horrid idea of turning All Souls into a kind of Indian Institute. Others thought of making it into an annexe of the Bodleian Library. It is an interesting and conclusive comment on such proposals that the sadder and wiser twentieth century has seen fit to set up in Oxford something like a second All Souls. Nuffield College derives its essential idea from All Souls : the union of academic research with the experience of the world. It might almost be called a daughter of All Souls.

And not on this side the Atlantic only. The Institute of Advanced Study at Princeton, of which Einstein is the most brilliant ornament, was conceived very much on the lines of All Souls. I well remember the period which Abraham Flexner, the founder, spent in college with us studying its nature and working, or, better, imbibing its atmosphere. It is more than pleasant to think of this close relation with that distinguished institution, perhaps also unique, in America : it is one more integument in knitting together the community of Atlantic civilisation.

(Yet Cambridge has not even one such college. What better form of national war-memorial could there be than to found a Cambridge All Souls ?)

As a matter of fact, All Souls came into being, you might say, as a kind of war-memorial. It was founded just over five hundred years ago, in 1438, towards the end of the long French wars, to pray for the souls of King Henry V, the

Duke of Clarence and all the lords and lieges " whom the havoc of that warfare between the two realms hath drenched with the bowl of bitter death ", and also for the souls of all the faithful departed.

Its founder was Archbishop Chichele, whom Shakespeare, following the Tudor historians, made responsible for egging Henry V on to the French war : a complete travesty of the truth, which has now been perpetuated upon the mob by the new film. Anybody who knows anything about Henry V knows that he was his own master and himself determined upon the conquest of France. Years after his early death, Chichele brought Henry's son, Henry VI, in with him as co-founder of the Oxford college he projected, giving it the added strength and security of a connection with the Crown as well as with the Church. That probably stood it in some good stead in the days of the Reformation, when the chantry side of the college's activities came to an end, or, rather, was commuted into a simple commemoration of the dead.

It is worth noting that in the very foundation of the college the chantry idea — the prayers for the souls of the departed — was essentially national, and not restrictedly collegiate. All the same, it was not the most important purpose of the college ; that was always the training up of clerks for the service of Church and State. There were no undergraduates from the beginning ; the members of the foundation were to be of three years' standing in the University on election. And as the colleges came in course of time to control practically all the undergraduates in the University, that has meant that the Fellows of All Souls have been nearly always recruited from the undergraduate members of other colleges. Dean Rashdall sums up : " Alone among the colleges of Oxford, All Souls still consists exclusively of Fellows without either scholars or non-foundation members ; and serves the function of reminding us that in their origin colleges were designed to be primarily bodies of students and not bodies of teachers ".

So it turns out that our peculiarity is not something that

we have developed by a later atrophy of the teaching function; All Souls is a survival of the medieval college — the sole example, I suppose, in the country. It is the other colleges that by their development of the undergraduate side, the enormous influx of commoners into them, have changed into something different.

From the first, All Souls was to consist of a Warden and forty Fellows, of whom twenty-four were to be artists and theologians, and sixteen were to be jurists. Chichele himself was a very distinguished ecclesiastical lawyer and had found the civil and canon law the path of promotion to high affairs and office in the Church. By the large part he gave to the study of law in his foundation he made it clear that his intention was to encourage a certain proportion of the Fellows to prepare themselves for service in public affairs. All through its history the college has stood in a peculiarly close relation to Lambeth, and to a lesser extent of the Crown. The influence of successive Archbishops of Canterbury, who are *ex officio* Visitors of the College and stand *in loco parentis* to it, has been to encourage and strengthen that side of the college. So that the element of public service in its constitution goes right back to the beginning and the intentions of the Founder. The eminent public servants, the Viceroys, the Secretaries of State, the Attorney-Generals, the bishops, who are or have been Fellows of the college have as much right to be there as the most academic of dons and researchers. But in truth, no Fellow of All Souls would wish things any other than they are. In a very imperfect world it seems to me that, of all human institutions, the University of Oxford, and in it the college of All Souls, come nearest to perfection.

What is the situation now? How is the college recruited? How does one become a Fellow? Who are the Fellows of All Souls? Such are the questions that are frequently asked of one.

There are several categories of Fellows — University Professors and Readers, Research Fellows, senior and junior, Law Fellows, Examination Fellows, and members of the college eminent for their service in Church and State. But the royal road to becoming a Fellow of All Souls is to sit for the examination, which in normal peace-time is held every October in time for the election of the successful candidates on All Souls' day (2 November) — the great day of the year for the college.

For many years the examination has been held in history, ancient and modern, and law. But in recent years, papers in philosophy, politics and economics have been added for the benefit of candidates from the Modern Greats School. Practically all the candidates then are undergraduates or graduates who have taken Firsts in Greats or History, Law or Modern Greats ; some of them have taken two or three Firsts. It is probably not much use your coming in for a Fellowship at All Souls unless you have a First in the Schools. Not that the college will have any prejudice against you, but you will come up against the competition of some of the brightest young men in the University and *they* won't let you get away with it.

So there is — though I am sure I ought not to say it — a certain *cachet* attached to becoming a Fellow of All Souls. It is true that the college has the choice of many of the ablest and most promising young men passing through the University. In these circumstances it is only to be expected that quite a number of them will make their mark later on in the life of the nation. To take a few examples in our own time : a Prime Minister in Lord Salisbury, three Viceroys of India in Curzon, Chelmsford, Halifax, an Archbishop in Lang, a Lord Chancellor in Simon, a number of cabinet ministers and bishops, two editors of *The Times*, Buckle and Dawson, who together ruled that newspaper for half a century. All of them promising young men once, who passed through the formidable ordeal of that examination we all remember so vividly, and were successful.

But in circumstances of such strenuous competition no one can repine at not being successful. Many Fellows of the college have had two, if not three, shots before being elected. And though it is a curious thought, it is not invidious to say that a college just as distinguished could be formed out of those not elected. It would be an amusing game to construct it : it would include Secretaries of State for Foreign Affairs, Dominions, Colonies, War, a Governor-General of Canada, many ministers and eminent lawyers and historians, and at least three writers who are far better known than any who *are* Fellows of All Souls. I leave you to guess who they all are. So much for the Examination Fellows, or Prize Fellows, as they used to be called. These are they that have entered in at the straight gate. They are the real thing. If there be any *snobisme* inside an institution where there is such an entire equality, it attaches to them. In the old days when Professors were first grafted on to the existing body they were supposed to be regarded as a kind of helotry and jokes were made at their expense in speeches at college gaudies. It was rather *de rigueur* to make fun of them. Nowadays the joke is completely lost on the younger Fellows who do not remember those days and have grown up with the professorial element becoming an increasingly important part of the body.

Before quitting the subject of the Prize Fellows, there is an interesting point to make. Elected as they are competitively from the ablest undergraduates from the other colleges, the All Souls elections give you something of a barometer to the standing of those colleges. During the great days of Balliol, from the time of Jowett up to the last war, there was an absolute majority of Balliol men in All Souls. And in fact for the last sixty years, since 1881, with the intermission of only a year when Lord Chelmsford was Warden, All Souls has been ruled by a succession of Balliol men as Wardens. The new Warden, Professor B. H. Sumner, is also a Balliol man and will, we hope, continue the tradition for a good many years to come. But since the last war New College has overtaken Balliol. Whereas in 1914 there was a majority of Balliol men — and Etonians — there is today a majority of New College men and Wykehamists.

Third in the list, but a long way behind, comes Christ Church ; one or two Fellows coming from Magdalen,

Queen's, University, Brasenose, Hertford, Corpus, and that is about all. The fact is that All Souls is three parts New College and Balliol in composition. I must not forget to add that there are four Cambridge men who have found a haven with us, three of them Trinity men.

Now for the Professors. The subjects of study in which the college has long been specially interested are Law and History. And a number of the most important chairs in these subjects have fellowships attached to them at All Souls. It would be logical and sensible, and very convenient for the holders of them, if all the important chairs in these subjects came under one roof. It would be very appropriate; for in the Codrington Library the college has a first-class Law and History library, far the best in the University; and it would be a great convenience to the professors in those faculties to be members of the same society, to be on the spot. But that was an opportunity which was lost by the University Commission after the first World War: the allocation of chairs to colleges was the weakest part of its work; if there should be another Royal Commission after this war — not that one is necessary — that should be rectified.

A number of the University professorships held at All Souls have been founded, or are substantially supported, by the college out of its revenues: one of the many ways in which it contributes generously, and increasingly, to University purposes. It may serve to bring the college more clearly before your mind if I cite a few names that may be known to you. Our Senior Fellow is Sir Charles Oman, known to several generations of schoolboys by his history books.[1] For many years he has held the Chichele Chair of Modern History founded by the college, and in that time has got through a prodigious amount of work — more than any other historian of our time. But in addition to the textbooks there are his two big works of research, the *History of the Art of War*, and the *History of the Peninsular War* in seven fat volumes. *A History of English Law* by Sir William Holdsworth, for many years Vinerian Professor of English

[1] This was written in 1945.

Law and an O.M., runs into a great many more volumes —
I forget how many. There must be something in the air of
All Souls that is very preservative, and renders these elderly
gentlemen so prolific; or perhaps it is the college port?
Anyhow, they provide younger Fellows with formidable, if
not somewhat minatory, examples; and as we do not come
up to their standards in the matter of port, neither do we in
the bulk of our books.

In recent years, with the expansion of our revenues, the
college has increased its contribution to the University and
much expanded the range of its interest in subjects of study.
The field logically marked out for expansion is that cognate
with our dominant subjects of study, law and history;
namely, politics and economics, and further afield in studies
connected with the Empire and government: in short, the
social sciences. There is our appropriate field: the proper
study of All Souls — as indeed of Oxford — is Man. (We
may leave Nature more to Cambridge.) Some time ago a
number of Fellows wanted to graft on to the college fellowships in natural science. The proposal had the interest of
going back to an earlier period in our history, when the
college made some remarkable contributions to science with
such figures as Linacre in the sixteenth century; Wren,
Sydenham and Mayow, the brilliant young Cornish physio-
logist, in the seventeenth century. But it is not the right
line for us to follow in the twentieth century, when we have
our work cut out to advance the study of the social sciences
and the path is already indicated for us by the nature of our
existing studies. And in fact the proposal was rejected by a
large majority.

Instead, All Souls has gone forward to expand its interests
in economics, politics, anthropology. To the chair of
Political Economy the college has itself added a full professorship in Economic History. The Gladstone Chair of
Political Theory and Institutions, recently held by Sir
Arthur Salter, has been turned into two professorships: one
in theory to which G. D. H. Cole succeeded, the other in
institutions with K. C. Wheare as professor, a distinguished

recruit from Australia. A new chair in Social Anthropology
has been created. All these come, either wholly or in part,
out of the funds provided by the college.

But this is by no means the full tale of its contributions
to the University. There is a growing category of Research
Fellows, senior and junior, who may in addition become
lecturers of other colleges and so add to the teaching facilities
of the University in general. The Bodleian Library and
the W.E.A. also receive handsome support from college
funds. Those junior Fellows who do not choose to remain
on in Oxford researching or teaching, lapse to the condition
of being fifty-pounders, *i.e.* they receive a token payment of
£50 per annum while still Fellows, and when their term of
seven years runs out they descend further into the condition of being quondams, *i.e. sometime* Fellows. There are a
number of them abroad in the world and the University;
but wherever they wander, they still belong to the company
of Chichele, and when they come home, they come home to
All Souls.

Such being the constitution of this peculiar college, unique
in its character and far from simple to explain, what is the
inner life and tone of the society like?

I am not letting you into any secrets, but you may guess
from its make-up that its conversation is dominated by
public affairs. The whole *stimmung* of the college is towards
politics in the widest sense, its interest in government and
public life. Anyone coming within its aura cannot help
being influenced by it: I was myself, and in my case, with
my working-class background, and in the circumstances of
the years between the wars, with the appalling leadership
the country got then, it led me to become a Labour candidate.
There was never any pleasure in it, and it went mostly against
the grain; but it was, I thought, a duty. And the influence
of the atmosphere in which I lived was a factor in that.
So too with other young men. It did not make us Con-
servatives or Liberals, but members of the body politic with
a responsibility.

I suppose in the days before the last war the classics

came second in the intellectual interests of the college. Now
it is probably history, but it comes a long way behind.
Myself, I could wish that there was more of a literary
atmosphere : it is curious that there should not be more in
a society of such well-read men. (But perhaps that is why :
they take it for granted.) The real explanation, I have no
doubt, is that the interest in politics and affairs comes before
everything else.

Academic ' shop ' is very much in the background ;
there is very little of the niggling about committees, personal
intrigue and so forth, which is such a futile waste of time
inseparable from so many academic, and other, institutions.
Wider horizons make for an easier atmosphere. And indeed
it has been true for many years that All Souls has been marked
by the complete absence of the quarrelling that smaller
bodies are apt to enjoy. In spite of its diverse character
there is entire harmony and agreement within the college.
We are sworn by our statutes to " brotherly love and con-
cord ", and that bond holds good outside the walls.

I do not think you would find two members of the
college, however opposed their political convictions, fighting
each other in an election. The college is a stronger tie. It
provides an example of the bonds there are in English life
that mollify the strains and conflicts of society, and make it a
gentler, a more comfortable, a more civilised thing.

I have no space to do justice to the history of the college,
or its customs and observances. The more's the pity, because
it provides an illuminating example of the way an old
English institution — in this case half a thousand years old
— changes in response to the changing needs of different
ages without breaking the mould ; surviving such cataclysms
as the Reformation and the Age of Reform and yet continuing to fulfil its old and most vital functions. It shows that
when Chichele founded, he founded well : a tribute to the
prescience of the Middle Ages insufficiently regarded in our
time.

All Oxford and Cambridge colleges with their long continuance have interesting histories and remarkable figures

to their record. But the history of All Souls is peculiarly interesting and its roll of great men rich and diverse; and it is in the concrete detail of history that institutions reveal their true character. The period of the early Renaissance yields us two figures of the first rank: Linacre, the " father of modern medicine ", first of the scientific humanists of his time, friend of Erasmus and More, founder of the Royal College of Physicians; and Leland, the first antiquary of the age and one of the greatest of English topographers.

The later Tudor time produced Privy Councillors, Secretaries of State and ambassadors, like Sir John Mason and Sir William Petre, and that fascinating Elizabethan traveller and adventurer, Sir Anthony Shirley, who perambulated Persia and the Levant. The seventeenth century gave us Jeremy Taylor, an endearing and enduring figure in our literature, and Sheldon, both Warden and Archbishop, that great ecclesiastical statesman who resettled the Anglican Church after the Restoration: he has left his mark on the history of the nation. Then there was the brilliant scientific outburst, which H. A. L. Fisher called " the real Oxford Movement ", of which Wren, Sydenham, Mayow were leading exponents. Wren was, I suppose, the man of the greatest genius the college has ever housed, and he housed here for some eight years until he became a professor. He was as distinguished a mathematician as an architect; choosing the latter, he has left his memorials upon the face of the country.

The Secretaries of State, the ministers, the ambassadors continue: them we have always with us. But the eighteenth century that was supposed to be such a dead time in the Universities, produced a more prolific crop with us than ever. There was Codrington, gallant young soldier and lover of letters, Governor in the West Indies, munificent founder of the great Library; the curious and brilliant genius of Edward Young, poet, author of *Night Thoughts*, which so fascinates the surrealists; above all, Blackstone, the great lawyer. It fell to him to be an influence on the world greater than any other Fellow — greater than Wren, who had more genius. For Blackstone's summing up of English law in his *Commentaries* — he was the founder of modern legal education —underlies not only American law, but the making of the American Constitution. His mark is upon All Souls : for many years he was its bursar, and to him we owe the completion of the great quadrangle and the decoration of the Codrington Library.

And so we come to the nineteenth century : to Bishop Heber and those romantic ambassadors, Sir Charles Vaughan and Charles Murray — for whom the young Victoria fell, though Lytton Strachey did not get on the track of the story. With Sir William Anson we reach the modern period of the college history : he piloted it through the period of Reform, remoulding it to what it is today and becoming almost a second founder. While Lord Salisbury initiates the system of Examination Fellows, which has produced Curzon, Chelmsford, Halifax; Henson, Lang, Headlam; Simon, Greene, Somervell; Buckle and Geoffrey Dawson; Oman, Amery, G. M. Young, and the moderns of our own time.

Nor can I tell you of the college customs. Everybody knows that the Mallard is the sacred bird of All Souls — our totem ; that at our gaudies we sing a song in its honour ; that an officer of the Common-Room is the Lord Mallard ; and that at the beginning of every century the whole college goes in procession round its roofs, following the Lord Mallard with the bird on a pole, by torchlight. There are medals in existence, of 1701, 1801, 1901, upon which you may see the scene depicted ; it has often been described, among others by Bishop Heber. I do not know the origin of this custom, and if I did, ought I to tell you ?

One thinks of all that past in a succession of images : Elizabeth, riding down the High, and casting her eyes upon the walls of the college hung with verses in her honour ; John Evelyn, listening to " music, voices and theorbos performed by some ingenious scholars ", and Pepys paying five shillings to see the chapel and Chichele's picture. The years, the decades go by ; it is a century later and Dr. Johnson is saying, " Sir, if a man has a mind to *prance*, he must study

at Christ Church and All Souls ''. A century more and
Froude steps into the quiet quadrangle from the bustle of the
High, to meditate under the spire of St. Mary's on the years
that had gone, on his brother Hurrell and Newman, and all
that agitation that had so strangely stirred his heart when
young. A few more years and it is our own time ; in a room
looking down upon the entrance, a youngish man with
strange fanatic eyes and tortured mouth lies out full length
upon the floor, hour after hour, writing a book : it is
Lawrence, the book is *The Seven Pillars of Wisdom.*

I think every All Souls man must carry at heart an image
and a dream. Always there are the sounds and summer
scents of those buildings set among the gardens of Oxford
that may come back to him at any moment, in a Cabinet
office, in the Embassy at Washington, patrolling in a
Sunderland off Norway, in a destroyer in the Pacific, or
eating his heart out on the coast of Cornwall. There are
the bells of St. Mary's, the regular accompaniment to dinner
in Hall on Sundays, the chimes of New College next door,
the silvery surf of Magdalen on mornings of May coming in
waves over the roofs. There are the great chestnuts in the
Warden's garden, mountainous masses of green and white
blossom, rich and festooned in the tapestry time of the year.
Or there is the scent of wallflowers stealing up in the night
from the old quadrangle, the aromatic fragrance of Cheddar
pinks from the pavement outside the Codrington ; in autumn
the secret figs ripening upon the September walls.

BISHAM AND THE HOBYS

As you come sailing up the Thames just beyond Marlow —
where Shelley and Peacock were once happy together — is
Bisham. You see it on the left hand : a church tower, little
red-tiled village, a picturesque great house with a turret, a
grange beyond, in a delightful situation among water-
meadows, at the water's edge, backed by the woods that rise
up the steep escarpment, all dusky-red now with the first
touch of spring before the buds break. Snowdrops, crocuses,
daffodils burst from the lawns and run along the banks ;
ahead is a pretty ridge of hills, Speen hill, Applehouse hill,
Ashley hill tallest of the three. It is still an unspoiled reach
of the Thames ; and up-river the right way to approach it, as
in earlier centuries people mostly did, the Thames the chief
highway. In old prints one sees the sailing barges passing
by these riverside houses mirrored in those remembering
waters.

Later in the eighteenth century a new road was made
through the parish, the bill promoted in Parliament by the
Marquis of Salisbury and the Earl of Essex, both sufferers
from gout, accustomed to take the waters at Bath every
year : one sees these gouty Georgian peers bowling along
in carriage or coach or chaise under the overhanging woods
until lost to view in the shadows of time. Their tougher
predecessors, the medieval barons, or the kings of England,
found this a convenient halting-place, or desirable retreat
in which to accommodate themselves or guests willing — or
unwilling, like the wife of Robert the Bruce. The Templars
established a preceptory here, nucleus of the present house.
Then the Montagu earls of Salisbury founded a priory hard
by the house, and many of that ill-fortuned family were
buried in the priory church : Earl John executed at Ciren-
cester, the great Warwick the kingmaker whose body lay
naked under the image of our Lady of Grace in St. Paul's

before being brought here, Henry VII's victim the young earl executed in 1499 : so much royal dust lying out there forgotten under those lawns. Margaret Pole, Countess of Salisbury, mother of the Cardinal, lived here from time to time up to her attainder and that last disordered scene upon the scaffold, running with blood and streaming white hair around the block : she is not here, but buried in the Tower.

All is quiet now, with the melancholy touch of spring upon the place. Nothing remains of the priory. There is the house that the Hobys made, out of the earlier mansion of the Salisburys : a cheerful, successful Tudor family, exorcising those medieval memories. Here is the parish church with its white chalk tower right on the edge of the river; the churchyard is planted with rose trees; there is a fallen trunk to sit on and meditate on the lives of those sculpted on the famous tombs within — of admirable workmanship by no common hand. Who are they all? They too have come to an end, like their medieval predecessors; but they have left these beautiful memorials of themselves, which fulfil their purpose, for, as long as they remain, the Hobys will not be forgotten.

They were an entirely new family, it seems; their fortunes made by Philip Hoby, one of those men whose education and talents made them so useful in the Renaissance state of the Tudors, and who now lies with his half-brother on the splendid marble tomb within. Philip Hoby was born at Leominster in 1505 — for all his quarterings, of no particular parentage. He was a secret, pleasant, cultivated man, able to keep his own counsel : what more promising for a gentleman of the privy chamber to Henry VIII? Henry trusted and rewarded him, in his will wished him to be one of the councillors to his son. Such a man was an invaluable diplomatic servant at a time when the needs of the state were expanding; and Henry made great use of him, sending him as envoy to Spain and Portugal, to the Emperor in Brussels, to France and Lorraine.

More important to us, he was one of the earlier conductors of the Renaissance impulse to this country, the latest to receive it, lagging behind in Gothic medievalism when Italy was illuminated by the bright light of the classical spirit. Abroad Hoby had met Titian and Aretino ; and presented the latter with a gratuity from the King in return for a dedication. He travelled abroad with Holbein on Henry's exacting commission to obtain portraits of possible royal brides — for example, the famous one of Christina Duchess of Milan, who refused the dangerous promotion. Among the figures of the Henrician Court portrayed by Holbein there are drawings of Hoby and his wife. If we can rely on the ascriptions, their features are well known to us : he with round Welsh head, grey-blue eyes and sparse beard, a kindly figure in that treacherous Court ; she long-faced and prim under her snood, the mouth shut tight.

So he became one of the intimates of the Edwardian circle governing the country during the King's minority, an indispensable diplomat. A respect-worthy man, he stands closest to Cecil. We find them exchanging news of their respective ailments — always a sign of mutual confidence. Hoby recommends rest and liberty to the indefatigable Secretary ; or he is against Cecil's taking the baths in England for his cold legs against winter ; he himself is going to the baths at Spa. In Brussels on embassy he receives a rose from the Secretary, which he ties to a lace and carries about his neck in token of his office. We hear of the servant who keeps his hawks. Then in 1553 we learn of the negotiations for the purchase of Bisham from the Crown. Hoby thinks the price demanded unreasonable. The greedy, grasping Anne of Cleves is after it. Cecil helps him in getting his documents signed, greatly to the Lady Anne's discontent. Mary's accession makes no difference to Hoby's employment abroad, in spite of his Protestantism : he is too indispensable. He is sent yet again to Flanders ; we find him trailing around after the Emperor in Germany ; an invalid now, he tries the waters at Liége, the baths at Pau, the doctors of Padua.

Little enough time remains to him for Bisham. He is there in 1556, beginning the new work on the house. Next year Cecil, a great builder himself, sends his man to view

its progress. Sir John Mason and Paget, the Lord Privy
Seal — both, like himself, men who have risen from nothing
to high office — are visiting him. He presses Cecil and his
wife to spend Christmas with him; the Mildmays will be
there. If the Cecils are holding back on account of little
Tannikin, they are not to leave her behind: she is to come
too. (This must be Cecil's little daughter Anne, who had
such an unhappy life as wife to Edward de Vere, Earl of
Oxford.) Then, we read in his brother's diary under 1558:
" The XVIII of April my brother went from Bisham to
London, there to seek the aid of physicians, where he made
his last will and testament and made disposition of all his
lands and goods. . . . Whit Sunday, the XXIX of May,
departed my brother out of this life to a better, at 3 o'clock
in the morning. . . . The IX day of June he was buried at
Bisham, being conveyed thither by water." He was fifty-
two years old; but childless, he had provided for the succession to his family; he had founded his house.

His heir was his half-brother Thomas, whom, twenty-
five years younger than himself, he treated as his son: we
find him in Tudor fashion referring to him as his son-in-law.
He had taken him in earlier years under his wing, sent him
to Cecil's college at Cambridge, St. John's, from which so
many of the Edwardian-Elizabethan circle came. Thence
abroad to learn languages and the ways of courtliness and
virtue. He was grounded in the last, first, by being placed
in the house of the Reformer Bucer at Strasbourg, where he
attended the lectures of Peter Martyr, Fagius and other
leading bores. After this came the delights of travel in
Italy — not that he seems to have availed himself of all of
them: he was rather a respectable young man. But we can
read in his Diary something of the excitement of travel in
Italy in these mid years of the century: masking and
murder in Venice, the reception of the Duchess of Urbino
in the *Bucentaur*, the sea covered with galleys and pinnaces
" and many other pretty vessels full of minstrelsy, dancing
and masqueries "; the sumptuousness and luxury of Italian
life, the furnishings of cloth of gold, silver work and rich

velvets ; everywhere the sense of beauty, art brought into the practice of life, the service of the dead — at Messina Giovanni d' Agnolo now sculpting the fountain with the story of Actaeon, in Rome the Farnese tomb being commissioned from Michelangelo. Everywhere we have the sense of how easily Italy grafted on to the classical reading of these Northerners : their dream of it rose up before their astonished eyes : here were the inscriptions on the portals they had read of, here were the places lived in and described by Livy and Cicero, Pliny and Tacitus. And we hear interesting news as we traverse the land in these years 1549 and 1550. The young Prince Philip of Spain makes a bad impression as he travels up through Italy : he holds himself aloof and makes small countenance to any of the ruling princes : they think him insolent. In Rome there is a papal election : the Englishman, Cardinal Pole, is the favourite candidate ; but he is thought a Lutheran ; the French Cardinals prevent his election. Hoby is impressed by the beauty and abundance of Naples and the Terra di Lavoro : " the city itself is replenished with all things, so good cheap in respect of all other cities in Italy, that it is wonder to see ". There are English gunners in the galleys there.

Thence he is summoned by his brother to Augsburg, where all the Hapsburgs are gathered together in the great family conclave to decide the succession to the Empire. Charles wishes to hand on his inheritance intact to his son Philip. His brother Ferdinand and *his* son Maximilian will not agree, as " a man might gather by their countenance, for they seemed to be always sad and pensive of the matter ". The decision they make there — to divide Germany and the Empire from Spain, the Netherlands and the Indies — determines the future history of Europe. Back in England he is received into the service of the Marquis of Northampton and accompanies him on a grand embassy to France to propose the hand of the young Edward for a French princess. It was while in France in 1552 that he undertook the task of translating Castiglione's famous book, *Il Cortegiano*, by which he has his place in our literature. This, perhaps the

most celebrated of books of manners and courtesy, is a key-
book to the Renaissance. It is a guide to the behaviour
and the lore of courts, a picture of the ideal courtier — and
the courts of princes were the chief conduits of these in-
fluences that had such a fertilising effect on the culture of the
time.

The English were very backward in these matters; the
leaders of their society were well aware how desirable it
was to catch up. When Hoby was settled in Paris, " the first
thing I did was to translate into English the third book of
the *Courtisan*, which my Lady Marquis [of Northampton]
had often willed me to do, and for lack of time ever deferred
it. And from thence I sent unto Sir Henry Sidney the
epitome of the Italian tongue which I drew out there for
him." The book appeared in 1561 and at once took its place
as one of the characteristic books of the age. It had four
editions during Elizabeth's reign; Sir Walter Raleigh tells
us that it is no accident that its vogue coincided with the
age, for its literature was essentially a literature of the
Court. The strong motive of cultural patriotism, the sense
of inferiority, the desire to catch up on abroad may be read
in Hoby's dedicatory letter to Lord Henry Hastings : " Even
so could I wish with all my heart profound learned men in
the Greek and Latin should make the like proof and every
man store the tongue according to his knowledge and delight
above other men in some piece of learning, that we alone of
the world may not be still counted barbarous in our tongue,
as in time out of mind we have been in our manners. And
so shall we perchance in time become as famous in England
as the learned men of other nations have been and presently
are." He had his desire : he won a name for himself and
in course of time the Elizabethans created a whole literature
of translation, putting into English virtually all the classics
and the best in the modern languages too.

All this is a far cry from Bisham. Thomas Hoby ac-
companied his brother once and again on embassy to the
Emperor, in 1554 paying a visit of courtesy to Cardinal
Pole, legate in Flanders, who had not yet received the final

summons home to restore England to the bosom of the
Church — work that turned out such a will-o'-the-wisp.
Hoby spent the midsummer of 1557 with his brother at
Bisham; they had company, Sir William Cecil, his wife
and her sister Elizabeth Cooke. These were two of the
formidable blue-stocking daughters of Sir Anthony Cooke,
learned in the classical languages, forceful of character, of
considerable acerbity. While Philip lay on his death-bed in
London, Thomas went up to Wimbledon, the Cecils' house,
" where I communed with Mrs. Elizabeth Cooke in the
way of marriage ". After his brother's death they were
married and spent the summer with the Cecils at Burghley.
He had entered the innermost circle of government with
this match. The Lord Keeper Bacon had married another
of the indispensable, or unavoidable, Cooke daughters; so
that the young Hobys would be first cousins of the Bacons
and the Cecils. The first of these to arrive was the young
Edward Hoby in 1560. In September there was very grand
company at Bisham: the Marquis of Northampton, the
earls of Arundel and Hertford, Lord Cobham, Lord Henry
Seymour, Lady Jane Seymour, Lady Katherine Grey (sister
of Lady Jane Grey, and destined to be hardly less unfortunate). The same year the turret was finished at Bisham.
Next year the new lodgings were finished : one sees today
the Renaissance influence brought home to Berkshire in the
classical set of the windows with brick pediments — as it
might be Bologna or Padua. In 1562 the garden and
orchard were planted and the gallery made with noblemen's
arms — the last have vanished under coats of paint or with
time, but the gallery at the end of the tall hall remains.
Next year the water was brought in lead to the house and
the fountain placed in the garden — it is there no longer.
The year after has the repairing of outhouses and barns ;
the record comes to an end.

Only two years more and Sir Thomas himself comes to
an end. He was no more than thirty-six. Following in his
brother's footsteps, fully equipped with knowledge of foreign
languages and experience of the Continent, brother-in-law

of the Secretary of State, he must have looked forward to a
long and successful diplomatic career with the promise of
the highest offices.   On his first embassy to Paris he was
struck down by plague, " leaving his wife great with child
in a strange country who brought him honourably home,
built this chapel and laid him and his brother here in one
tomb together.   *Vivat post funera virtus.*" — So the magnificent
alabaster tomb within, on which the brothers lie in gilded
armour, to the accompaniment of Latin verses by the learned
widow and doggerel English from which we learn that
Thomas Hoby was good-looking :

> Thomas in France possessed the legate's place,
> And with such wisdom grew to guide the same
> As had increased great honour to his race
> If sudden fate had not envied his fame.
> Firm in God's truth, gentle, a faithful friend,
> Well learned and languaged, Nature beside
> Gave comely shape, which made rueful his end.

The verses, continuing, express the sorrow and celebrate the
good deeds of the widow, who was never slow to declare
either herself.   She received comfort from a magnificent
letter of condolence written in the Queen's own hand, from
amid the academic junketings of the Court's first visit to
Oxford :   " Although we hear that since the death of your
husband, our late ambassador, Sir Thomas Hoby, you have
received, in France, great and comfortable courtesies from
the French king, the Queen Mother, the Queen of Navarre
and sundry others, yet we made account that all these laid
together cannot so satisfy you as some testimony and spark
of our favour. . . . We let you know that the service of
your husband was to us so acceptable, as next yourself and
your children we have not the meanest loss of so able a
servant in that calling. . . . And for yourself, we cannot but
let you know that we hear out of France such singular good
reports of your duty well accomplished towards your
husband, both living and dead, with other your sober, wise
and discreet behaviour in that court and country, that we
think it a part of great contentation to us, and commenda-

tion of our country that such a gentlewoman hath given so
manifest a testimony of virtue in such hard times of adversity.
. . . And so we would have you rest yourself in quietness,
with a firm opinion of our especial favour towards you.
Given under our Signet at our city of Oxford the . . . of
September 1566 : the eighth year of our reign. Your loving
friend, Elizabeth R."

Lady Hoby picked herself up and went on undaunted to
face a long life of bitter disappointments, considerable
troubles and some success. To this last the royal road was
a grand marriage; and this she made when she managed
to catch Lord Russell, heir to the most opulent of the new
earldoms, that of Bedford. For her first child by him —
disappointingly a daughter — she secured the Queen as
godmother. Her lying-in and the christening were accomplished in great state at Westminster, where the Dean was
complaisant enough to grant her lodgings because of the
plague in London. " In the chamber was set up a rich bed
of estate for a countess, and also a rich pallet covered with
a rich counterpane; also a rich cupboard, and a secret
oratory for necessaries appertaining to such estates. In the
second chamber was a cloth of estate for an earl, and a
traverse which was not to be drawn up till the purification
be passed; in the outer great chamber a cupboard for the
ewery." What a changed world it reveals : in place of the
monks, the Russells and the fuss of a grand child-birth. The
christening took place in the Abbey, the child borne in in a
mantle of crimson velvet with laces of gold and powdered
with gold and white flowers. The magnificent Leicester
was godfather, Lady Warwick deputy for the Queen ; Lady
Bacon and Lady Burghley, Lady Russell's sisters — all
touched with the same Cooke characteristics — bore the
train; from the chapel of St. Edward came Mr. Philip
Sidney with the towel on his left shoulder.

Alas, Lady Russell, for all her care, never became a
countess : her consort failed her, dying in his father's lifetime in 1584. He must have been rather an inept Russell,
with none of the family ability, to have left so little record

of himself in his time. We hear of him giving the Queen a
New Year's gift in 1581 — a watch set in mother-of-pearl
with three pendants of gold garnished with sparks of rubies
and an opal in every one of them and three small pearls
pendant : which was intelligent of him. Three years later
he was dead. His widow had him buried in the Abbey : a
grand Renaissance tomb with marble sarcophagus and alle-
gorical figures, Latin and Greek inscriptions from her own
pen, herself lying expectantly on a shelf below him. Their
little boy had died before, so that she was disappointed even
of the hope of the earldom coming to her progeny. She was
left with two daughters, always more trouble than they were
worth to an ambitious mother. She took firmly, sourly — in
the Cooke manner — to her widow's weeds ; henceforth she
always signed herself — with a faint suggestion of reproach
at the Deity who had treated a pious servant so scurvily —
Elizabeth Russell, Dowager.

What meanwhile was happening to her Hoby children ?

The two sons were growing up not much to the liking
of their virtuous, unpleasable mother. Edward, the elder,
was at Eton, where his great friend was John Harington —
not that that did him much good in his mother's eyes.
Harington was the Queen's godson — clever, cultivated,
witty, infinitely amusing, naughty, a light-weight, per-
petrator of puns and practical jokes. At Oxford, Hoby had
Lodge, the future novelist and dramatist, as his servitor
waiting on him. There followed two years of travel on the
Continent, like his father before him, to equip himself for a
career at Court. We have a portrait of him at this time —
the year 1577, aged eighteen : a youth in a high-crowned
French hat, with ornaments stuck in it and a feather at the
side, exquisite ruff of figured lace, white slashed doublet ;
the face long, eyes narrow-slitted and intelligent, sly and
amused, prominent sensuous nose, mouth weak : a foppish
young man. His interests were in the arts, connoisseurship,
painting, scholarship ; but above all in the art of life and its
enjoyment. It is interesting to watch the Renaissance
influence in the third generation : he is a genuine Hoby in

his tastes, without the moral stiffness, the rectitude of the makers of the family fortune. He is out to enjoy it.

All this must have recommended him to James of Scotland, to whom he was sent with Lord Hunsdon, Elizabeth's cousin, on a special mission in 1584. His qualities much impressed the King's susceptible heart, who after his leaving wrote him a letter expressing how much he longed for his company and how he had commanded his ambassador to sue for it. The Earl of Arran wrote to the same effect, enclosing a small token for Hoby to wear in testimony of their brotherhood. These amenities were less pleasing to Elizabeth : it was not her idea that her envoys should enjoy the confidence of those to whom they were sent, rather than of her who sent them. It was twenty years before he saw James again — not until he came to England as King. He was allowed to feel in disfavour and that he had better not appear at Court. He stayed on at Berwick with Hunsdon, whose daughter he had married — he does not seem to have given her a child or, indeed, much happiness. He enjoyed the pleasures — and the advantages — of correspondence with his clever cousin, Robert Cecil : the news is that Lord Lindsay is under arrest — him of whom the Queen of Scots used to say that she felt his cold dagger pass by her cheeks when Rizzio was murdered ; he has a dispute with Humphrey Gilbert ; Walsingham is his enemy ; there are squeals about property — for of course he is unthrifty. There is a long dispute about some land with Dean Nowell and Brasenose College, which, if he loses, thirteen years' service will have gone for nothing : *operam et oleum perdidi.* Back at Bisham, " I humbly beseech your honour to bear with the rudeness of my paper and pen, being in a place where it is scanty and naught, and of the hand, the weakness of my stomach not permitting me much to stoop, and most of all of the enditement, my wits being weak and feeble, and, through absence many months, unacquainted with a courtly style worthy of your virtues ". Clever little Robert was now virtual Secretary of State, source of power and influence, dispenser of all good things.

Hoby was hardly ever at Bisham: his redoubtable mother was too much in possession. He preferred the life of the Court, the delights of Queenborough Castle, of which he was made Constable and where he made a collection of portraits of the keepers, including his own. His letters to Cecil are intimate, uninhibited, full of his troubles, of demands for help, of chat about women, private allusions to which we have lost the key. Brasenose is winning the long legal struggle with him: he owes a rent of eight score and eight quarters of sweet straw-dried malt. The keeper of Queenborough is under restraint in his own castle; his friend Sir George Carew has him in custody; there is gossip of his girl friends at Court. " I will yield caution of a privy chamber lady to be with you before the first of the term, if that may suffice. Brasenose knoweth I have goods and chattels and will not fly. . . . I cannot be permitted by my gaoler to write to Winefrid. I beseech you to answer for me to her, and let her know what is become of me. I assure her I am a true man to her peradventure." Or Sir Robert is bidden to supper at his house in Cannon Row, " where, as late as it shall please you, a gate shall be open for your supper, and King Richard present himself to your view ". Or there are private allusions to Sir Walter Ralegh (the Guiana knight) we cannot now unriddle. " Methinketh out of the grates of this castle I behold how patiently Sir W. R. carrieth his attending hope and how gravely George Carew standeth before your lordships, but neither of them with much hair on their heads to be able to bear out so great a storm." The weather that stormy summer had confined Sir George Carew for four days at Queenborough: " It shows what he deserveth if he had his right and how your honour should use him, the heavens having concluded him worthy of a gaol. This proved a double prison unto him, both for his fast as that he was *in domo luctus* with a comfortless lady."

One sees something of Hoby's charm and gaiety in the letter he wrote to excuse himself when he stole away from Court to join the expedition to Cadiz, without a word to

anybody for fear the Queen would stay his going. For once
he had his mother with him in bidding farewell to none.
He writes from aboard the *Ark Ralegh* " in the Sound of
Plymouth, from whence, I think it is too truly derived. . . .
If I perish in this action I beg you to sue that George Carew
may have the keeping of Queenborough Castle. Though it
be nought worth, yet as it delighted me, so do I think for my
remembrance it would be agreeable to him. But what ! I
mean to come home again and play the wag once more.
But no more writing of books."

His younger brother, not to be out-done, was in the
Ark Ralegh too this summer. Most of the young gallants of
the Court — not that Thomas Posthumus was one of them —
were in the fleet with Essex and Ralegh bound for Cadiz.
Posthumus was the child Lady Hoby was carrying when her
husband died in France. The boy grew up undersized,
spindle-shanked, a hunch-back ; from his characteristics of
temper — self-righteous, self-important, virtuous yet spirited,
a Cooke rather than a Hoby — he makes a comic figure in
the company. For all his virtue his mother had no joy of
him. Rather than be placed in the Inns of Court as a youth
he ran away : even the Treasurer of the Inn entreated her
" both in respect of his own credit and the house, I would
forbear till he were bigger, for that he should be reputed as
a child. . . . On the other side, for travel : the sequel of
his brother's travel and example of Anthony Bacon doth
make me resolute in no wise to consent to his going over the
sea. . . . The certain fruits daily found of young men's
travel nowadays nothing but pride, charge and vanity in
deeming better of their own conceits than wisdom would.
And though I will never be found unnatural, yet will I not,
while I live, beggar myself for my cradle, if I may prevent
it." If only Burghley would take him into his service she
would allow him £100 a year ; let him gad to my Lord of
Leicester, or who living, he shall have but £40.

The only solution for him, wanting preferment, was to
marry him to an heiress. All the wheels of the powerful
family connection were set in motion to find one for this

unlikely candidate. They found him one in Yorkshire —
Margaret Dakins of Hackness near Scarborough, an only
daughter. Only a fortnight after her young husband's death
the great Lord Burghley was commending the charms of his
nephew : " his mother hath provided a good portion of
livelihood to be left to him and will deal very honourably
and kindly with him to enable him to make to his wife a
convenient jointure ". But the Huntingdons were after the
heiress for their nephew, Thomas Sidney, and they in the
North were on the spot. Lady Russell was all for action :
" Posthumus. Now, child, it standeth you upon for your
own credit's sake to try your friends." She would try something even better : her postscript runs, " Let Anthony
Cooke help to steal her away. She hath her father's consent
to match where she list." But Margaret's affections were
already settled on Sidney and she married him. Lady
Russell blamed the failure on her son.

Within five years Margaret Dakins-Devereux-Sidney was
again a widow. The news brought mother and son together
again. Posthumus was dispatched north with an influential
member of the Council of the North to plead his cause. He
needed it, for the young widow could not or would not take
to him. In the autumn Posthumus rode north again, this
time with a good store of fair jewels and pearls, and letters
from Lord Burghley to the Earl of Huntingdon pressing the
match. The widow was still cold, the prize inaccessible ;
but, wrote her suitor, " I have learned a former lesson of
audaces fortuna juvat, whereby I am led continually to exceed
good manners in being more ruled by my love than reason ".
What proved more persuasive was that the new Earl laid
claim to the forfeiture of Margaret's estates. She was assured
that only the powerful connections of her persistent suitor
could save them. Love had its reward. Lady Russell had
the pleasure of inviting Sir Robert Cecil and his wife to the
wedding at her house in Blackfriars. There would be " no
solemnity but only a private meeting of good and honourable friends " ; no music, as she did not wish it, and no
dancing, wrote Posthumus to his somewhat saturnine cousin

Anthony Bacon, for dancing was far from his own humour,
so that he would " have all let alone, and seek only to please
the beholders with a sermon and a dinner, and myself with
beholding my mistress ".

Lady Russell was at length rid of her younger son.
After the ceremony he betook himself north with his bride
to their estates, where he lived more or less happily ever
after. His rough, rude neighbours laughed at the little man ;
they found him ridiculous ; they called him the " busiest
saucy little Jack in all the country, and would have an oar
in anybody's boat " ; they said that he was not able to get
any children — nor apparently was he. They came and
kept up a commotion in his house, helping themselves to
the drink. He made a great fuss about this — he was very
conscious of his dignity — and took the matter before the
Council of the North, Star Chamber and what all. He was
rather a ridiculous figure, but he was spirited and served the
government well in that area, keeping an eye on Recusants,
maintaining order and the established religion. Old Burghley
had been right, after all — as he always was. And, funnily
enough, Posthumus and his wife *were* happy after their
fashion. When she died, many years after, his will was to be
buried there in the North in Hackness Church, " next unto
the dust of the body of my late most dear and only wife, the
Lady Margaret Hoby ".

His mother was free to advance the interests of her
daughters, to interfere with everybody's business, to point
out everybody's faults and her own virtues, to lay about her
right and left, to let her personality rip, uninhibited, released, without fear or consideration, like some rich, rank
vegetation running to seed with an acrid odour in the air.
She was one of those old women : a perfect specimen of the
female egotist, domineering, not without her good qualities
— plenty of courage and always ready to step into any
breach — whom everyone conspires to circumvent since
there is no dealing with them, hence often checked, never
wholly defeated. Since she was literate and very expressive,
she stands out naked in her letters, fully revealed. There are

frequent, interminable letters to the long-suffering Burghley and her nephew Robert. A neighbour at Bisham, a Cornish Borlase, wants to be let off being sheriff. Like everyone else in that age she has interminable legal business, but she directs it all herself. She wishes Lord Burghley to direct the Judges, in the case of her daughters' inheritance, to deliver their opinions individually to the Queen and not give a collective decision, so that " her Majesty shall receive their reports to better purpose ". This was more than the Crown itself could command within a few years. Her lawyer, her cousin Morris, has been with her this afternoon, poor man : he has had a set-back, could not Robert Cecil, in his father's absence, solicit the Queen to recompense him by making him Master of the Rolls ? He did not get the office.

Her neighbours, the Lovelaces, were a constant source of trouble ; though they were only small gentry and she a great lady, they were always ready to take advantage of a poor widow. When their servants trespassed on her property, she took the law into her own hands and imprisoned the men. Attorney-General Coke has to intervene : " the causes be so intermixed as on the one day they cannot punish Lovelace but on the other they must sentence against my lady. For, albeit an honourable lady being so abused as she was could hardly (all circumstances considered) brook such indignities, yet her stocking and imprisonment of his men is not justifiable in law, and seeing there is so great inequality of persons, I would not have them suffer equal punishment." Years after, similar troubles recur. Anne Lovelace refused to enter her service, in spite of her ladyship being willing to have gotten Mr. Latten for a husband for her. Not content with that, the girl had beaten her at law over a tenement she had got by her favour. Evidently she had lost that easily exhausted commodity : " neither list I while I breathe to be thus bearded by a girl's tearing out of my teeth what I meant to her preferment in my own parish if she had kept my favour ". Keeping Lady Russell's favour was no sinecure. " Think that it toucheth you in honour in the face of the world to see your aunt, a noblewoman that hath made petition in a most just cause to the Council table to have redress ", etc. etc. Judge Warburton, who had sentenced against her, should be sent for and carpeted by the all-powerful Secretary. Judge Warburton was in for it : it was the beginning of a long feud. He does not seem to have taken it too seriously : there was not so much bite after all in the old barker. " Compound it to my honour and equity as yourself " think best. . . . " This done I am going to Donnington." She flounced off to Donnington in a huff.

Elizabeth had been good to her and granted her the constableship of Donnington Castle, near Newbury — the shell of the keep remains looking down upon the pretty water-meadows of the Lambourn. It was a pleasant place to retire to in the country, away from her house in the crowded Blackfriars with all its *tohu-bohu* of theatre men, foreigners, jewellers, craftsmen of all sorts. It gave her a home of her own, if her son should come back to Bisham. On the rumour of a royal progress that way in 1602 the " poor desolate widow " offers to put up Robert Cecil and his friends, the Worcesters and the Shrewsburys. They should have " three bed-chambers, with inner chambers, castle fashion, the best I have. (But soft, I do not say for yourself and your lady one.) " Robert Cecil was now a widower : the proprieties must be observed. Lady Russell was in a gentler mood than usual.

Ten years earlier she had had the honour of entertaining the Queen at Bisham, on her progress to Oxford and back to Rycote. As the Queen reached the top of the hill going down to Bisham, the cornets sounding in the woods, a wild man came out of them to greet her with a speech full of the conceits the time so loved : none could tell who was passing that way — the nymphs and shepherds were fearful of the music in the woods — " none durst answer or would vouchsafe, but passionate Echo, who said ' She '. And She it is, and you are She, whom in our dreams many years we satyrs have seen, but waking could never find any such. . . . Your Majesty on my knees will I follow, bearing this club,

not as a savage but to beat down those that are." Half-way
down the hill a pretty scene was enacted: Pan with two
shepherdesses sewing their samplers. A charming pastoral
dialogue followed — like something out of *As You Like It* or
Love's Labour's Lost — in honour of virgins who became god-
desses for their chastity and so made Jupiter blush and dismayed Juno, as wounded at her Majesty.

" This way cometh the Queen of this Island, the wonder
of the world and Nature's glory, leading affections in fetters,
Virginities slaves. . . . By her it is that all our carts that
thou seest are laden with corn, when in other countries they
are filled with harness; that our horses are led with a whip,
theirs with a lance; that our rivers flow with fish, theirs
with blood. . . . Jupiter came into the house of poor
Baucis, and she vouchsafeth to visit the bare farms of her
subjects. We upon our knees will entreat her to come into
the valley, that our houses may be blessed with her presence,
whose hearts are filled with quietness by her government."
Pan offers: " During your abode, no theft shall be in the
woods; in the fields no noise, in the valley no spies; myself
will keep all safe ". At the bottom of the hill, at the entrance
to the house, the Queen was met by Ceres with her nymphs
in a harvest cart. After singing a song, Ceres lays her
feigned deity at the feet of the Queen, promising for the
Lady of the Farm " that your presence hath added many days
to her life, by the infinite joys she conceives in her heart, who
presents your Highness with this toy and this short prayer,
poured from her heart, that your days may increase in
happiness, your happiness have no more end till there be
no more days ".

It is like the masque of Ceres that comes into *The Tempest*.
Whoever penned this entertainment had a pretty wit and a
touch of true poetry — can it have been Lodge, Hoby's old
servitor at Trinity, author of *Rosalind*, dramatist as well as
novelist? But no: it has been identified as by Lyly, the
author of *Euphues* himself, who wrote the speeches for the
Queen's entertainment at Rycote.

Lady Russell's lengthening days were not without in-

cident : she continued to be vexed by neighbours, the way-
wardness of her children, the general wickedness of the
world. Other people's affairs were specially troublesome
to her : it seems they were sent to plague her. Burghley
and Cecil were still the patient receptacles of her con-
fidences, complaints, reproofs. Not that they got much
credit for their patience. She intervened with Burghley
about his granddaughter's jointure. She badgered him
about episcopal preferment, an apt subject for such old
women : " Since your father and you set so lightly by so
grave and worthy an old servant, I have done. I desired
that he might have been of London, which happening not,
your father in his wisdom set down with his own hand and
nominated to Durham, wherein more than your young experience yet thinketh on, he, I say again, in his great wisdom
discharged himself with nominating Day to Durham . . ."
and so on interminably. It seems that her candidate failed
to get either. Shortly after, " I have been to see her Majesty
when going to God's house, not being able through malice
to see her face else ". Elizabeth, no doubt, knew how to
keep her at arm's length. " I am maliced thus through your
father's mutterings, which stick fast by me, and yet he con-
siders it not, nor knows what I have endured for him, to my
undeserved shame." There was no peace for the old man
this side the grave.

Now all her guns are trained on Robert. Could he not
make the Earl of Kent Lord President of the North in place
of the Earl of Huntingdon ? " There cannot be a fitter
supply for the good of God's church and that country."
But — " I would not have it known to proceed from me,
because he is a widower and I a widow, but being entreated
thereto, I could not do but thus much in respect of my duty
to my dead. I beseech you *quod facis fac cito*, or else I fear
one of the tribe will be before him *Hercules Furens*. . . . Your
aunt, that thought on Wednesday that you should never
have heard her speak more in faith, Elizabeth Russell,
Dowager." The Earl of Kent did not become Lord President
of the North, or of anything else. Now she is very busy

with her lawyers — and, of course, with her tongue and her pen. Could not Dr. Dale (a Fellow of All Souls) be made a Master of Requests? — certainly *not* Dr. Caesar, " who hath enough already, if these days could acknowledge what is enough ". Dr. Caesar became Master of Requests. It never seems to strike such old persons that the more they ask for the less they get.

When Robert Cecil loses his wife, his aunt sends him Latin verses and intolerable religious consolations, mingled with sharp good sense. He is not to give himself up to melancholy : " it will bring forth the fruit of stupidity, forgetfulness of your natural disposition of sweet and apt speeches, fit for your place ; and, instead thereof, breed and make you a surly, sharp, sour plum, and no better than in truth a very melancholy mole and a *misanthropos* hateful to God and man ". She ends with a postscript about the Islands Voyage, the great enterprise of the year 1597 : " I in no wise like of the enterprise toward. It may have good beginning, but I fear ill success in end." Unfortunately she proved right, as such people sometimes do.

Now, upon report of the quarrels between Cecil and Essex, she will come to Court to do him any good offices she can. But the Queen must give her lodging there within the house, " otherwise, upon the least wet of my feet or legs by long clothes or cold, my pate is so subject to rheum that my hearing will be so bad as that I am fit for no company or other place than my own cell. — Your aunt that ever deserved the best." Down in the country she hears that Mr. Moon has been made a knight, and — " I pray you for my credit's sake make my neighbour, Mr. Rogers, a knight, here by me dwelling this winter time. He is husband to Lady Mary, the Duke of Somerset's daughter. . . . Either I would have it done by your own procurement, as token of your remembrance how much your father was beholden to her father, or else in truth I desire it not. — Your loving aunt, poor and proud."

Now she is in trouble again : " Friend me so much as to procure me a lodging in the Court in this time of misery.

Here I remain where none be left but artisans; myself a
desolate widow without husband or friend to defend me or
to take care of me; my children all in her Majesty's service;
myself so beggared by law and interest for relief of my
children as that I was forced to break up my house more
than a year since, and to live here with only six, a very few,
and those necessary persons . . . if God deliver me out of
this plunge of danger and misery alive, though I be both
blind, deaf and a stark beggar, yet will I by the experience
of this tribulation and discomfort, I will take me to a mischief
and marry to avoid the inconvenience of being killed by
villains." This was on the news of the approach of the last
Spanish invasion fleet, and she a woman nearing eighty:
she does not seem to be in any doubt about finding a partner.
Now she has heard something dreadful about Sir Robert,
something she is not willing to commit to paper: " it is
brought to my ears here in my very cell that most vile words
have been openly uttered of you at an ordinary. Thus I
manifest it to be true, long since written, *Naturam expellas
furca tamen usque recurrit.* . . . In the meantime, I sorrow in
my heart my sovereign's hurt, your peril, I fear, and danger
to come, to her Majesty's disquiet and trouble. I can but
pray, which, I am sure, is most devoutly done here day by
day in the Friars in the most reverent manner, for her
Majesty and her Council."

But she was not above a joke at her clever little nephew's
expense. There was an interesting scene one day in 1596
at Essex House, when she went to effect some reconciliation
between her equally sharp nephew, Anthony Bacon, and
the Cecils, his uncle and cousin. The Bacons, for all their
wits and ambition, were carefully kept out by old Burghley
in the interests of his son, and not unnaturally had transferred their abilities to the support of his rival, the Earl of
Essex. At this moment — it was just after the Earl's triumph
at Cadiz — the Cecils were feeling a little queasy and a
feeler for a reconciliation was put out. Lady Russell was the
all too willing instrument. " Good nephew," she began,
" are not you much bound to your aunt, that will make such

a posting journey, only with one gentlewoman, first in a coach to Paris garden, and then in a wherry over here to you " — Essex House was between the Strand and the river, on the site of Essex Street — " to visit you and to perform a very kind office ? " The *maladif*, somewhat Machiavellian Anthony replied that her merit and his own obligation were very great, but not greater than the thankfulness of his heart. " Marry, nephew," said she, " it is the same heart that must ease my heart, which is almost choked with grief to hear what I do." She paused, " looking wistly upon him, probably to see whether he was dismayed ".

But that very clear head, not a bit dismayed, gave a good account of itself. Lady Russell passed on the Lord Treasurer's complaints that he was too intimate with the somewhat serpentine Lord Henry Howard — James's confidant, there was the danger-point for the Cecils — and with Philip's exiled minister, Antonio Perez. At that moment a message came to say that Lord Henry was below : he made haste to be off when he learned who was above. Lady Russell said : " The daily resort of these unto you makes you odious. You are too well known and beloved in Scotland to be a true Englishman ; and busy yourself with matters above your reach, as foreign intelligences and entertainment of spies. You have not only abandoned the kind old nobleman, but you do him ill offices, not only with the earl here, but in France and Scotland." This was true : Anthony Bacon was running a foreign service of his own for Essex, which was making him a power in government, rivalling the Cecils. Bacon replied directly : when he came home from his years of travel and experience abroad, " he found nothing but fair words, which make fools fain, and yet even in those no offer or hopeful assurance of real kindness, which he thought he might justly expect at the Lord Treasurer's hands, who had inned his ten years' harvest into his own barn, without any halfpenny charge ".

Anthony Bacon was no fool ; was it surprising that he had transferred his affections to Essex ? He proceeded to drive home his advantage and prejudice her against Robert

by telling he how Cecil had sworn a feud against her sister
and his, Anthony's, mother, Lady Bacon. " Vile, wretched
urchin," said the credulous old lady, " is it possible ? "
Anthony referred her to his mother, to whom he had said
when she herself told him of it, in the words of a Gascon
proverb, " Braire d'âne ne monte pas au ciel ". " By God,"
Lady Russell replied, " he is no ass." " Let him go for a
mule then, madam, the most mischievous beast that is."
" At this she laughed heartily and seemed to be very glad to
understand such a monstrous insolency, which brought her
into very good temper, and altered her style quite from
censures and reproaches to praise." And in a good humour
she went off, having done, as usual, little good.

She was more successful in this same year in stopping a
theatre from being built on her doorstep in Blackfriars. Her
town-house was within the precinct : she was a leading
inhabitant. At the Dissolution the great church was pulled
down, and in its place Sir Thomas Cawarden, Master of
the Revels, kept his tents and stores for masques and plays
at Court. What more natural than that theatre people
should gravitate to the spot ? Among them James Burbage,
who had bought some property there and was proposing to
establish a theatre. Lady Russell did not propose : she got
up a petition with her neighbours, the Hunsdons, against
any such thing as " a common playhouse, which will grow
to be a very great annoyance and trouble, not only to all
the noblemen and gentlemen thereabout " — an authentic
touch — but also to the general inhabitants. The precinct
had already grown very populous and this would increase the
sickness in time of pestilence ; and besides, " the same playhouse is so near the church that the noise of the drums and
trumpets will greatly disturb and hinder both the ministers
and parishioners in time of divine service and sermons ".
Among the petitioners — her ladyship's name comes first —
is that of Richard Field, publisher of Shakespeare's poems.
It was some time before Burbage could make use of his
property for what he intended, and then as a private playhouse. Among the lessees was Shakespeare ; later on he

owned the house over the gate. The site of the playhouse is now occupied by *The Times* office. Lady Russell survives erect upon her tomb at Bisham.

The great concern of her later years was to provide for her two Russell daughters; they were called Elizabeth and Anne, like the two little Hoby daughters who had died within a few days of each other in 1571. Their grandfather the Earl of Bedford had left them ill provided for, she complained; now that they are grown up she has no fit place for them, she tells Burghley, unless she should make them nuns. And where, she asks him, is she to leave her eldest daughter now she is going out of town and how will the diet for herself, her maid, groom and footman be provided? The answer, of course, was the Queen's service: they became maids of honour. The Queen may expect a New Year's gift for accepting her daughter: she proposes to give £20 in a purse. "I have many enemies and can only serve her Majesty by prayers." That haven of refuge was not without its storms. Just before the Islands Voyage in 1597, the Queen boxed the ears of the fair Mistress Bridges — who was Essex's girl-friend — and turned her and her friend Anne Russell out of the Coffer Chamber. "They lay three nights at my Lady Stafford's, but are now returned again to their wonted waiting. . . . The cause of this displeasure said to be their taking of physic, and one day going privately through the Privy Galleries to see the playing at ballon." That — and, it may be added, the jealousy of an ageing woman for the young, of the Virgin Queen for Essex's mistress.

It seems that the young Lord Herbert, the Earl of Worcester's heir, had fixed his affections on Anne Russell. But her mother was not paying too high a price for the match. "Her virtue, birth and place, joined to the hundred pounds of inheritance presently enjoyed . . . with £200 yearly after my death till £2000 be come out in ten years to her own good . . . will be a sufficient portion for an Earl of so small revenue and so many children as the Earl of Worcester." Negotiations languished. Meanwhile she quar-

relled with her daughter Elizabeth, who, not having a marriage in prospect, was prepared to sell Russell House for cash.
Her sister agreed. This ran up against her mother's real
religion, worship of the dead, *her* dead. " I had ever told
Bess and her sister long since and often, whensoever they
weeded out their father's name out of Russell House they
should root out my heart from them. . . . But I must either
consent or bring the burden of a mighty Councillor my
nephew upon me, God reward Mrs. Elizabeth. Much good
shall she get by her presumptous disobedience herein. . . .
I cannot be content to dishonour the dead, or not to give
all due to my dead darling while I breathe. . . . I think
that I go upon my last year. Some will kill me, and therefore my kingdom is not of this world." The old girl lived
for ten years more yet. The young people could see no
reason for so much fuss about what her son called " an old
rotten house of Russell ". They had not her loyalties.

Bess was, of course, forgiven and soon we find her mother
lobbying for an extension of her lease of Donnington from
the Crown " for Bess Russell's good. It cost me truly, twelve
years since, a gown and petticoat of such tissue as should
have been for the Queen of Scots' wedding garment; but I
got them for my Queen, full dearly bought, I well wot.
Beside, I gave her Majesty a canopy of tissue with curtains
of crimson taffeta, belited gold. I gave also two hats with
two jewels, though I say it, fine hats. . . ." And so on.

In 1600 the marriage negotiations are taken up again.
Lady Russell has to make a better offer: Lord Herbert is to
have £2000 in money, £150 a year in land with a reversion
to 1000 marks in land, with his fair bride. The news is that
Lady Russell has gone to Court to obtain the Queen's leave.
Everything must be done in order: she wants the Queen's
leave to have the banns called in the royal chapel before
she will sign assurances; that done, she will seal them. The
Earl and Countess of Bedford come to town for the marriage;
Lady Russell is making exceeding preparations for it — it
is a contrast to the simple dinner she gave for the wedding
of poor Posthumus. The Queen is expected to attend the

D

ceremony. Everyone is waiting : the news letters go over-
seas, Rowland White to Sir Robert Sidney, John Chamber-
lain to Dudley Carleton ; but the Queen will not appoint a
day. She has always had great difficulty in stomaching the
marriages of others, particularly of her own circle, most of
all of the young, who seem to be happy to spite her, leaving
her an old and famous woman, alone with her fame. The
delay troubles many of Anne's friends " that stay in town
to do her service ". " Tomorrow my old Lady Russell goes
to Court and hopes the next day to bring her fair daughter,
Mistress Anne, out of Court and so to go on with the celebration of the marriage."

The visit of the dowager has its effect. Elizabeth,
capitulating, determines to do things in the noblest style.
" Mistress Anne went from Court upon Monday last with
eighteen coaches, the like hath not been seen amongst the
Maids. The Queen, in public, used of her as gracious
speeches as have been had of any, and commanded all the
Maids to accompany her to London ; so did all the lords
of the Court. Her mother brought a great number of
strangers to Court ; all went in a troop away. The marriage
will be upon Monday next ; her Majesty will be there, as
it is hoped." The preparations are the talk of London.
The Queen is to lie at Lord Cobham's to be near the bride-
house. " There is to be a memorable mask of eight ladies ;
they have a strange dance newly invented ; their attire is
this : each hath a skirt of cloth of silver, a rich waistcoat
wrought with silks and gold and silver, a mantle of carnation
taffeta cast under the arm and their hair loose about their
shoulders curiously knotted and interlaced. These are the
masquers : my Lady Dority, Mrs. Fitton, Mrs. Carey, Mrs.
Onslow, Mrs. Southwell, Mrs. Bess Russell, Mrs. D'Arcy,
and my Lady Blanche Somerset. These eight dance to the
music Apollo brings, and there is a fine speech that makes
mention of a Ninth, much to her honour and praise. The
preparation for this feast is sumptuous and great, but it is
feared that the house in Blackfriars will be too little for
such a company."

It may be surmised that Lady Russell was equal to the occasion. She calls on all her friends. Her all-powerful nephew, the little Secretary, is to command the house at the bride's home-coming " as my husband ". Only near relations are bidden to supper that day : the earls of Worcester, Cumberland and Bedford with their countesses, and Lady Warwick — so powerful with the Queen : all Russells and Herberts — the Hobys are left out of it, disposed of. Then on the marriage day, 16 June 1600, " if the poor widow can provide meat for a widow's marriage dinner, no feast comparable to the Earl of Shrewsbury's, or fit for a Prince, for then I would look that they should be beholding to me to be bidden ; but now they shall take pains which come, and deserve my thanks. For six messes of meat for the bride's table, and one in my withdrawing chamber for Mr. Secretary and myself, is all my proportion for that day's dinner. . . . You thought that I should never have bidden you to my marriage. But now you see it pleases God otherwise. Where I pray you dispose yourself to be very merry and to command as master of the house. For your welcome shall be in the superlative degree. Your most loving Aunt."

The great day is described to us by another hand : " The bride met the Queen at the water side, where my Lord Cobham had provided a lectica, made like half a litter, wherein she was carried to my Lady Russell's by six knights. Her Majesty dined there and at night went through Dr. Pudding's house (who gave the Queen a fan) to my Lord Cobham's where she supped. After supper the masque came in, and delicate it was to see eight ladies so prettily and richly attired. Mrs. Fitton led, and after they had done all their own ceremonies, these eight lady masquers chose eight ladies more to dance the measures. Mrs. Fitton went to the Queen and wooed her to dance. Her Majesty asked what she was. ' Affection ', she said. ' Affection ! ' said the Queen, ' Affection is false.' Yet her Majesty rose and danced."

The Queen's mind was full of forebodings. No wonder she had delayed in naming a day for her presence at the marriage. She and Cecil had other things to think about. Essex's career was rushing headlong to a catastrophe. The Irish campaign had been a disaster; he was in touch with James, her successor: what was he planning? Only ten days before, he had been dismissed from all offices of state and sentenced to remain a prisoner at the Queen's pleasure. At this moment he was a prisoner, not far away, at Essex House. Affection was false indeed; yet she rose and danced.

She danced because she must; the masque of state must continue.

It is of this scene, her visit to Blackfriars, that we have the celebrated picture painted by Gheeraerts. There is the Queen going by in her chair of state, with plumed and decorated canopy, carried by six knights, her old knight Sir Henry Lee, her Champion, in the foreground. Before her are the officers of her household — one recognises Lord Admiral Howard; and there is the Secretary: the gartered and ribboned legs of the men move in rhythm, the rhythm of the masque of state to which they all move. Following behind are the maids of honour, with the bride in white at their head. Up aloft sits the old woman, in more dazzling white, jewelled and coroneted, painted to look like a girl of twenty. Nearing seventy, she was within a year or two of the end of that long and fabulous reign.

Such was the high point of Lady Russell's life. Everyone said that the entertainment was good and plentiful, and she was much commended for it. Within a week one of the young masquers was dying: Bess Russell, the bride's sister. The world said, " If she go, she will mend the new bride's marriage ". Great lamentation was made for her " by my lady her mother, my Lady Warwick and my Lady Herbert ". It was long before Lady Russell could bring herself to come to Court, " to fill every place I there shall come in with tears by remembrance of her that is gone ".

Little remains to complete her story. She nourishes a grievance against the Queen for not giving her daughter an honourable burial, as meaner maids have had. " Since my farewell from Court hath been every way so uncomfortable,

it hath killed a courtier and Parliament woman of me."
She consoles herself with translation, publishing in 1605 her
version of a French treatise on the true *Nature and Substance
of the Body and Blood of Christ in the Sacrament*; with that and
the composition of epitaphs for her monuments, the gathering together of her dead. She was engaged in ordering her
own funeral, writing a long letter, just before her death, to
Garter King of Arms to know " what number of mourners
were due to her calling . . . the manner of the hearse, of
the heralds and church ". The ordering of the Hoby chapel
at Bisham must have been her doing in these last years.

For, until his mother died, Sir Edward seems hardly to
have been there at all. He held the fort at Queenborough.
But, writing to Cecil for favours — " Men in great place are
thrice servants ", wrote the keenest intellect among these
cousins — " if I die tomorrow next, my wife has never a
house to put her head in ". Soon it was not necessary.
Though he had neglected her in life, he put up a monument
of great beauty and rarity of design to her when she died.
There it is at the east end of the chapel, with the rich
tapestried colours of the Hoby window behind, mostly gold
with black and blue and silver lattices. It is more like a
garden ornament from some Roman villa than a funerary
monument : an elaborate square base for an obelisk, with a
flaming heart on top, and clustering round the obelisk with
outstretched wings four great swans, the Carey supporters ;
on one side the word *Silentium*, on the other *Fuimus*. The
Hoby sense of style had not deserted him ; one sees it in
such a sentence, written of course to Cecil — now Lord
Cecil : " My ambitions be not great ; it is but to keep what
I had when my late Queen died, pay my debts and make
myself ready to go to that last home, whereof my years now
bring me to the vespers of the day ".

The accession of James increased his favour : the King
had not forgotten the charm and gaiety of the attractive
youth of twenty years before. He made him a Gentleman
of the Privy Chamber and came to visit him several times
at Bisham. Such entertainments were not without expense ;

James was more generous than Elizabeth had been, forgave him £500 arrears of rent, gave him licences to enable him to make ends meet. There are mementoes of James's visits in the house : his arms and Anne of Denmark's in a window of the Council Chamber upstairs, that with the oriel window looking upwards to the woods of Bisham ; a portrait of the King on wood — no beauty — in the gloomy panelled study. They shared similar interests, bookish and theological. Hoby had carried on the family tradition with his translation from the French of Coignet's *Politic Discourses of Truth and Lying*, and of Mendoza's *Theorique and Practice of War* from the Spanish. Now he embarked on the theological controversies so dear to James, with their Corinthian Jacobean titles : *A Counter-Snarl for Ishmael Rabshacheh, a Cecropidan Lycaonite* (1613). To which the gentleman similarly replied. Hoby countered with *A Currycomb for a Cox comb . . . In answer to a lewd Libel lately foricated by Jabal Rachil against Sir Edward Hoby's Counter-Snarl* (1615).

Other interests of his the King did not share. Hoby had no children by his wife, but he left a natural son, Peregrine Hoby, by one Catherine Pinkney. Over the hill from Bisham and down the other side towards Maidenhead are Pinkney's Green and Maidenhead Thicket, with Robin Hood's Arbour in the midst : presumably there, sporting in the woods, he found her. Peregrine was left to the care of an Archbishop, and in the days of the Restoration, when a very good time was had by all, became a baronet. Through him the family continued until the male line came to an end in mid-eighteenth century with another Sir Thomas and another Sir Philip — ending as it began — who was Dean of Ardfert. He is the last of them lying in the chapel.

The presiding spirit there — almost its tutelary deity — is Lady Russell. To her worship of the dead, her fidelity, her tenacity we owe the visual scene awaiting us. She had brought them all together, steered them safe into harbour at last. There she is in her wide cavernous weeds, immensely widowed, but not omitting the coronet on top of all, her life's unrealised crown. She kneels at her prie-dieu, as so often in the little church in Blackfriars (did the drums and trumpets disturb her devotions in the end, I wonder?), or more quietly in the chapel here. Under the great columned canopy are brought with her her dead : the little Russell boy, a bundle of child's clothes with black shoes peeping out, with whom her grand hopes foundered : behind her, Bess Russell and her two little Hoby girls. Outside the canopy kneel the living, who now to us are as long dead as those within : the Hoby sons in gilt and coloured armour. Sir Edward and Thomas Posthumus, small and spry, but undeformed. Facing her ladyship, but outside, kneels her daughter, ruffed and coroneted, for she is a peeress. Here they all are, no longer reluctant, protesting, but grouped submissively around the masterful old lady who planned and made this place for a perpetual memorial to her dead — and to herself.

HILLESDEN IN BUCKINGHAMSHIRE

IF you take a map of Buckinghamshire and look a few miles south of the old county town, between it and the Claydons — that have their memories now for all lovers of English letters — you will find a name that means nothing to you : Hillesden. It is indeed a forgotten place : hipped up there on its little hill, the fat pastures and flat water-meadows all round it, isolated from any main roads, with only one little road winding up to it : a dead end. And yet it was far from being that in its heyday ; only its heyday was three centuries ago, the time of the Civil War, which left such a mark upon it and on the lives of all that lived there. Now, hardly anyone ; just a cottage or two, a church, a farm, where once was all the bustle, the coming to and fro of a great house, with the family, important, numerous, ramifying in every direction, affecting the life of all this countryside. Now all vanished and gone ; where the house stood but an open space in the fields, the fields revealing under the grass the slopes of the former terraces.

It was on a November day, the first of the month, that my friend and I set out in pursuit of this place. We were walking from Steeple Claydon, the way that so many generations of Verneys had gone to visit so many generations of Dentons. There in the village was the big Camp Barn around which Cromwell's small army, some two thousand men, was encamped and from which they advanced to the attack on Hillesden House : March 1644, three hundred years ago. Over the Planks we went, directed by a superb young soldier newly returned from the wars : duly we negotiated the duck-boards laid across the low-lying water-meadows and out into the open, lonely country beyond.

Sitting on a gate at the foot of the slope we ate our sandwiches, looking up to the corn-yellow haystacks moulded firm and clear by the November sun. There was a mellow-

ness in the colouring, a water-clear purity in the air; the
autumn fruits in the hedges glowed red and gold.

So we approached the place, the same way that Cromwell
came. Drawing near we observed the remains of the park, a
few oaks, the great ruined trunks of elms, the rich red-brick
wall that bounded what had been the enclosure. Inside,
nothing but space, every vestige of the house gone, except for
the falling terraces under the grass, going down to the
ornamental water that had now — saddest touch of all —
become a cow-pond; to the east, the great avenue running
down the slope and away into the blue Buckinghamshire
distance; on the horizon, the spire of Steeple Claydon
whence the attack came; the dominant colour here the
lemon-yellow of elm leaves lying everywhere.

We entered the church, dedicated (I noticed) to All
Saints — and this was All Saints' day on which we had
come. I took it as a good omen, that was at once in part
fulfilled, for on throwing open the door a splendid interior
was revealed: a late Perpendicular masterpiece in this
sequestered spot, a jewel of a church with its high, graceful
arcade, the nave so light and airy, with a continuous
clerestory admitting the white November light. It was like
being in a glass-house, but, all the same, with what richness!
One was transported with its loveliness — one held one's
breath — and at the same time there was the unspeakable
poignancy of a place that had kept watch through all the
ages and that was now left high and dry like some shell cast
up by the retreating ocean, now unregarded, unvisited,
empty and alone. Something was listening in the silence;
perhaps the silence itself was listening: something that
could not get through, that could not be said in words.
The spell was not broken, only deepened by the comfortable
noises of the afternoon outside; the clatter of the hens in the
farmyard, a cock-crow further away, the lonely sing-song
voices of children calling to each other across the fields.

I went up into the chancel and there were all my friends:
all the people that had lived here and loved this place in
centuries gone by, to me so many living individuals with their

troubles and their memories, the things that had happened
to them thronging in my mind. For a moment it was too
much : to find them all here just like that. I sat there a
moment reflecting on an easier plane how odd it was that
I a stranger should come into this place, knowing so much
about the men and women buried there, when, I suppose,
they mean little or nothing to the living whose place it is.

There on his altar-tomb in the chapel lies Thomas
Denton with his wife, the founder of the family, a lawyer who
did well out of the Reformation and got this manor from the
Crown on the crash of the Courtenays. There they are, two
fine alabaster effigies, he in armour, she in close-fitting head-
dress and costume of the mid-sixteenth century, the impulse
of the Renaissance in the motifs on the pilasters on the sides
of the tomb. But the figures have been deliberately slashed,
evidently by Cromwell's common soldiery, the sort of people
that in all ages hate what is beautiful because it is beyond
them. The hands of both figures joined in prayer have been
cut off at the wrists, one leg of the man and the cushion on
which his head rests, so decapitating a pretty little lion
creeping up to him. (I remembered the similar lion on the
tomb in Hereford cathedral, that splendid Elizabethan
affair on which Thomas Denton's son lies with his first wife,
though his body is here with his second.) There are dents
on the cheek and on the chin, evidently slashed with a
sword or a pike ; yet traces of colouring remain on coat
and cushion. How brave and fine — and annoying to
Puritan Philistines — it must have looked three hundred
years ago, when they descended on the place.

Not far away is the Elizabethan limestone monument,
with its sarcophagus, to his eldest son Alexander Denton
and his second wife : very different from the magnificent
altar-tomb on which he is depicted at Hereford, wearing a
double chain round his neck and holding a cross in his
hands. He evidently thought to lie there by his young wife,
who died in child-birth at the age of eighteen. But life
gained renewed hope for him, and here he is at last, gathered
to his father and his descendants. These are many : they

lie all around one under the flags, or under their slabs, their monuments upon the walls. One cannot hope to go into them all : sufficient to note two : the plain white and dove-grey monument to Dr. William Denton, with coloured coat of arms and flowers and fruit at the top — the most appealing member of his family and the one of whom by far the most has come down to us.

The second is a splendid work, a masterpiece by that admirable eighteenth-century sculptor, Sir Henry Cheere, of whom Roubiliac was a pupil, and who executed the statue of Christopher Codrington at All Souls and the series of busts that decorate the bookcases in the library there. Here he has a fine bold composition : a sarcophagus of a rare dark-grey veined marble, slotted or grooved, with beautifully carved great lions' feet supporting ; above, an urn in white marble ; on either side a portrait-bust, of Judge Denton and his wife ; the whole built up on a base and backed by a tall diminishing shaft of dull grey. The portrait of the Judge is of a speaking character : in cap, ermine and bands, a full heavy face, of an amiable, kindly man, well-liking and pursy, a face troubled with grief; his young wife, a small well-shaped head poised on an elegant slender neck with one curl coiled round. The whole thing is a noble piece of work with its gradations of colouring from dark green-grey to dove-grey and white, and of texture from plain stone to highly polished marble.

He was the last male of his line : Justice of the Common Pleas and Chancellor to Frederick Prince of Wales, of an excellent reputation for bounty and hospitality. His youngish wife died before him : *Siste et defle*, etc. After them came heiresses who in two generations carried the place away to the family of Coke of Holkham, who pulled the house down and sold the land.

But before that the house had had its vicissitudes, above all during the period of the Civil War. We derive a fairly full account of events there, and of happenings to its inmates, from the *Memoirs of the Verney Family*.

These neighbouring Buckinghamshire families formed, as

in every county, a close-knit, well-defined cousinage, with
their own friendships and feuds, their quarrels and joys.
Verneys of Claydon, Dentons of Hillesden, Hampdens of
Great Hampden, Temples of Stowe, Grenvilles of Wotton :
one sees the picture moving through the conflicts, the Civil
War, of the seventeenth century into the serene calm,
well-established and secure, of the Whig oligarchy of the
eighteenth. It is the connection between the Verneys and
the Dentons that is closest and to that that we owe so much
of our knowledge of their common family-life. Though they
are all gone now, the fields remember them. The tradition
is that two black trumpeters in red used to sound a reveillé
from the hill at Hillesden to be answered by two trumpeters
from the other hill. In the intervals left by passing planes
one can hear those echoes still.

The foundation of the close relations that subsisted for a
century between the two families was the marriage between
Margaret Denton, eldest daughter of the house, and Sir
Edmund Verney, the King's Standard-bearer, who fell at
Edgehill, torn between loyalty to his master and his inner
conviction that Parliament was in the right. Margaret's
mother, Lady Denton, was a Temple of Stowe : a formidable, dominating old dowager with all the cross-grained
character of her family. But like such women she was an
excellent manager, a tower of strength to her numerous
family, and she had a way with children down to the third
generation : in her time Hillesden was a matriarchy. Her
daughter always came back to her mother for her confine-
ments and almost always one or other of the Verney children
was with the grandmother for the benefit of " Hillesden's
sweet air ". Stern with everybody else, the old lady was
gentle with her great-grandchildren, and we find her pleading with Ralph Verney that his little Mun should not be
whipped for being rustic and shy. " i heare he is disliked, he
is so strange. Sonn, you did see he was not soe, nor is not
soe, to any where he is aquanted, and he must be wone with
fair menes. . . . i pray tell him [Ralph's father] from me,
I thought he had more witt then to thinck a childe of his

adge woulde be a quanted presently. He knowes the childe
was feloe good a nofe in my house. i praye shewe him what
I have written abought him, and be shore that he be not
frited by no menes; he is of a gentel swet nature, sone
corrected." " Spare the rod, spoil the child " : the horrible
adage throws light on the ways of our forefathers : life was
apt to be a strenuous struggle for survival for the children.

Troubles of another sort came over the marriage of a
younger daughter, another Margaret, who, having been left
a rich widow, was much sought after. Her mother objected
to one well-qualified suitor because he did not live in Bucks ;
the daughter observes tartly, " it was knowne before ever
he came to the howes where his estate laye ". It was quite
a good one : £2500 a year in demesne, £800 p.a. parsonage
land held of the Church, subject only to £300 old rent and
his mother's jointure of £100 p.a. Old Lady Denton could
hardly gainsay that : "for the man, my mother sayes she
canot as far as she sees Dislike him, & for my owne part
god send me a good hus:, & I care not wher his land lies ".
The truth was that her mother favoured a nephew of Lord
Falkland's, with a still larger estate, " but i am soe much
against it that I will for no conditiones in the world here of
it. . . . Suer I am not so fond as to be in love with any at
tow days sight." Fortunate for her that, being left well-off,
she could choose for herself.

These two suitors, cancelling each other out, were followed by Lord Howard of Escrick, a widower with five
children. This was no recommendation to Lady Denton,
for though she recognised that " he is honorablye desendede,
& upon report is onest & worthye ", still " i wil speake it
to you I should never ventar upon so many children as 5,
althoughe the ware wel provided for, for you know it is a
grate family ". However, she did not dare to oppose the
match, pressed as it was by Lord Pembroke and other great
personages at Court.

Her daughter took the matter in her own hands and
married somebody off her own bat : the son of Lord Eure,
a North Country Catholic peer of no particular fortune.

She had evidently been looking out for someone she fancied. Having been married once before, she knew. At once alarm and despondency spread throughout the family. Ralph Verney wrote to his father, the Standard-bearer, now on the Scottish expedition with the King : " Oh Sr shee is married, shee is married, and therefore now tis past recall. this unlucky deed was don before I mistrusted ever twas." His father replied from the campaign : " This woman laye soe neare my heart that I shall find her folly ther whilst I have an hower to live ". She must have been an attractive girl for them to feel like that about her ; but no doubt the thought of a fortune slipping out of the family had something to do with their grief.

Old Lady Denton was furious and in her anger blamed her grandson, Ralph Verney : " Your mother writes me word about a samite gowne, i remember i did here before of such a thinge, but now i pray tel her if she would provide sack cloth and line with asshis, then I mought morne for the folie of my wise disobedient children ". Only Ralph's father, Sir Edmund, was spared from this general commination : " for she often saith you have dealt wisely and honestly and lovingly in this businesse, but all the rest of her children are fooles, and the night before I came from Hillesdon she told me that (except you) wee had all dealt unfaithfully with her ".

There was in fact nothing against the young man, who was a gallant handsome fellow, save his religion. It was his Catholicism that the old lady had taken so much against — and the disappointment of her own projects. But a visit from the repentant, but safely married couple did a world of good ; and Mrs. Eure's sister writes : " the party [*i.e.* the old lady] is beter contented a great dell, and showes him more respecke then I thought she would a done ". She even went so far as to be willing for the young couple to live with her at Hillesden ; but her daughter was not inclined to risk that : " I must confes to you I like it not by aney meanes, nayther do I thinke as he will ".

Her intention was, " to youse all the meanes I can to

convert hime, for if I live neere London I can have the best
devines to my own house, and besides I intend to keepe on
myselfe ". Actually it was she that was converted : not
surprising considering that she was much in love with the
husband she had found for herself. When he was killed, in
the autumn of the year 1644, that brought such disasters
upon the house at Hillesden, one of the women wrote of him :
" a gallant man, the whole nasion has a lose in him ; he
had but one fault ". That was his religion, for both the
Dentons and the Verneys were strong Protestants. Lady
Sussex wrote to Ralph : " Your ante is I believe a very
sad woman for the lose of her fine husbande — I belive he
hath not left her so good a wido as he founde her ". The
young Royalist colonel evidently had the suffrage of all the
women ; his inconsolable widow wrote of him as " the
galentest man that ever I knew in my Life ".

But within the year she consoled herself with another
husband. Her brother, the delightful Doctor, writes to
Ralph : " I hope for the best, for I have great reason to
believe she will quickly marry & (which is my comfort) to
a Protestant this time ". Her third husband was the second
son of Lord Sherard, another soldier, captain in the army
of the Dutch States. Within a year he too was dead. She
certainly had an improvident way with husbands. But by
this time her mother was no longer there to impede or
advance her marrying again. Old Lady Denton died before
the Civil War brought ruin upon the house.

Her figure loomed so large in the family that we hear little
of her husband ; but that Ralph Verney was much attached
to him we learn from a passionate letter of regret : " The
greate God in whose hand is the soull of every livinge thinge
hath by death taken my grandfather into an endlesse life ".
His friend advises him to console himself and divert his
thoughts with *Breerwood's Logicke* and *The Figures and the
Tropes Rhetoricall*. Shortly after, his mother died : " Let me
be buried in leade att Claydon next where yr ffather porposes
to ly himselfe, and lett no strandger winde me, nor doe nott
lett me bee striptte, but put a cleane smoke over me . . .

and lett my fase be hid and doe you stay in the roome and see me wounde and layed in the firste coffin. . . ." (It is just like the last instructions that Elizabeth Henchard, in *The Mayor of Casterbridge*, left after her death: evidence of the absolute fidelity of Hardy to the old country life.)

After the death of Lady Denton — much concerned to the last about the disposition of her large fortune — her son Alexander reigned in her stead. He married Mary Hampden, a cousin of the great John Hampden; and we hear of a family gathering at Claydon for the christening of their son. At Hillesden a large family were gathered in the house in the first years of the Civil War: not only Alexander and his wife and children, but his sister Mrs. Isham and hers, and his unmarried sister Susan.

Such was the household upon which disaster descended in the year 1644.

The Dentons were Royalists; the convictions of Ralph Verney and his father, as we have seen, on the side of Parliament. But this did not break the good feeling that subsisted between the two houses. At the beginning of 1644 Mrs. Isham complains of having soldiers quartered upon them: " one hundred men in our one House, which my thinkes is very harde to be put in one house, and we being allmost 50 in family ". Hillesden lay in an awkward strategic position out there in the no-man's-land between the King's headquarters at Oxford and the Parliament's forces at Aylesbury, covering the north road to London.

Early in 1644 the Royalists decided to fortify the place. Colonel Smith took command, dug a trench half a mile in circumference, enclosing the house and church. Forage parties from both sides swept the country round; and one day Royalist troopers drove off cattle belonging to a tenant of Mr. Hampden's. There was a characteristic dispute as to the rights and wrongs of it — in the middle of a Civil War — and the injured tenant carried his complaint from the Royalists at Hillesden to the Parliamentary commanders at Aylesbury. This woke them up to the danger of allowing the place to be turned into a strong-point; and a surprise was attempted by a force of three hundred horse and foot. It was driven off and the Parliamentary commanders prepared for a regular attack in strength. Half the forces were under the command of Colonel Oliver Cromwell — ominous name, if the Royalist defenders had known.

For with his usual dynamic drive, he caught them in the midst of their preparations to stand a siege. Colonel Smith was still engaged on his trenches, and throwing up a mound on which to mount the small ordnance he had obtained from Oxford, when out of the March dawn, from over the hill at Claydon, Cromwell appeared with overwhelmingly superior forces. A parley was sounded and unconditional surrender demanded. When this was refused, the place was carried by assault. From the first the defenders were overpowered, and driven into the house and church. A second assault followed and the church taken : you may still see the bullet-holes in the old oak door. Seeing the hopelessness of any further defence, Colonel Smith surrendered the house on promise of quarter.

The Parliamentary forces had certainly made a good haul at Hillesden : a store of ammunition in the church — to think what a narrow escape it had from destruction — the cellars of the house full of beer, the stables full of horses, the yards of oxen and beasts. In the house a large sum of money was discovered behind the wainscot and in the roof. There were some forty casualties among the defenders. Sir Alexander Denton and his brother were marched off into captivity, the former protesting that he had only come to the house two days before to remove his family thence on the King's placing a garrison there. It was of no avail : off he was marched into the imprisonment from which he did not emerge. Next day, on the rumour of large forces approaching from Oxford — as usual, too late — the house was fired and burnt down : a Cromwellian touch. Having accomplished his purpose, he retired on Buckingham.

It was a melancholy procession of women, with such belongings as they could collect together, that made across the fields to take refuge at Claydon with their relations.

E

Penelope Verney was among them and wrote: " We were not shamefully used in any way by the souldiers, but they took everything and I was not left scarce the clothes of my back ". Mrs. Isham described how " Hillesden park pales be every one up and burned or else carried away, and the Denton children like to beg ". On his way to the Tower, Sir Alexander wrote to his steward to " take a viewe of the house that was burnt upon Tuesday, that I may have some certayne information of what destruction is fallen upon mee, and whether it bee possible to rebuild those walls that are standing if the distractions of the times should settle ". Ralph Verney wrote to his brother: " Suffer me to tell you how much I am afflicted for the ruine of sweet Hillesden and the distresses that happened to my aunt and sisters. God knowes what has become of my unhappie brother that was there taken."

The taking of Hillesden had its consequences in two romantic episodes to which the stress — and the excitement — of war gave opportunity. One of the Parliamentary assaulters, Captain Jaconiah Abercrombie, fell for one of the distressed Royalist ladies, Sir Alexander's unmarried sister, Susan, already well on the way to becoming an old maid. Like his commander, the Captain must have been very prompt in action. Three days after, John Denton writes: " My sister Susan, her new husband Captain Abercromy is quartered at Addington ". But in June we hear from gossipy Mrs. Isham — now silent enough under her slab in the chapel — " My sis: Susans marage is to be accomplished very suddnly if her captive be not killed, it tis him as did first plunder Hilsdon. . . . The Capt. his land is in Irerland, he is half Skotts, half Irish. I think fue of her frinds lik it, but if she hath not him she will never have any, it is gone so far." What is the explanation ? Are we to conclude that the impetuous Ulsterman carried his woman off with him as part of the spoils ? Anyway, their brief happiness, snatched out of the chances of war, was soon at an end : next year he was killed by a party of Cavaliers from Boarstall and was buried at Hillesden among the family whose house he had plundered and whose daughter he had married.

A second match was not much longer in train. The Royalist commander, Colonel Smith, had in the course of the operations fallen in love with Sir Alexander's young daughter, Margaret. His imprisonment in the Tower along with Sir Alexander advanced his suit. In August we hear from Mrs. Isham, who was sharing imprisonment with her men-folk, her brother and her husband, in order to look after them : " I thinke it will be a happy mach if these ill times doth not hindre it, but he is still a Prisenor. So you may thinke itt a bolde venter, but if these times hold, I thinke they will be non men lefte for woman." She at any rate was determined to do her best, and with the aid of Susan Verney procured the Colonel's escape — for which they earned a spell of incarceration on their own account. Truly did Dr. Denton declare that " women were never soe usefull as now ". As for Colonel Smith, he died in his bed, a baronet.

Sir Alexander's troubles were not yet at an end. There was his eldest son, John, a gallant fighting fellow who was shot through the thigh " endeavouring to gett my house then in the parliaments possession ". In August he was killed in leading the assault on a Parliamentary outwork at Abingdon. He seems to have been a well-loved young man — " that good young man whose very enemies lament him ", one account says. " I must ever account it as on of my greatest and particular afflictions to loose the man that you and I did love soe well," wrote Ralph Verney to Sir Alexander, " but this is our comfort, hee lived and died most gallantly, and questionlesse is now most happy." What a consolation — that is not for us — it was to them in their day to be so sure of a better world ! Not long after, Sir Alexander received his quietus : he was not yet fifty, but the succession of blows had worn out his resistance. He died in captivity on New Year's day, 1645, and was brought home at last to Hillesden.

He had borne his troubles with all submission, in the spirit of his contemporary, Herrick :

Rapine has yet took nought from me :
But if it please my God I be
Brought at the last to th' utmost bit,
God make me thankful still for it.
I have been grateful for my store,
Let me say grace when there's no more.

This was far from being the spirit of Aunt Isham — as
she was known to all the family : she did not cease to
complain of her misfortune to all her relations : " For our
clothes we must sew fig leaves together, we lost all by fier,
and since I have had but one gown. I could wish as it would
last me forty yeres as the childrenes of Iserells did, but,
however, now I am come to town, I have not where withal
to buye another." She had not lost all interest in the world's
affairs, however, when she adds : " Ye fust of May but
never so dull an one, and so fue chases [chaises] in hide
Parke as I heare ".

With the end of the Civil War, affairs became more
settled and people began to make the best of things, whether
they liked them or no. They began to reconstruct their lives
on the old foundations in the old places. Already in 1648
we hear of Hillesden " they are building there againe and
intend to sett upp a little house where the old one stood ".
In spite of Ralph Verney's lament, under the rule of Cromwell's major-generals : " I confess I love Old England very
well, but as things are carried heere the gentry cannot joy
much to bee in it " — or perhaps rather because of it, there
was a tendency for the gentry to draw together, whether
Royalist or Parliamentarian, in self-defence against the new
order. It was the foundation upon which the Restoration
came about. We find one of the Isham correspondents
writing : " In these degenerating times, the gentry had need
to close neerer together, and make a banke and bulwarke
against that sea of Democracy which is over running them :
and to keep their descents pure and untainted from that
Mungrill breed, which would faigne mixe with them ".

In reaction to their exclusion from politics and power,
and to the social dulness of Puritan rule, the gentry went in

more and more for horse-racing and gambling : already the
gracious wind of the Restoration is blowing. Life has
returned to the house of Hillesden, and Aunt Isham, who
dearly loves a little gambling, complains that she is quite
worn out by the late hours her rakish soldier-nephew, Harry
Verney, keeps : " he will never give one over as Longe as
one is able to sit up ". Visits are resumed ; the connection
between the families is as close and affectionate as ever.
The chief bond is between Ralph Verney and dear Uncle
Doctor away in London. But now the Ishams are staying
at Claydon ; now Ralph is with his cousins at Hillesden.

His sister Penelope married another Denton, John Denton
of Fawley in Oxfordshire. They were always in trouble.
Now her husband is in prison at Oxford Castle for debt,
and Pen is " almost brought to deth's dore . . . this 3 days
I have not eate more then a mess of milk and a negg. I
must sell myself to my sking, goods & all to defray this great
chargis." Their three children died young. And then it
turned out that her husband was cracked : " Mr. Denton
has bin so outragious with me, that he has run after me with
his knif in his hand and vowed to stob me ". It throws an
odd light on the attitude of earlier centuries towards insanity
that at a wedding feast at Claydon an elaborate practical
joke was played on him : a letter was composed telling him
that his mother was labouring to have his younger brother
made a lord, but that if he would part with £500 he
should have the honour himself; that his kinswoman, Lady
Studdall, was working so successfully for his interests at
Court that it was thought he was to be made a Lord of
the Privy Council, and so on. There this cruel jest remains
among the Verney papers, carefully endorsed " A Sham
Letter to John Denton that is crackt ".

But a year or two and he was dead. He had not been
an unlovable man : he had had something of that quality of
the Dentons. Sir Ralph wrote to his sister : " though you
have been unhappy in him, yet hee was a Gentleman &
your Husband, & twill be your Honour to conceale his
faults ". Pen put on handsome mourning for him, but she

was not inconsolable. She set up house in London with her gallant racing brother, Harry, whom she adored; there was not much love lost between her and the Dentons.

Before the Restoration the young squire at Hillesden died. He had never been able to get upsides with the devastated inheritance he took over from his father: the losses had not been made good, debts accumulated, he ran through his wife's fortune: he was no manager, things were too much for him. Shortly after, the bells of Claydon and Hillesden rang out and bonfires burned on the hills for the return of the King. Pen Denton expressed everybody's thoughts in her woman's way: " I pray God send we may live to see peace in our times, and that friends may live to in joye each other ".

Aunt Isham, who had for so long been a feature of the landscape, was next to go, scattering little bequests to all her female relations: to one " my little silver grater and my silver measure ", to another " my diamond Bodkin but first put a stone in it ", to a third " my little gold ring with a posie Ever Constant ". Except for her brother, the Doctor, she seems to have had most personality of all her family; " she lived & dyed a good Xstian ", he wrote of her, " and the best of us can doe no more ". There is a genuine tribute to her personality behind the formal phrases of her Latin epitaph in the church where she worshipped from her girlhood and where she had witnessed such vicissitudes: " Pia Mater! Certa Amica! Optima Conjux! Hic jacet quae virtute sua praelucet vivis sibique fit superstes matrona tam tenax, amicitiae tam jurata cultrix. . . ."

So long as Sir Ralph Verney and the Doctor lived — and they both lived well into their ninth decade — relations between the two families continued close. But there was a new generation at Hillesden, where another Alexander, grandson of him of the Civil War, was growing up in the reign of Charles II. On the King's death we find him consulting his great-uncle, Sir Ralph, " whether it be my duty for to goe into mourning . . . being in the Country, or if it be necessary for me, then whether my wife must doe the like, & whether it must be black cloth or Crape. I would not be singular."

His wife was Hester Harman, only daughter of Nicholas Harman of Middleton Stony in Oxfordshire : beautiful and an heiress. Her pathetic story is told by John Verney : " After she had had 7 children, on Thursday 29 March 1688, she left his house and him, & Monday 17 September 1688, she was delivered of a girle, which he would not own, named Eliz. who soon died. This his wife Hester died in Aug. 1691 about Spittlefields & was buryed in Stepney Ch. meanely." The poor woman's fortune he had apparently already squandered. Sir Ralph wrote once to let Alexander know that he had heard of Hester in London ; he only replied that he wished her at Jamaica. Within a few years he too was dead : like her, still young. The Diary of Narcissus Luttrell gives us the clue to their melancholy story. In June 1689 he writes : " A tryall was this term at the common pleas barr between Mr Denton of Buckinghamshire and Mr Thomas Smith (son of Sir William, late a justice of peace of Middlesex), for enticeing away and lyeing with his wife ; which being proved, the jury gave Mr Denton £5000 damages ".

With these later generations it seems the Denton stock was failing ; they had never been long-lived. And with the deaths at length of Sir Ralph and the Doctor the intimacy goes out of the relations between Verneys and Dentons, that had subsisted so long, and with such fortunate results for posterity. A slightly hostile note creeps into the references of one to the other, exacerbated by politics. For after the Revolution of 1688, young Sir Edmund Denton came under the influence of the Whig Lord Wharton and marched along with the Temples in Buckinghamshire politics ; while the Verneys adhered to the Church and Tory interest : a curious transposition of roles from earlier days. We hear of Sir Edmund become " rich and great " ; perhaps by marriage, for he married the daughter of a Court official who was Clerk of the Board of Green Cloth. He held some office himself, which he lost on Queen Anne's accession and promptly quarrelled with his wife. He too died young, and is buried under a finely cut slate slab in the chancel of the church.

It is pleasant to record that in later years relations improved and neighbourly visits were paid between the two houses. In October 1709 we read of all the Verneys being invited to Lady Denton's, " and a fine entertainment we had ; it was a Leaven dishes the first course, and a Doe killed on purpose upon this occasion ". Alas, that we cannot keep up the standards of our forefathers ! There was a large company to enjoy the Michaelmas venison.

Judge Denton succeeded his brother : the last of the male line at Hillesden. He was evidently a hospitable, agreeable, easy kind of man, a very worthy representative for the family to end with. He had scholarly inclinations and was a friend of Browne Willis and Parson Cole of Bletchley, who describes a visit to Hillesden in the autumn of 1735. He calls the house a good old one, on a beautiful hill, commanding a delightful prospect ; before it a large parterre ; below, a canal ; below that, a very bold terrace ; and through the gardens, charming vistas terminated by groups of trees and windmills. It must have been delightful. But " the best thing belonging to this place is its master ; to speak of whose humanity, probity and bounty, would be like telling the world that the warmth of the sun produces the fruits of the earth ". The Judge was — have we not guessed it already ? — a martyr to the gout. " I cannot say that I am much better for the country," he writes to his neighbour at Claydon, " though my spirits and appetite are better but my pains are very violent." His neighbour replies wishing he may find benefit from " Hillesden's sweet air " — the long correspondence between Verneys and Dentons ends on that appropriate note — and with the hope that " your pains will cease quite ". With the spring, they ceased for ever.

So much for the Dentons at Hillesden.

But half the richness of English history lies in the way layer upon layer is to be descried under the surface by the discerning eye. Before the Dentons there were the Courtenays. And there lies a very nice point about the nature of the Reformation changes in this country. As the result of them, eligible estates like Hillesden were apt all over the country to fall away from the great absentee nobles consuming their substance away at the Court or in some great house, and to come into the hands of smaller families who made their homes on the spot, cultivated them for all they were worth, identified themselves with them, prospered or declined with the place itself. In fact we may say that the heart of those changes, the permanent upshot of them, was the rise of the gentry; the symbol, some such thing as here at Hillesden — the arms of the Dentons painted on the east wall where once stood the statue of the Saint.

The fabric of the church, save for their monuments, knows nothing of the Dentons — except that it holds their dust. It belongs to the century before they came, itself a moving memorial to the sense of beauty and the art of the late medieval craftsmen. The parishioners of Hillesden, all those coloured medieval tillers of the soil, those ploughmen and peasants in from the fields, and the distant Black Canons of Notley who owned the rectory and so were responsible for the chancel, must have been determined to do themselves proud. Look at the magnificence of the chancel: high up under the roof a choir of angel-figures, elaborately carved in stone with traces of their colouring still remaining, red and blue, ending up with angel-musicians playing upon their organs, their viols, lutes and pipes. How it speaks of the certainty of the world of faith, the unity of all things visible and invisible!

What this chancel must have been like in the first flourish of its beauty with all the glass in its windows — that forgotten art — red and blue and green and gold! There are lights remaining in only one window to tell us something of what we have lost — wonderfully vivid scenes in the life of St. Nicholas, patron of sailors and all in peril on the sea. Here is the boy in red falling into the sea, the sailors hoisting sail: the inscription, *Cadit puerulus quem mox*

salvat Nicholaus. Here again is a three-masted ship, with
rigging and sails furled, at the quayside with men unloading
corn and tying it up in sacks : the whole full of life and
action and that naïveté of spirit which enabled the medievals
to transmit their vision so powerfully to the world. (Our
dreams have no permanence, no lasting quality, in com-
parison.)

I wonder if we owe the theme of this window to that
John Courtenay, an earlier owner of Hillesden in the
thirteenth century, who was once in great peril on the sea
by reason of a tempest rising at night. The mariners
expected shipwreck ; but he bade them have courage and
labour one hour more, for that would be the time when his
monks of Ford rose for matins and they would be praying
for him, and by their prayers they would be preserved from
danger. One of the company said that there was then no
hope for they were all still asleep. Courtenay answered that
they interceded day and night, and " because I love them,
and they love me, I know and verily believe that already
they are interceding to God for me and mine, in safety and
in calamity ". And immediately the tempest ceasing, they
all came safe to land.

So, our minds teeming with memories, half in a trance
so strong was the impression that forgotten place had made
upon us, we went down the little winding road to where
the pastures opened at the foot, on either side. Looking
at the velvety emerald-green of shadow resting on the
ploughed land — suddenly the All Clear sounded across the
countryside. Astonished, we could not believe our ears —
the war now sometime over and behind us. For a moment
we stood there incredulous, struck-still, in the road, the
familiar nightmare once more returned. Then a few steps
forward around the bend and a David Cox scene presented
itself : the corner of a plaster cottage, a little girl pushing a
wheelbarrow, with a red hat to punctuate. The siren went
again across the fields of Hillesden, now behind us.

We went on our way to Buckingham, the road trodden
by so many Dentons in the past — one disquieted, troubled

mind turning backwards from the nightmare of our time to the troubles of theirs, and before them to the troubles and the bloodshed of the Courtenays, and before them the de Veres and the Boelbecs, who held Hillesden from the Giffards, who got it from the Conqueror ; and before that, to Alric the thegn who held if of the Confessor, and so back to the original Saxon settler who gave his name to this place on the hill, standing above the swirl and conflict of peoples out of which we came.

DEAR DR. DENTON

AN ENGLISH GENTLEMAN OF THE
SEVENTEENTH CENTURY

OF all the gallery of portraits with which the *Verney Memoirs* present us, there is none more appealing than that of Dr. William Denton. There is Sir Edmund Verney, the Standard-bearer, brave, impulsive to a fault, torn between conflicting claims of conscience and duty; or old Lady Denton, generous, dominating, indomitable, between whom and her son-in-law there was great mutual respect; or gossipy, chirpy Aunt Isham with her love of cards, her courage and resource; gallant young Mun Verney, among those put to the sword at Drogheda, or Jack Denton, killed on the bulwark at Abingdon; or the poor mad lady who brought the White House at Claydon into the family — does she haunt it still, I wonder? Then there is Ralph Verney, sensitive and scrupulous, with his courtesy and consideration for others, a pillar of kindly strength to his family and all his friends. But his uncle, the Doctor — dear Dr. Denton — surpasses them all in the vivacity, the naturalness, —so life-like and homely, like an old and cherished garment with its comfortable creases and folds — with which his character comes across to us.

His letters are a complete revelation of the man he was, if they are not — at least in the fragmentary way in which they necessarily appear in the *Verney Memoirs* — of all his interests of mind. For, as we shall see, he was deeply interested in the public affairs of his time, and had contributions of his own to make to its political and religious thinking. These letters we owe to the abiding love there was between the Doctor and his nephew, that lasted unbroken all their lives: that friendship which makes the backbone to that vast, and otherwise rather disparate, family correspondence.

In his letters the Doctor depicts himself for us : shrewd, whimsical, humorous — as full of character as an egg is full of meat; for ever busy and bustling, infinitely kind-hearted and in consequence badgered by everybody to do them good turns — which he usually manages to do. Now he is neglecting his own business for his nephew's, looking after Ralph's interests while he is away in exile in France, running down to Claydon to see to this and that, buying books for him in London and sending them over, keeping him in touch with everything. Or he is helping to place young John Verney as an apprentice to a merchant in the City; or finding preferment for discontented Betsy Verney's parson husband. Now he is sick in bed with a bedful of books — for the Doctor is very much a reading man, and given to writing too. Or he is chaffing Ralph for " a hob-nail clowne ", because he won't come up to town, or he is laughed at himself for being robbed in his coach by highwaymen — all the family thought that a great joke. Now he is buying land in the Fens and losing on every transaction. And always when people are in trouble they turn to the Doctor, for under that cheerful, busy exterior there is a very tender heart. The griefs of the world, the sorrows with which he was brought professionally so much into contact, never hardened his responses or deadened his humanity. What a friend said of Ralph Verney was no less true of Dr. Denton : " You are now become, I think, the Generall Trustee of all that know you ".

There is a portrait of him at Claydon that confirms these traits; rather finer-looking than we should have expected and certainly more handsomely dressed. But then, he was a gentleman of good family, and he would naturally put on his best clothes to have his picture painted. There he is with his silk cloak thrown round one shoulder, the broad masculine wrist supporting the hand hidden under a fold of the voluminous material; the pointed cravat tied high up at the throat, his doublet buttoned so as to reveal a slash of white shirt. The head has an aristocratic poise with an interesting sidelong look at the world; fine wide-apart eyes under the high arched brows, that give the dominant

expression to the face, a humorous, quizzical look; the
nose long and fleshy, the lips full. The Doctor seems to
be wearing his own hair curled over his shoulders, a light
moustache and a little goatee beard such as was worn at the
time of the Civil War.

He wrote a neat, precise hand; his letters were short
and to the point, as was suitable for a busy over-worked
doctor with a large practice in London. And that leads us
to another side of him which the *Verney Memoirs* do not
present. He was a good deal of a scholar, and a writer
of some interest. Anthony Wood tells us, " he hath written
several things ", and then adds wryly, " but nothing of his
faculty ". Wood could hardly approve of the Doctor's
writings : he was a high Tory, the Doctor a Whig. The
fact is that his main line of interest was in current affairs :
in the controversy between Protestantism and the Romanis-
ing tendencies of the monarchy under Charles II and James
II, in the struggle between the authoritarianism of the time
in Church and State, monarchical absolutism with its
corollary in the doctrine of Passive Obedience on one side
and the Protestant standpoint of liberty of the individual
conscience and the rights of the people on the other. It is
fascinating to observe how in the course of the struggle,
which expressed itself in the heated party-politics of the
time, in its violent polemics and controversies, a scion of a
strict Royalist house like the Doctor, who also happens to
be a physician-in-ordinary to both Charles I and Charles II,
is driven more and more to take a line contrary to the
monarchy and emerges in the end as a convinced supporter
of the Revolution of 1688.

The Doctor was a moderate; a plain Church of England
man holding to the middle way, humane and sensible. He
hated Popery and he hated autocracy : he lived at a time
when the growing shadow of Louis XIV's domination lay
across half the Continent and threatened dangerously our
own security. He believed in people being allowed to think
things out for themselves; he had no undue regard for
monarchs : he believed in the rule of Law, by which kings

were as much bound as peoples. He held that government existed for the benefit of the ruled, not the pleasure of the rulers. He was a very characteristic Englishman; his were the convictions of the great majority of English people.

And indeed he has a certain historical importance, in that his writings — even if few seem ever to have read them — express the plain man's point of view, though tricked out with a good deal of contemporary erudition. From shortly after the Restoration to the time of the Revolution he put forth some half a dozen tractates on political and church questions, in which we can trace very clearly the way the middle body of opinion moved away from the Stuart kings, playing about as they were with Romanism and ideas of autocracy, completely contrary to the plain sense of the country. It was the last that prevailed and got rid of them in the end, and Dr. Denton expressed it. He wrote an admirable prose style, direct and simple, in the new manner of the Restoration; even if he overloaded himself with citations of learned authorities, also after the manner of the seventeenth century. Perhaps he was a bit old-fashioned even in his day, and that accounts for his having been insufficiently regarded. But his character comes through his writing : his moderation, his sense, his plain Protestantism, his humanity, his whimsical humour. And a writer who in one of his tracts replies effectively to a work of Milton's and in another provides an interesting parallel to Locke's *Treatise on Civil Government*, has his place. He deserves not to be forgotten. But, in fact, he has to be called back from oblivion. With such a personality it is a pleasure to bring him back to life and give him once more a name.

William Denton was the youngest son of the numerous family of Sir Thomas Denton and Susan his wife, who was a Temple of Stowe. The child was born at Stowe in April 1605, and perhaps he took after his mother's family, that interesting stock, for nothing in the Denton heredity pointed to what he would become, with his intellectual interests and humours. There were among his brothers and sisters several characters whom we already know : Sir Alexander Denton, his eldest brother; Margaret his eldest sister, mother of Ralph Verney ; Mrs. Isham, the much-married Mrs. Eure, and Susan who went off with the Puritan captain.

At the usual enough age of sixteen he was sent to Oxford, where he matriculated from Magdalen Hall in November 1621. In the very next term Edward Hyde came up to the Hall : so it is likely enough that they knew each other. These years were the heyday of the Hall ; it had a prominent and successful tutor who gave it a decidedly Puritan tone, and so, many leading Puritan families sent their sons there. It is an influence that must be remembered in the make-up of the young Denton. Three years later he took his B.A., his M.A. in 1627. But he remained on in Oxford to study physic, living with and ultimately practising under a noted physician, Dr. Ashworth. He took his medical degrees and was licensed to practise medicine in 1634, " the only pro-ceeder in his faculty this year ". Meanwhile in 1630, his nephew Ralph, only seven years his junior, came up to Magdalen Hall, and it was at Oxford that their friendship was made fast.

After taking his doctorate he left Oxford to practise in London, and in 1636 was sworn physician-in-ordinary to the King. Three years later he attended Charles I on the Scottish expedition — the unfortunate Bishops' War that set the subsequent landslide in motion. Sir Edmund Verney was also with the King, and both the Doctor and Ralph were alarmed for him, knowing his impetuosity in action. The Doctor wrote, with his usual good sense, reflecting on the folly of the Court which had brought things to such a pass : " Ralph, wee have noe neede of foolinge, wee have an enough of that here ; if the wisest were not a little guilty of it, wee might bee happier then now we are likly to be. . . . I pray buy me Dr Read his treatise of wounds and send it to me as soone as you can ; it is a thinn booke in 4°, & if it be only stitched it will be noe more then 2 quire of paper." Young Ralph fears for his father and replies : " Oh Dr if my father goes to the Borders he is lost, I know his corrage will bee his distruction. Did he beget us to noe other end but to make us the sad spectacles of the world? Will noething moove him? Deare Dr: try, & try againe & set all his freinds uppon him, be more then earnest, night & Day perswade him, give him noe rest till hee hath yielded to stay." The Doctor did his best. He now wants "a paire of harbinge sissers . . . yr father is yett well in body & att a good distance from the borders. Be confident that I will leave noe stone unmoved that I conceave may knocke yr ffathers fightinge designes on the head & preserve him; if I can but keepe him from goeinge out in parties, I hope he will returne with safety." The very next day Ralph's father was one of a band of horsemen in a fair way to be cut off in an ambush. The Scottish expedition came to an end in fiasco and defeat; but such a man was fairly certain to fall early in action, and in fact he was killed at Edgehill, in the first battle of the Civil War.

Thus Ralph Verney was left at the head of his family and connection, with all its responsibilities, in this time of danger. He shared his father's inner sympathy with the cause of Parliament and refused to fight on the King's side, as against his Royalist relations, the Dentons. He remained on at Westminster, a member of the House of Commons; and then, at the end of 1643, surprised everyone by refusing to take the Covenant, part of the engagement with the Scots into which Pym had entered for the sake of victory. He was the only member of the House to refuse. It was a dangerous and lonely course that he was now pursuing; but he was determined to follow only the dictates of his own conscience. It is very revealing of the times to observe the reactions of his friends. A cousin wrote, "In my opinion you steere a course wherein there is almost no hope of indemnity on either side, but certaynty of great losse and blame from both. If you shall say there is much to be disliked in ether partye, my thinkes that should not seeme strange, or alienate you totally from ether, for in these publicke divisions, where religion and liberty are indangerd all men ought to adhere

F

to that cause which is dictated to them to bee ye better and ye more harmless by ye light of nature and the most forcible indications of reason." Now we know the kind of principle that weighed in most people's minds in those distracted times. Ralph's brother, hearty, sporting Harry Verney, put it more bluntly when he urged him " to take the Pitt one way or other . . . these times are likely to hold very long, and beelive it, non will bee in soe sad a condition as those that stand newters ".

There is the plain horse-sense of the horsy man, and there was a good deal in it. But Ralph was a man of finer fibre, and he held on his way. It involved exclusion from Parliament and sequestration of his estates ; much searching of his conscience and the decision to go with his family into exile in France. "The separation of friends I find to be worse than the sequestration of estates from the continuance of which I daly implore our good God with a piece of our old Latany."

During Ralph's exile the Doctor took charge of his interests and affairs, kept him in touch with all that was going on, advised him as to his course of action, sent him books to occupy his mind. These were many and interesting : Milton's *Iconoclastes*, Prynne's book on Parliament, tracts on the Levellers, impeachments of Cromwell and Ireton, Bishop Andrewes and Hooker. Evidently the list represents the character of the Doctor's own reading — Church and State affairs and history. At some point during the war the Doctor had married — an agreeable, rather vulgar woman of the middle-class, with whom he was happy enough. But he entertained a great affection for Ralph's wife, Mary. He called her pet-names, " Landlady " and " Mischief " and " Devil-do-thy-worst ". And now he writes recommending Sclater to " Landlady's reading . . . it treats or rather indeed mencions Anti Xst . . . tell her it is now time to leave her Romantz : to please me it is one of the best bookis I ever read ; he is strangely piquante and short and strangely convincinge ". He recommends Ralph to occupy himself by translating Laud's *Book against Fisher* and Chillingworth into French, " for certainly never any books gave a greater blow to papacy than those two ". That was a cause the Doctor had very much at heart.

But the great business, as the war drew to a close, was how to get the sequestration off Ralph's estates. In this, involving endless lobbying and persistent pressing, the leading part fell to the Doctor. The difficulty was that in order to compound for the sequestration, Ralph had to acknowledge his delinquency, *i.e.* confess that he had assisted the King. This, Ralph could not and would not in conscience do : " if they make me petition as others doe that ' A. B. humbly sheweth hee hath assisted the King ', etc, 'tis a notorious lye, for I never assisted him in my life ". The Doctor's advice was that, since it was a question of making interest with those in power, Ralph should send over his wife : " though you should be my agent and sollicitour of all the men I knowe yett I am confident if you were here, you would doe as our sages doe, instruct your wife, and leave her to act it with committees, their sexe intitles them to many priviledges, and we find the comfort of them now more then ever ".

So Lady Verney came over, and the Doctor and she bustled about, interviewing lawyers and waiting upon the great. " Coaches are most infenett dear, and there is noe stirring forth without one or a chaise, the towne was neavor so full as tis now." The fact is that during the Civil War London was the safest place of residence in the country and was growing fast, while other towns languished and lagged behind. The Doctor tried to search out the reasons for various cases of sequestration ; he was encouraged to learn of someone being let off " whose only fault was that he went a woinge to his mistress att Woodstock before Eghill fight ". He thought this promising.

In addition the " honest Doctor ", as Mary calls him — we must remember that the word meant more to them in the seventeenth century — was anxious about her health : she was delicate and her pregnancy was advancing. The Doctor came to see her at least twice a day. In June she was brought to bed of a lusty boy. In July the Doctor writes,

" Landlady is churcht & well, but lookes ill enough ". He
put her on a course of steel, but the poor lady thought —
truly enough, when one thinks of seventeenth-century
medicines — " good broths and a good diett will doe me
more good then phissic, though the honest Dr will nott
beleeve itt, his love to us both makes him have soe much
care of me, and I tell him hee has toe much apprehention ".
In October came distressing news from France : Mary's
little girl had died and the Doctor had to break the news.
Ralph wrote, " Oh Dr. Dr. my poore Peg is happy but I
am your most afflicted and unfortunate servant. Tell mee
how and when this shall bee made knowne to her mother."
Meanwhile at Claydon the baby had died. The Doctor
found Mary " in her bed lamenting and very inquisitive of
me alsoe how her children did, expressinge that you had
sent her noe worde of them for a month or longer. I thought
it best to make but one business of both and soe I lett her
know how happy her gerle was."

For a time Mary was distracted with grief, her mind
wandering so that she hardly knew her friends. The fit
over, she recovered and came up to London to prosecute
Ralph's suit. " Your wife I thanke God is very well . . .
she hath not ben abroad since I told her of her daughter,
but I expect her this hour to come and eat a goose : for all
you condemned me to plum pudding and puddie all yet I
believe landlady will tell you she hath found good nappy
all to be very comfortable and to fatten her." The suit
was prospering too ; and at last the Doctor got Ralph's
petition through the House, through the good services
of Francis Drake, who had married the Doctor's niece :
" Deare Ralphe, I told you in my last that I would drive
on the naile furiously, and I have been as good as my
word, for the very next day I drave it beyond all the Pikes
of the house against the advice of most ". He thought
there was *digitus Dei* in it, for it was a very unpropitious
day, full of Scottish and Army business, and he was laughed
at for his pains. But things took a good turn and the
petition passed. " We have had some of our good frends

with us att dinner, our bellies are full and I have noe more
to say."

Before Mary left for France, her mission accomplished,
she was chief guest " att the honest Dr.'s, att his wife's
eldest daughter's wedding, whoe is married to Mr Gape the
apothicary . . . there is none of Dr.'s kindred there, butt
myselfe and Frank Drake and uncle John Denton ". On
Valentine's day the good apothecary entertained his grand
relations at his house. The Doctor to Ralph : " We are
all a house-warminge and you must not expect much ".
When the time came for Mary to go, he missed her sorely ;
he would have travelled down to the coast with her, but for
his wife's jealousy. " I have with much regret (pardon my
passion for her, for if she be so worthy of yr love, you cannot
blame me if I thinke her soe of mine) returned yr Jewell. . . .
I shall want her here to helpe sollicite, to rost me apples,
and poide me bread and sassages and make pottage, and
above all her good company, which I would envy anybody
but yr selfe." And later, " I have not eat one morsell of
good bread since mischief went. . . . Tell her that Prag-
maticus is for her owne proper use and not for yours, without
a capp and a knee and a kisse for me."

Public events did not cease to impinge on their lives ;
the distraction of the times had taken toll of both Dentons
and Verneys and was to do so again. Ralph's young
brother Mun was left penniless in London, and as usual it
fell to the Doctor to befriend him : " he hath neyther cloathes
to his back nor money to buy them, and is neyther able to
live in this town, nor able to set foot out of it, except somebody relieve him, and if I cannot or doe not, I doe not know
who will here ". Mun was anxious to serve under Ormonde
in Ireland : " You are the loadstone that may draw me all
over the world, and I am in paine untill I am with you ".
It drew him onwards to his death : he was killed in the
massacre after the storming of Drogheda. The Doctor to
Ralph : " My hart hath beene so sad since the newes of
Mun as I thinke hath not beene since Edgehill, but we must
not repine, it is God not the Sabeans, that takes all away,

let him do best what seems in his eyes ".

With the year 1648 affairs moved to a terrible crisis. The breakdown of negotiations between the King and the Army led to the Second Civil War and the invasion of England by the Scots. The Army was convinced that the King had been only playing for time with them, which was indeed true, and they determined to arraign him for blood-guiltiness. There was a general atmosphere of crisis and consternation among the people; opinions fluctuated daily, until the crisis was reached with the execution of the King. His blood ran for ever between the Puritan Revolution and the bulk of the English people. All these events and their reactions may be read in the Doctor's letters to Ralph away in France : they communicate the excitement of the time, the fluctuations of feeling day by day.

He had foretold the year before that if either party, Parliament or Army, could prevail without the King's support, they would clip his power. Now the Army were settling accounts with both. The Army are at the Parliament doors, and secure all the members they can light on that they suppose will obstruct their proceedings : it is Pride's Purge in progress. Frank Drake is among the members arrested. There is a strange consternation of spirits amongst all people. " I doubt before this comes to you our Kinge will be defunct, and it is feared the sword will govern instead of the crowne." In January the scaffolds are going up in Westminster Hall for the trial of the King : " it is almost every man's opinion that nothing will satisfie but his head ". As that day came near, " the confusions & distractions are everywhere soe greate that I know not where to wish my selfe but in Heaven ". After the King's execution : " We are now in the maddest world that ever we mortalls sawe, and have great reason to feare we doe but now begin to drinke the dreggs of our bitter cupp ".

That bitter moment over, the King's execution and his demeanour throughout his trial produced their inevitable reaction. The women generally were in mourning for him ; the men dared not, only some few. The King's book,

Eikon Basilike, made a most powerful impression upon the public; the Doctor promises to send it, but there is a prodigious demand for it. " The kinge's book, with his deportment, indurance, att his tryal and on the scaffold, hath amazed the whole kingdome, to see soe much courage, Xstianity and meekness in one man." After that, the Puritan Revolution could never put itself right with the English people : it held on to power only by the sword.

The development of the Doctor's views has a greater interest for us than it might appear. For it is too often taken for granted, even by students of the seventeenth century, that in the grand division between parties, Tories and Whigs sprang simply out of the Cavaliers and Parliamentarians of the Civil War. But the Whig Doctor came from a completely Royalist family; while the Verneys, whose sympathies were with Parliament against the Court, became Tories. Things are more complex and perverse in life than they look from the books.

The Doctor's solicitude for Ralph's wife proved only too much justified : in exile in France, at their house at Blois — in spite of visits to Avignon, a move to Montpellier, to Bourbon to drink the waters — she languished more and more of a slow consumption. Bravely she kept up her chaff with the Doctor, sending him waggish messages. From this side the water he sent injunctions, reproaches, remedies. Then the fatal words are pronounced : " I doubt my poore landlady will have *febrem lentam* which may in time consume her ". That time was nearer than they conceived. In Ralph's diary are the entries : " 5 May, 1650. I writ Dr. word I received his letter, but could write of no businesse, Wife beeing soe ill. 12 May, 1650. Oh my . . . my deare deare." Ralph was distracted by his loss ; his mind was grieved by the thought what sins of his had brought upon him such punishments. In the manner of the time, but with a meticulous scrupulousness characteristic of him, he examined his past and laid bare all the faults he could find to the Doctor.

The Doctor, who was a humble man of heart himself,

deprecated the role of confessor, though he thought it " not
to be monopolised by the priests only, but everyone is left
at libertie to whom to doe it ; but wherefor to me, who have
swallowed downe soe many & mighty sinns without remorse
or acknowledgment that I cannot but thinke these of yours
Peccadilloes. Oh that my soule were guiltie of noe higher ! "
The only fault the Doctor could find in Ralph, which he had
intimated " even soe longe agoe as when we were Academians
. . . is that you have beene ever thought to take pett upon
very small occasions against many, & then very hardly
reconcileable, which hath beene used as an argument to
me as inconsistent with love ". The Doctor used his
advantage to press Ralph to be reconciled with the parson
at Claydon, with whom there had been some bickering,
and with his brother Harry Verney, from whom he had
received much unkindness. Ralph was very amenable and
wrote back : " Dr. you are a right peace-maker, & cannot
misse of the reward, for you doe not only endeavour to
preserve peace where it is, but to restore it where it is lost.
I doubt I am too guilty of beeing hardly reconcilable . . .
wherfore I often strive against it in my praiers."

The more one reads of these family correspondences of
the Civil War and before, the more it is brought home to
one what good and conscientious people these were — particularly when one goes into their inner motives, as we can
through the evidences of their private letters. One is more
and more impressed by the modesty and goodness of these
men and women, by the careful watch they kept on their
actions, the scrutiny of their motives, all under the eye of the
religion in which they were brought up, which sustained
them in their troubles and enabled them to fashion such a
fabric of society with its standards of duty and service.
Today, now that it is passing — though not without handing
something of its own element on to a new order — we can
at least pay tribute to what the old was at its noblest. After
the turbulent world of the Tudors, the violence of the
Middle Ages, there was a delicacy, a moral refinement
among the early Carolines, such as one can see in their

portraits and in the portraits they involuntarily drew of themselves in their letters. Something of all that was lost from the world of the Restoration: a gay and cheerful society, full of *bonhomie* and enjoyment, of rips and rakes, with its strain of cynicism and its deflation of ideals — a world in which Clarendon and Evelyn, those survivors from the old, felt themselves not at home. The society that emerged from the stress of Civil War and the rule of the Saints lived its life on a lower plane: it had had too much high-mindedness: it was post-war: it was content to live. Ralph and the Doctor breathed the air of a purer, happier clime.

The Doctor was anxious to have Ralph come home; but things were too unsettled for one who could not subscribe to either party or any, and who had a scruple against Cromwellian government resting on force. At the same time Ralph could not be happy with the Royalist *émigrés* in Paris, with their intrigues and cabals and plots. He decided to go on a grand tour of Italy, taking his little son, Mun, with him. " I hope you have bussed the Lady of Loretto and have taken a Doctorshipp at least at Padua ", wrote the Doctor. Meanwhile Ralph asked him to go down and look into affairs at Claydon, which were giving cause for worry. " You need not go to Stow, for want of roome at Hillesdon, for you well know Claydon is neare & big enough, and therefore I pray let your summer quarters be there." The Doctor went down, but " to as little purpose as one would wish besides eatinge and drinking ". The steward's accounts were all in disorder, indeed he could give no statement of them. " He & I are at as great a lose about the accounts, & when he was no plus'd then he would get home & fetch those papers to rectify it (O that he would), & went againe & againe and fetched paper after paper, & ne'er a one to the purpose." One sees the scene, and how well one understands the situation — the absence of the master : it was the strongest argument for his return.

In this time of confusion, it seemed, everybody's troubles came to rest at the Doctor's door. After the destruction of Hillesden and the death of his brother, Sir Alexander, in the Tower, the charge of the orphaned children — a small flock of them — fell upon the Doctor and his lawyer brother, John. Things gradually sorted themselves out. The eldest boy provided for himself agreeably by an early marriage with an heiress. Within a few years he too died, leaving a small family to be brought up by their great-uncle, as he had cared for the generation before them. There were the natural troubles that befell from having young women unmarried hanging about without husbands, the situation aggravated by the upset of the times. Nor was it helped by the rule of the Saints, who took the opportunity to pass an Act against fornication, with severe penalties attached to such pleasures. (Saints, it seems, are always against pleasures not their own.) While under the Doctor's roof Mary Verney had been got with child by Robert Lloyd, and the Doctor had great difficulty in bringing them together in matrimony. Meanwhile, Mary was in some danger; her sisters were incensed against her; the Doctor sheltered her under his roof and kept her secret. In the end, though not apparently too soon, Mary and Robert were married at Paddington, and lived — unlike some of their more virtuous relations — happy ever after.

By this time Ralph was back in England: he returned in 1653. The Doctor had the job of looking for lodgings for him in London. He heard of a house " on the right hand going towards Russell St., with a faire dining Roome, little lodging chamber, and a good closet of a Floore, and the same againe over head, and a garret or two with chimnies above ". The price 20s. a week : " the people are very good and dresse meat well and simply; use only the lower Roomes for themselves, and have no children only one Neece ". O those fortunate, happy days, when life was easy and tolerable ! The friendship of Doctor and nephew continued firm and unchanged through the alarms of state and public vicissitudes. " Yours body and bones, Wm D.", writes one. " I confess Meum and Tuum devides most men," writes the other more sedately, " but by the grace of God it shall never devide us." Nor did it.

Ralph's son, another Mun, was now home from abroad : aged twenty, tall and rather handsome, but — in spite of his French education — gauche and careless of dress and appearance, which distressed his too precise father. " Much more will be expected from Mun ", he wrote, " than from such youths as have gone noe father than Oxford or Cambridg, or at most the Inns of Court." Such expectations asked to be disappointed. Young Mun left home for London, where, the Doctor reported, " methinkes Mun lives wonderful orderly here. I doe not see that any one comrade hath been with him since he came. He keepes at home all day till candle-light, and then we have his comppany till bed time and much more free and merry then formerly." But soon Mun was to be heard of all over the place — unlicensed expeditions under assumed names. To the father's protests Mun replied with the kind of home-truths fathers are apt to find insolent : " mais c'est que votre naturel est tel " — his letters are in French — " que vous aimez à prolonger les choses ". Father was furious. Evidently the Doctor had to step in. He pleaded for more liberal treatment of the lad in money matters, said all the kind things he could of him to Ralph, while pressing the boy to submit to his father. Such judicious diplomacy did not fail to patch matters up.

But getting Mun married was a more difficult business. The Doctor wished to introduce him into polite society, but found him " in most pitifull equipage, noe trappings at all ". This remedied, the Doctor found him a most desirable match. His father's opinion was that " Mun is not at all nice either in point of Bewty or of Breeding, nor must that woeman bee soe that marries him ". But though the Doctor very much fell for the promising heiress, the young man refused to be stirred. He did not wish to marry ; he preferred to go on with his education. " I beleeve myselfe of that temper ", he wrote, " that I can easily break off, without heavy sorrow, when I see I cannot love with any conveniency." The two old friends had indeed great trouble in getting the young man into the marriage-bed. Then he fell in love at last with a cousin who would not marry him.

Before he was provided for, the Restoration had come about : the country was disposed of before he was.

From London the Doctor's letters came down to quiet Claydon, full of the excitement of the time : on Cromwell's death, " the souldiers are not so quiett as I could wish, they would fayne a generall, as distinct from the Protector [*i.e.* Richard Cromwell] ". Next year, the Doctor was elected a member of Richard's Parliament — though his name is missing from the Official Return of M.P.s. " I can tell you noe newes but that I graced the Parliament House by makinge a simple speech in it." In answer to Ralph's expression of surprise, he writes : " Soft Sir soft. It is not for Plebeians to know why we made our learned speech in the House." Soon it was : " We all wished ourselves with you last night ; this place was never so neare aflame, bussell, confusion, which you will, as last night by the Judgment of all, & what will be the Issue a few more houres I guesse will declare ". The only possible issue, it soon became clear, was the restoration of the monarchy and the old known ways. Neither Ralph nor the Doctor was returned to the Cavalier Parliament ; but this did not damp the rejoicings : " Such universall acclamations of wilde and sober joy I never yet saw ; we had our Bonefire too & Bells ringing even at Claydon ". Only one lonely great man, a blind poet, wrote : " By returning of our own foolish accord, nay running into the same bondage, we make vain and viler than dirt, the blood of so many faithful and valiant Englishmen, who left us in this liberty ; losing by a strange after-game of folly all the battles we have won, all the treasure we have spent ". Such eloquence was no use against a landslide ; the country had had too much of all that ; it wanted normality ; the rule of the Saints was over.

With the Restoration, something of the interest and excitement goes out of the correspondence between the two friends. It was a new world, and they were elderly men, growing old. The Doctor did not lose interest in events, indeed his concern with politics grew stronger. It took the form of argumentative and learned tracts and treatises on the issues of the time, with long titles after its manner. As I write I have under my hand two of them in quarto: the first, *Horae Subsecivae: or a Treatise shewing the Original Grounds, Reasons and Provocations necessitating our Sanguinary Laws against Papists made in the days of Queen Elizabeth,* etc., published in 1664. The argument of it is correct enough. The second tract, *The Burnt Child dreads the Fire,* came out in 1675: it is an examination of the claims of Papists to toleration and a justification of the Test Act excluding them from office. There followed a folio from the Doctor's pen in 1681, a treatise on Independency, Presbytery and the sects, and their place in the state. As the struggle with the Stuart monarchy and its Catholicising tendencies and leanings towards absolutism sharpened, the Doctor became more Whiggish, came out more strongly for the rights of the people. He had always had the kindly egalitarianism of his profession and had written long before, in the days of the Levellers: " If ever I had found that God had respected the person of Princes or of the riche, more then of the poore, I had long sinse been confounded in my selfe ". Now he turned his indefatigable pen against James II, whose stupidity and subversion of the country's laws corroborated the Doctor's warnings and proved him right. Another long folio, *Jus Regiminis: Being a Justification of Defensive Arms in General,* justified the Revolution to a world that no longer needed the Doctor.

For he and Ralph were old men now. But the Doctor was equal to giving Ralph a banquet, of which a bustard (O Restoration days, O days of Pepys and City Feasts!) was the central feature. " All ye gange was here last night drinking Sir Ralph's health & preying on a goodly formidable beast out of ye Fens called a Bustard, which was more then a whole round table & by standers could devoure. When will Barley yard or Knowle hill produce such a beast? " The Doctor still bustles about and sends news of town home to Ralph at Claydon: there were the seven bishops, " they are most mightily visited, courted highly by the multitude at Whitehall craving their benediction, as they took water, and so again as they landed at the Tower so that they could scarce get into the Tower ". Never before or since have bishops been so popular in England. Then came James's flight: " We are all in a strange confusion, abandoned by K. Qn. & Pr. all gone *cum pannis*, confounded be all they that worship graven Images & boast themselves of idols ". Soon, having delivered himself of his last folio at the age of eighty-six, the Doctor was to go on a longer journey. Ralph came up from Claydon to be with him in his last hours, on 9 May 1691, so that what they said to each other is for once unrecorded. But the epitaph in Hillesden church is borne out by all that we know of him : " He was blessed with that happy composition of Body & mind that preserved him chearfull, easy & agreeable to the last, & endeared him to all that knew him ".

I have said that the Doctor has his place in the history of the political thought of his time. Shall we go into the long and tedious expositions of doctrine, the citations of dreary texts, the arguments forwards and backwards, the controversies that were always boring and are now defunct ? I think not : the world has had too much political theory of late. It is the life that matters — the kindness and goodness of heart, the spirit with which men support their misfortunes or come to the aid of others, the love between friends, their humours and their capacity for enjoyment, even of a bustard — not what they think they think.

THE MILTON COUNTRY

THE name and fame of Milton are so strongly associated with Cambridge — and rightly — that people are apt to forget that he came of purely Oxfordshire stock, that his family associations were with Oxford and that his native neighbourhood, where some important events in his life took place, was right on the threshold of the city. The Milton name indeed goes back in those parts to the Middle Ages and the first taking of surnames : it comes from the place-names of Great and Little Milton, villages some eight or nine miles to the east of Oxford. Closer in, only four and five miles away, is the broken, hilly country that once was the royal Forest of Shotover : still wooded in parts, and with the magnificent green slopes of Shotover Hill, the ridge along which ran the ancient highway to London : haunts and coverts familiar to all Oxford men. There are the villages of Stanton St. John and Forest Hill, so closely associated with Milton's forbears and his own life. This is the Milton country.

Milton's forbears were of good Oxfordshire yeoman stock. A Roger Milton was collector of tenths and fifteenths for the county in 1437. We are on firm ground with Milton's great-grandfather, whose will is in the Bishop's Registry at Oxford. It is a typical will of a small yeoman, made on 21 November 1558. Elizabeth was already Queen ; but nothing had been changed as yet and the Miltons were Catholics. " I, Henry Milton of Stanton St. John's, sick of body but perfect of mind, do make my last will and testament in manner and form following : First, I bequeath my soul to God, to our Lady St. Mary and to all the holy company of heaven, and my body to be buried in the churchyard of Stanton. I give to Isobel, my daughter, a bullock and half a quarter of barley, and Richard my son shall keep the said bullock until he be three years old. Item, I give to

Roland Milton and Alice Milton, each of them, half a quarter of barley. I give to Agnes Milton, my wife, a gelding, a grey mare and two kine and all my household stuff, whom I make my executrix." It is the kind of will that Shakespeare's forbears — similar stock — would be making in the neighbouring county of Warwickshire. Richard Milton, the eldest son, would evidently succeed to the farm and its stock. Three years later and Agnes, the wife, was dead, bequeathing her soul likewise, in Catholic form, " to God and to all the celestial company of heaven ", and her body " to be buried in the churchyard at Stanton at the belfry end ".

So Richard Milton reigned in his father's stead. He married a wife from Holton, by Wheatley, a couple of miles away across those pleasant fields sloping to the east and looking out across the low-lying woods of Buckinghamshire. In 1563 a son was born, the poet's father, John Milton : almost exactly contemporary with John Shakespeare's son, William, at Stratford. This John Milton was a person in his own right : an accomplished musician, he contributed along with the most famous composers of the day, to the collection of madrigals, *The Triumphs of Oriana*, brought out in honour of the Queen in 1601. In this same year the father, at Stanton St. John, was fined £60 for three months' non-attendance at church, and another £60 later in the year, " neither having made submission nor promised to be conformable, pursuant to the Act ". In short, Milton's grandfather was a Catholic Recusant. He does not seem to have been penalised ; for all his life he held an official appointment as under-ranger of Shotover Forest. In the State Papers of the time one comes across orders for the felling of so many hundred oaks to build ships for the Royal Navy. From that Forest, where the oaks are few enough now, there grew one oak as tough and seasoned as any timbers in the Navy.

Milton's grandfather was a stiff-necked Catholic : the stock was obstinate. All the early Lives of Milton have the story that he disinherited the son for conforming to Pro-

testantism while at Oxford. So it seems that the poet must
have been proud of the tale and fond of relating it. Aubrey
tells us that Milton's father " was brought up in ye Univty
of Oxon at Christ Church and his gr. father disinherited
him because he kept not the Catholique Religion. Q. he
found a Bible in English in his chamber. So thereupon he
came to London, and became a Scrivener (brought up by a
friend of his, was not an Apprentice) and gott a plentiful
estate by it." It was a good thing for Milton's father that
he had a friend to look after him; for certainly he took no
degree at the university, was unable to complete his studies.
It has often been asked why the poet should have been sent
to Cambridge, when all his associations were with Oxford.
Need we look any further for the explanation?

We do not have to suppose that Milton's father ceased
to have any connection with his native countryside, indeed
we have an indirect piece of evidence that he did not; nor
that the young Milton was unacquainted with it — we have
several bits of direct evidence connecting him with Oxford
and the neighbourhood. The scrivener prospered in London,
accumulated enough to keep his son at Cambridge for seven
years without an exhibition of any kind (himself must have
been a servitor at Christ Church) and to leave him a com-
petence sufficient for the poet to retain a proud republican
independence throughout life. In addition, the virtuous
father was enabled to retire to enjoy the delights of country
life. He bought a small property at Horton in Buckinghamshire, down by the Thames next Datchet, with the serrated
ridge of Windsor not far away on the skyline: a place perhaps half-way between London and his native Oxfordshire.

Here the young Milton came in the vacations from
Cambridge; it was to this place that he longed to retreat
altogether and bury himself in unbroken study, solitary and
uninterrupted. For he had no very great liking for the
university; he never looked back with any affection on it;
once he had left he seems never to have returned to it. It is
only fair to add that he had no very high opinion of the
university of Oxford either. This serious young man had

G

nothing in common with *l'homme moyen sensuel*, and of course
less than no sympathy with average human foolery. He was
a perfectionist; it was the source at once of his greatness
and of his despair.

At last the time came when he was free of the university,
its wearisome impositions and endless logic-chopping, free
to give himself up to the studies he longed to devote himself
to — poetry, theology, history. It was the year 1632 — that
blissful quiet time before the Civil War when, Clarendon
said, England had never known greater happiness and
prosperity. Milton was twenty-four. He mapped out a
course of study for himself that practically meant his taking
all knowledge for his province. To his great friend, Charles
Diodati — his friend from schooldays and perhaps his only
intimate friend — Milton confided his settled intention.
" My own disposition is such that no delay, no rest, no
thought or care for anything else can divert me from my
purpose, until I reach my goal and complete some great
cycle of my studies. . . . Ceres never sought her daughter
Proserpine (as the legend tells) with greater ardour than I
do this Idea of Beauty, like some image of loveliness; ever
pursuing it, by day and by night, in every shape and form
(' for many forms there are of things divine ') and following
close in its footprints as it leads. . . . What am I thinking
about? you ask. So help me God, of immortality. What
am I doing? Growing wings and learning to fly." All this,
of course, in Latin; Diodati replied in Greek. They make
an interesting pair : the one so extravert and sociable, gay
and high-spirited; the other lonely and self-absorbed, with
illimitable ambition of mind and soul. Yet — it is not surprising — it seems to have been the latter who was the
pursuer. Milton appears always to have needed a touch
of the Italian temperament to release him.

They had been at school together at St. Paul's. Three
years before Milton went to Cambridge, Diodati went up
to Oxford, to Trinity College. But they did not cease to
keep touch : they wrote to each other, they saw each other
in the vacations in London and at Horton. Diodati went

to Cambridge to be incorporated M.A. *ad eundem* in 1629, while Milton was still up. In 1635 Milton went to Oxford to be incorporated M.A. similarly. It is not likely to have been his only visit. When Diodati went to the North to practise as a doctor, Milton sent him news of the progress of his studies. His study of Greek history has brought him, by steady work, to the point at which they ceased to be Greeks. He is now engaged on the obscure history of Italy under the Lombards, Franks and Germans. He intends to follow the history of each independent state : will Diodati lend him Giustiniani's *History of Venice* ?

So, in these quiet years at Horton, reading alone and far into the night — with only occasional visits to London to the booksellers or for concerts of music, with at least one visit to Oxford — Milton built up the extraordinary body of his learning in ancient history and literature, in the Bible and Jewish history, in Italian and English poetry, in philosophy and religious thought. It was this that enabled him, when the Civil War began, to pour forth volume after volume of prose, on political and ethical theory, on questions of divorce, education and freedom of thought, on Christian Doctrine and the institutions of the Church, not to mention a History of Britain and a History of Muscovy. All this in addition to the learning that went into his poems : he is the most learned of our poets. To Milton his prose works were as essential a part of his total work as his poems : we owe them to the long midnight hours at Horton, that nothing disturbed.

> Or let my lamp, at midnight hour,
> Be seen in some high lonely tower,
> Where I may oft outwatch the Bear,
> With thrice great Hermes, or unsphere
> The spirit of Plato, to unfold
> What worlds or what vast regions hold
> The immortal mind that hath forsook
> Her mansion in this fleshly nook.

But characteristically it is the poems of these years that are remembered : *L' Allegro* and *Il Penseroso*, *Arcades*, *Lycidas*

and *Comus*. They are all country poems, full of the sense of
the countryside and of joy in its life : the mingled countryside of a poet's imagination, in which the low-lying walks
by the Thames at Horton lie alongside the upland hamlets
and the sheep-walks of Forest Hill, the woods and brakes of
Shotover. It is not fanciful perhaps to see the upland
country reflected in *L' Allegro* :

> Sometimes, with secure delight,
> The upland hamlets will invite,
> When the merry bells ring round,
> And the jocund rebecks sound
> To many a youth and many a maid
> Dancing in the chequered shade. . . .

> Oft listening how the hounds and horn
> Cheerly rouse the slumbering morn,
> From the side of some hoar hill,
> Through the high wood echoing shrill.

This is clearly not the countryside of Horton ; nor

> Sometimes walking, not unseen,
> By hedgerow elms, on hillocks green,
> Right against the eastern gate
> Where the great Sun begins his state . . .

It exactly describes the situation of Forest Hill, perched
half-way up against its eastern hillock.

> Straight mine eye hath caught new pleasures,
> Whilst the landscape round it measures :
> Russet lawns, and fallows grey,
> Where the nibbling flocks do stray ;
> Mountains on whose barren breast
> The labouring clouds do often rest. . . .

There surely is Shotover : just what it looks like from
Stanton St. John and Forest Hill, those high upward slopes
with the nibbling flocks, the long green crest to the sky, the
church bells ringing in the villages below. Is it fanciful to
see in Shotover Forest the wooded wilderness in which the

Lady is lost in *Comus*? — it was possible to lose one's way in Shotover then.

> I know each lane, and every alley green,
> Dingle or bushy dell, of this wild wood,
> And every bosky bourn from side to side,
> My daily walks and neighbourhood . . .
>
>   might we but hear
> The folded flocks, penned in their wattled cotes,
> Or sound of pastoral reed with oaten stops,
> Or whistle from the lodge, or village cock
> Count the night-watches to his feathery dames,
> 'Twould be some solace yet, some little cheering,
> In this close dungeon of innumerous boughs.

Others have thought so. In the eighteenth century, Sir William Jones, the great Oriental scholar, went out one day from Oxford for a ramble around these villages and noticed the aptness of the description : " the villages and turrets, partly shaded with trees of the finest verdure, and partly raised above the groves that surrounded them, the dark plains and meadows of a greyish colour, where the sheep were feeding at large ". What pleased him was that there was then a living tradition of Milton among the villagers ; one of them could not remember his name, but knew about " the poet ". There is something convincing about that — it is extraordinary how tenacious these memories are.

It is more usual to recognise the banks of the Thames or Cam in such verses as

> Oft, on a plat of rising ground,
> I hear the far-off curfew sound,
> Over some wide-watered shore,
> Swinging slow with sullen roar. . . .

or

> Meadows trim, with daisies pied ;
> Shallow brooks, and rivers wide ;
> Towers and battlements it sees
> Bosomed high in tufted trees,
> Where perhaps some beauty lies,
> The cynosure of neighbouring eyes.

Surely this is Horton, with Windsor not far away on the skyline, its towers and battlements rising above the wide-watered shore ? For this is how poetry is made : the images of place may be intermingled or even fused, but they are always actual.

Now it is Horton again, some centuries later. It is Trinity Sunday, the year after the ending of the war. There is a thrush calling loudly across the trim meadows. A disconsolate group of German prisoners of war watch the parish coming out of church — one young Nazi instinctively stands to attention to the young English officer as we pass by. The young Englishman blushes — as it might be the undergraduate Milton, the blushing " lady of Christ's ". Beyond the church we go down the road to the ' Five Bells ' inn ; opposite is a farm with an orchard — you see the church tower through the orchard blossom in spring. Next is the plot where the Miltons lived — the house was rebuilt in the last century. It is a little estate defined by a shallow brook that runs down one side of it and in front along the road, like a moat. Inside there are planes and tall chestnuts, a lime-tree, ash and acacias. Outside, dog-rose in bloom hangs over the hardly moving water. Everywhere there is the characteristic June scent — elder-trees in flower, blue speedwell, little June daisies, poppies out in the grass verge along the road, the white flowers of nettles.

As we go back there is a rain-cloud black behind the flint and brick tower of the church, thick-set and squat, that looks out over the meadows to Windsor Great Park on the ridge. The proximity to Castle and Court of the sober high-minded family living its Puritan life down here amid the meadows — its greatest extravagances music-making and books — must have made sharper to the uncompromising young poet the conflicts of the time, encouraged the reformer in him. The cloud breaks, deluging the land. After the shower the birds are sweeter than before, the thrushes singing contentedly to each other, the humbler birds cheep-

ing. We enter the churchyard : it has a big old yew, old
enough to go back to Milton : perhaps he knew the yew
and remarked it ? At any rate, the church is not much
changed : it is much as he knew it : we enter by the Norman
door, a thing of beauty, of elaborate design and alternat-
ing coloured stones, blue and brown. O the placid quiet
of the place ! Silence, the service over, the smell of snuffed
candles, the heavy clock ticking in the tower, the birds
cheeping in the churchyard outside. The Bible is open at
the Lesson for Trinity Sunday, Isaiah vi :

" In the year that king Uzziah died I saw also the Lord
sitting upon a throne, high and lifted up, and his train filled
the temple.
"Above it stood the seraphims : each one had six
wings ; with twain he covered his face, and with twain
he covered his feet, and with twain he did fly.
"And one cried unto another, and said, Holy, holy,
holy is the Lord of hosts : the whole earth is full of his
glory."

Within the chancel is the long blue slab under which
lies Milton's mother : " Heare Lyeth the Body of Sara
Milton the wife of John Milton who Died the 3rd of April
1637 ".

A year after his mother's death Milton set out on the
Italian tour which made such an impression on his mind —
and in the course of which he made such an impression,
both by his scholarship and his good looks. He was rather
small in stature ; but, as dear Aubrey says, " his harmonicall
and ingeniose soule did lodge in a beautifull & well pro-
portioned body — In toto nusquam corpore menda fuit.
Ovid." One can see the impression he would make on
cultivated Italians. While he was away, his dearest friend —
half an Italian himself, Charles Diodati — died. Milton
came home to write the most moved — and moving — of
his personal poems in his memory : the *Epitaphium Damonis*.
It is only the accident of its being in Latin that has prevented
this poem being as well known as *Lycidas*, to which it is
superior in personal feeling and emotion, as an expression

of grief. It is perhaps characteristic of Milton that it was in Latin he should have chosen to let himself go :

> Ah ! certe extremum licuisset tangere dextram,
> Et bene compositos placide morientis ocellos,
> Et dixisse " Vale ! nostri memor ibis ad astra ".

It was not until some time after his friend's death that Milton married ; and most people have found his marriage inexplicable — as certainly it seemed sudden and ill-considered. The primary source for it is Milton's nephew, Edward Phillips : " About Whitsuntide it was, or a little after, that he took a Journey into the Country; no body about him certainly knowing the Reason, or that it was any more than a Journey of Recreation : after a Month's stay, home he returns a Married-man, that went out a Batchelor ". His other nephew, John Phillips, adds a convincing touch, to the effect that he courted, married and brought home his wife all in a month's time, " according to his practice of not wasting that precious talent ". It was the Whitsuntide of 1642, the threshold of the Civil War. He was now thirty-four, his bride not yet seventeen. She was the eldest daughter of the squire at Forest Hill, a Royalist and Cavalier.

It always has been thought surprising, and of course the affair was unhappy. But need we be so much surprised now that we know the background ? Milton was only going home to his native village for a bride. He may have known her since she was a child. For there were business transactions between the two families. Richard Powell of Forest Hill was interested in the timber in the Forest. At some point, many years before, he had contracted a considerable debt to the Miltons, which had been settled on the young John from the time of his going to Cambridge. At the time of his marriage it amounted to £500 (multiply by fifteen for contemporary values). Mr. Powell engaged himself to pay this debt and to give his daughter a dowry of £1000. The dowry was never paid. Nor is this so surprising in the circumstances of the Civil War. What is so are the consequences that followed, the curious sequel to the marriage that made such a deep mark upon the life of the greatest of English poets (save only one).

The plain fact is that Milton was marrying above him — as has happened in other poets' families : John Shakespeare, for example, married into the Ardens, a family of Catholic gentlefolk. The grandson of a small yeoman of Stanton St. John, under-ranger of the Forest, was marrying the daughter of the squire of Forest Hill. One can see visually what it meant : from the roads about Stanton one can still see the chimneys of Mr. Powell's diminished mansion at Forest Hill dominating the village in the distance.

As I write, I have under my hand the inventory of that house and its belongings. We can visualise just what it was like : the hall with its long table and ten joined stools, its court cupboard, its wainscot chair and leather chair for the squire and his wife — they had ten or eleven children. In the Great Parlour there was a new tapestry carpet, carpets and cushions with green silk fringes — in those days carpets covered the tables, as we can see in the pictures of the time ; in this room there were eleven pictures in frames ; the window curtains and carpets were green. The Little Parlour had an oval table, carpets and cloths of striped stuff, fourteen leather chairs, green cushions. There was a still-room, a cheese-press house, kitchen, pantry, bake-house, brew-house, dairy, saddlery, wash-house. The best bedroom was a matted chamber, with green taffeta curtains and valances, embroidered chairs and stools. There were bedchambers over the hall, the parlours, the pantry, dairy and wash-house. The study had a bed in it, with green curtains, laced valances and a yellow coverlet, an old horseman's coat with silver buttons — which must have been Mr. Powell's. Most of the linen was in Mrs. Powell's lodging over the dairy-house and wash-house — this was after the family was dispersed ; we read of her red velvet mantle with gold lace, her camlet coat with buttons and loops, lined with black plush. What was of greatest value was the timber stacked in the backyard. The family kept two coaches. No books are mentioned, except one great Bible kept in a chest ; but there are red and taffeta waistcoats and petticoats with silver and gold lace.

We have seen enough to recognise it for what it was : the home of a jolly family of Cavalier gentry, inclined to be extravagant and completely Philistine. No Samson among the Philistines could be less at home than Milton in such an atmosphere ; no Dalila find her husband's home more uncongenial than Mary Powell the sedate Puritan household in the little house in Aldersgate.

And so it turned out. Milton's nephew tells us that some of the bride's family accompanied her to London, where there was several days' feasting in celebration of the nuptials ; then they returned to Forest Hill, leaving their sister behind : " probably not much to her satisfaction, as appeared by the Sequel ; by that time she had for a Month or thereabout led a Philosophical Life (after having been used to a great House, and much Company and Joviality) ". After a month of it she went home to her people to spend the rest of the summer, on the understanding that she would return at Michaelmas. At Michaelmas there was no news of his wife's return and Milton sent letter after letter to her to come back. " At last he dispatch'd down a Foot-Messenger with a Letter, desiring her return ; but the Messenger came back not only without an answer, at least a satisfactory one, but to the best of my remembrance, reported that he was dismissed with some sort of Contempt." That summer the Civil War had broken out ; the prospects of the Royalists were good and the Powells " began to repent them of having Matched the Eldest Daughter of the Family to a Person so contrary to them in Opinion ; and thought it would be a blot in their Escutcheon, when ever that Court should come to Flourish again ". Mrs. Powell, who had been something of an heiress herself, seems to have been mainly responsible : no doubt she considered her daughter too good for the scrivener's son.

But the scrivener's son was John Milton, and he was furious at such treatment — " so incensed ", according to his nephew, " that he thought it would be dishonourable ever to receive her again, after such a repulse ". There are

those who think that the trouble was that Milton's young
wife refused to consummate the marriage. He was as much
of a virgin as she was — for what that was worth. He was
humiliated : his pride — the essential element in Milton's
nature, along with his genius, which was bound up with it
and depended on it — was deeply wounded. Earlier,
Milton had written (in Latin) of the transcendent prizes
that rewarded learning, the recompense that awaited cul-
tivation of the intellect : " then at last most of the chances
and changes of the world will be so quickly perceived that
to him who holds this stronghold of wisdom hardly anything
can happen in his life which is unforeseen or fortuitous ".
Only the very remarkable make that sort of mistake ; and
Milton had made it in its most intimately wounding form.
So far, up to his marriage, Milton had maintained an extraordinary rational control — too much so — over his life.
On his very first and most important venture into the open
sea he found he had put himself at the mercy of the irra-
tional ; he had become the victim of the unforeseen and
the fortuitous. What more humiliating for a man so intellectually proud — and so sensitively ignorant of life ? He
had been made a fool of by a recalcitrant and foolish girl.
He was to bear the consequences of that month in the
country at Forest Hill to his dying day. It is deeply imprinted in his greatest work ; the blow must have had the
effect of deepening and ripening his genius.

In addition to the shock to his pride, Milton was now in
an intolerable situation : neither married nor unmarried ;
or rather married, but without the supposed advantages of
that state — which he set such store by — but being contracted was now not free to obtain them. (It is this that is
difficult to understand. Milton was one of those men who,
rather feminine in appearance, was determinedly, perversely,
provokingly masculine ; who are apt to over-insist on their
masculinity all the more because they are a little doubtful
at bottom. At any rate, now that he was awakened belatedly
to the pleasures of sex, he fell in time into the incomprehensible vice of uxoriousness.) Anyone more ordinary, or

more sensible, would have gone elsewhere, or tried an alternative. Not so Milton : he wanted lawful pleasures : to be

> Locked by the law in wedded chastity ;

for, of course, he was immensely respectable — as a Non-conformist, a Republican, a bourgeois would expect to be.

It was this that made his dilemma so acute ; it was rendered absolute by the law, which allowed of divorce only in case of adultery, and even then made it practically impossible to effect. Marriage was a sacrament and inviolable. To anyone of Milton's independent, proud spirit, set on leading opinion, not following it, this was a call to action. In the year before his marriage Milton had made himself a public man of mark with a series of tractates against the Church and its government. The immense reading at Horton was beginning to bear fruit in a series of works developing a consistent system of thought : democratic in a sense (oligarchical in effect), rational in its appeal, modernist in theology ; always, of course, virtuous. Intolerably unjust as these tracts were to the bishops — for Milton remained always the perfectionist — they brought him great favour with Parliament and the Presbyterians. Henceforth he was a public name.

Now, brought up against the horrid facts of life, Milton turned his attention to the divorce law and boldly appealed to Parliament for a reform of it. He made the case general ; it was in no sense a personal appeal — too proud for that. People always generalise from their own particular circumstances ; but it would seem that in Milton's case he held these views before — they are consistent with his passion for the liberty of mankind and the rights of the individual. In August 1643 he published his tract, *The Doctrine and Discipline of Divorce Restored, to the Good of both Sexes*. It was a plea for a sensible, contractual idea of marriage and divorce, arguing that obstinate incompatibility of mind and temper between husband and wife should be as lawful a ground for divorce as infidelity ; and that unsuitable partners, especially where there were no children, should be free to separate and marry again. This seems very reasonable to us, though it took some three hundred years to arrive at it. It caused a great hullabaloo at the time, especially with the humbugs of the Westminster Assembly, the canting Presbyterians who were far less tolerant than the Church they had overturned.

Milton was undaunted; he followed it up in the next two years with three more tracts on the subject — until the bulk of his writings on Divorce was even greater than that on Church government. In those days, it was necessary to argue the common sense of the matter through a fog of Scriptural nonsense and an ocean of texts and disputes, Old Testament and New Testament, Mosaic Law, Church Fathers, authoritative Reformers : one whole tract, for example, is devoted to the judgments of Martin Bucer on the matter — though why that dreary divine should be regarded with such respect it is difficult to see.

All this had no influence whatever on the divorce law. Its only effect was to cut off Milton from his original background and friends — he was too independent and original a man for them — and to bring him into line with the Independents and Oliver Cromwell, of whose personal dictatorship, resting on military force, Milton became the official, the famous, propagandist. Such is the irony of human actions : this is where intellectual pride, reacting to events, brought him. The literary consequences of the *fracas* were a couple of fine polemical sonnets and a splendid phrase:

> I did but prompt the age to quit their clogs
> By the known rules of ancient liberty,
> When straight a barbarous noise environs me
> Of owls and cuckoos, asses, apes and dogs.

(Well, what else could he expect?) What he had discovered from the experience was that

> New Presbyter is but old Priest writ large.

But, of course. Enough of these dreary public matters : back to the more endearing, and enduring, delights of the private and the personal.

We have an insight into how Milton viewed his own situation in various phrases, in passing, in the first Divorce tract : he speaks of " a luckless and helpless matrimony ", " a mute and spiritless mate ", " unconversing inability of mind " — from which we see what the trouble was, and its consequence, " the disturbance of her unhelpful and unfit society ", " a worse condition than the loneliest single life ". To those people who say one should be more careful in one's choice, he replies with a direct reference that is pathetically revealing : " for all the wariness that can be used, it may yet befall a discreet man to be mistaken in his choice, and we have plenty of examples. The soberest and best-governed men are least practised in these affairs ; and who knows not that the bashful muteness of a virgin may oft-times hide all the unliveliness and natural sloth which is really unfit for conversation ? Nor is there that freedom of access granted or presumed as may suffice to a perfect discerning till too late ; and where any indisposition is suspected, what more usual than the persuasion of friends that acquaintance, as it increases, will amend all ? " What could be more revealing of the circumstances of that hurried wooing at Forest Hill ? — the family careful not to grant too much access for the suitor to see how null the daughter was — " mute " appears to be Milton's frequent word for her ; the scrivener's son not presuming on more access than he was granted. Milton concludes, " it is not strange though many who have spent their youth chastely are in some things not so quick-sighted while they haste too eagerly to light the nuptial torch : nor is it therefore that for a modest error a man should forfeit so great a happiness, and no charitable means to release him ; since they who have lived most loosely, by reason of their bold accustoming, prove most successful in their matches, because their wild affections, unsettling at will, have been as so many divorces to teach them experience ". That, to the mind of the Puritan, was no argument for enjoying oneself.

So three years passed, filled with the momentous events of the Civil War. Mary Powell remained at Forest Hill ; for

Milton there was still no remedy. Early in 1645 he thought
of providing a remedy for himself. " If the Law make not
a timely provision," he had written, " let the Law, as reason
is, bear the censure of the consequence." He was not the
man to be deterred by the opinions of ordinary fools. Edward
Phillips tells us what was afoot ; he refers to " a grand Affair,
which was more than probably thought to be then in agitation : It was indeed a design of Marrying one of Dr. Davis's
Daughters, a very Handsome and Witty Gentlewoman ".
It is this lady who is thought to be the object of the sonnet,
" To a Virtuous Young Lady ", written at this time :

> Lady, that in the prime of earliest youth
> Wisely hast shunned the broad way and the green,
> And with those few art eminently seen
> That labour up the hill of heavenly Truth . . .

Evidently her conversation left nothing to be desired ; the
only thing that was wanting was the virtuous young lady's
acquiescence : she was " averse, as it is said, to this Motion ".

But the news of it, or perhaps rather the upshot of the
Civil War, made its impression at Forest Hill. At Naseby
this year the King's cause was irretrievably ruined. Meanwhile, the Powells had reason to reflect, their son-in-law
was a person of importance with the victorious side in
London. They determined on a reconciliation between
husband and wife ; and friends on both sides hit on a
stratagem. Milton was in the habit of visiting a bookseller,
who was a relation, in St. Martin-le-Grand, and " upon this
occasion the visits were the more narrowly observ'd. . . .
One time above the rest, he making his usual visit, the Wife
was ready in another Room, and on a sudden he was surprised to see one whom he thought to have never seen more,
making Submission and begging Pardon on her Knees before
him ; he might probably at first make some shew of aversion
and rejection ; but partly his own generous nature, more
inclinable to Reconciliation than to perseverance in Anger
and Revenge ; and partly the strong intercession of Friends
on both sides, soon brought him to an Act of Oblivion, and

a firm League of Peace for the future." In short, Milton's
wife was to come back.

This extraordinary scene is paralleled in both *Samson
Agonistes* and *Paradise Lost*: it had its effect in Milton's
imagination :

> SAMSON. My wife, my traitress ! let her not come near me !
> CHORUS. Yet on she moves ; now stands and eyes thee fixt,
> About to have spoke ; but now with head declined,
> Like a fair flower surcharged with dew, she weeps,
> And words addressed seem into tears dissolved,
> Wetting the borders of her silken veil :
> But now again she makes address to speak.
> DALILA. With doubtful feet and wavering resolution
> I came, still dreading thy displeasure, Samson,
> Which to have merited, without excuse,
> I cannot but acknowledge : yet, if tears
> May expiate (though the fact more evil drew
> In the perverse event than I foresaw)
> My penance hath not slackened, though my pardon
> No way assured.

Anyone who has witnessed this scene in performance can
testify how moving it is, how dramatically effective. Dalila
is not forgiven, Eve is :

> She ended weeping, and her lowly plight,
> Immovable till peace obtained from fault
> Acknowledged and deplored, in Adam wrought
> Commiseration : soon his heart relented
> Towards her, his life so late and sole delight,
> Now at his feet submissive in distress,
> Creature so fair his reconcilement seeking,
> His counsel whom she had displeased, his aid ;
> As one disarmed, his anger all he lost,
> And thus with peaceful words upraised her soon.

Which was more or less what happened in Mr. Black-
borough's bookshop in St. Martin-le-Grand. One sees that
being engaged in life has, after all, as against its penalties,
some rewards for the spirit.

For the moment, the disadvantages were to the fore. No
sooner had Milton's wife returned and he had moved into

a larger house in the Barbican to accommodate her, than all her family descended on him : " her Father and Mother, and several of her Brothers and Sisters, which were in all pretty Numerous ".

The fact is that the Powells' affairs were now in inextricable confusion. During the siege of Oxford, Richard Powell and his sons had been in the city, leaving the house at Forest Hill to take its chance. They were liable to the full extent of Parliamentary fines on active malignants and the sequestration of their property. But the squire of Forest Hill had not the wherewithal to pay the fines. He was some £3000 in debt by the end of the Civil War ; he had never been the owner of the Forest Hill estate, but held a lease on it. Now, the mortgagor, Sir Robert Pye, took over the estate. Meanwhile, the Parliamentary Commissioners were sequestrating the Powells' goods to meet the fine. Hence the inventory we have quoted, with its indication that in the absence of the menfolk of the house, in Oxford, Mrs. Powell had occupied the rooms over the dairy and wash-house. During the week that the inventory was being made Cromwell had been next door at Holton to see his daughter, Bridget, married to Ireton.

At the end of the month, the Powells, having nowhere to go, were given a pass by Fairfax to go to London, where Milton took them in and gave them a refuge. No tribute is needed to the nobility of his character, but here is testimony to its essential generosity. For he had been taken advantage of by the Powells throughout. No doubt they thought it a condescension in them, to judge from their behaviour in his hard-working house. Richard Powell was conscious of the obligation he was under to his son-in-law; it is doubtful if Mrs. Powell had any such sense. At the end of the year Powell died, his affairs quite uncleared up. In his will he expressed the desire " that my daughter Milton be had a regard to in the satisfying of her portion, and adding thereto in case my estate will bear it ". Poor Richard Powell did not even know what the true state of his affairs was : it was so bad that the son refused the executorship. Not so Mrs.

H

Powell : she was going to see it through. It was after her
that Milton's first child, Anne, born amid the troubles of
that July, was called. His mother-in-law did not cease to
be a liability : Milton made her an allowance out of the
small Wheatley property which he took over as one of the
creditors of Richard Powell for the past twenty years. But
for many more the widow and her affairs were to give him
nothing but trouble.

What Milton felt about it all may be seen from the
touching letter he wrote to Carlo Dati, a friend he had made
at Florence in the blissful years before the war. Once more
it is to an Italian, and in Latin, that he really opens his
heart. By the uncertainty of the time Dati's letters had been
lost and Milton had never received them. The thought saddened him. " But an even more saddening thought came
into my mind, a thought which often makes me lament my
fortune, namely that those who are closely bound to me by
the fact of propinquity or by some other tie of no real importance, either by chance or some legal claim, though they
have nothing else to commend them to me, are with me
every day, deafen me with their noise and torment me as
much as they choose. While those who are so greatly endeared to me by sympathy of manners, disposition and tastes,
are almost all separated from me either by death or the
cruel accident of distance, and are as a rule snatched from
my sight so swiftly that I am compelled to spend my life in
almost perpetual loneliness." And then he says, with a
humility all the more affecting in him, " it gives me great
satisfaction to hear that since I left Florence you have never
forgotten me, and to find that the feelings which I had, perhaps perversely, imagined to be mine alone, were in fact fully
reciprocated ". Indeed, he had never been forgotten in Italy.

He was now a celebrated poet. For that same year of
his wife's return saw him put forth, very belatedly, all his
earliest poems, in English and Latin, by which he would
have a high place among English poets even without
Paradise Lost. He was no less careful of his fame as a prose
writer, and had presented his collected works, both prose

and verse, to the Bodleian Library through his friend John Rous, who was Bodley's Librarian. A pleasant episode, connecting Milton with Oxford, occurred over the presentation. Rous and Milton were on friendly terms; before the war Sir Henry Wotton, writing to Milton, had referred to " our common friend, Mr. R." It seems that Rous, whose sympathies were Parliamentarian and who had not hesitated to refuse, under the statutes of the Bodleian, to lend the King a book out of the Library, had requested Milton for all his writings up to date. Milton complied with a Latin inscription to the prose works, welcoming their reception into the university's ancient and celebrated Library, " as into a temple of perpetual memory, and so, as he hopes, into a merited freedom from ill-will and calumny ". On the way down to Oxford the little volume of poems disappeared from the parcel, and Rous wrote again asking that it might be replaced. This Milton did, adding a fanciful mock-heroic Latin " Ode to Rous ", about the loss of the little book, with polite compliments to his friend, the great library in his care and the university of Oxford. Cowper has translated the characteristic last stanza :

> Ye then, my Works, no longer vain
> And worthless deemed by me,
> Whate'er this sterile genius has produced,
> Expect at last, the rage of envy spent,
> An unmolested happy home,
> Gift of kind Hermes and my watchful friend,
> Where never flippant tongue profane
> Shall entrance find,
> And whence the coarse unlettered multitude
> Shall babble far remote.
> Perhaps some future distant age,
> Less tinged with prejudice, and better taught,
> Shall furnish minds of power
> To judge more equally.
> Then malice, silenced in the tomb,
> Cooler heads and sounder hearts,
> Thanks to Rous, if aught of praise
> I merit, shall with candour weigh the claim.

There the little volume now lies along with the others —
cum aliis nostris in Bibliotheca Publica — one of the most
cherished treasures of the Bodleian.

Milton and his wife lived together after her return,
according to John Phillips, " in good accord till her death ".
We hear nothing of her except the births of her children,
save for one phrase to say that it was her mother who had
been responsible for her desertion of her husband. Mute she
must have been, and no intellectual companion for Milton.
But Milton did not expect much of women intellectually,
and he undoubtedly grew fond of her; indeed the very
strength of his reaction to her desertion may be an indication that he was in love with the girl. In the six years in
which they lived together she bore him four children, and
died on the birth of the fourth, in May 1652. She was still
only twenty-six.

It is now thought that Milton's famous sonnet " On his
Deceased Wife ",

> Methought I saw my late espousèd saint,

was addressed to her memory :

> And such as yet once more I trust to have
> Full sight of her in Heaven without restraint,
> Came vested all in white, pure as her mind.
> Her face was veiled ; yet to my fancied sight
> Love, sweetness, goodness in her person shined
> So clear as in no face with more delight.
> But, O, as to embrace me she inclined,
> I waked, she fled, and day brought back my night.

For Milton was now blind.

Mrs. Powell, with a pertinacity one can only praise
rather than appreciate, kept going her suits for the execution
of her husband's will and the return of what she claimed
as due to her, until even before the Restoration she had won
a large measure of success. (Mrs. Powell was restored before
the King was.) One has hardly the head to follow the
legal tangle ; but not for nothing was her son brought up
at Inner Temple, and in addition Milton's lawyer brother,

Christopher (a Royalist, who lapsed back in the end to the old faith of the family), was called into use, and Milton himself, now Latin Secretary to the Council of State, was both used and abused. Mrs. Powell was one of " the women who clamour upon the Council upon the pretence of debts due to them from the Parliament ", from whom the badgered Council sought protection from the officers of their guard. In the end, she got her way. She first got a decree of restitution of her husband's goods at Forest Hill, on the ground that their sale had been a violation of the Articles of Surrender at Oxford — which had been notoriously generous to the Royalists. No-one quite understands the ins and outs of her dealings with regard to the estate itself; but it looks as if its occupation by the Pyes was an act of neighbourly collusion. She did not cease to put in claims for compensation at their very highest, and her income at its lowest. Milton allowed her out of the Wheatley property one-third of the revenue in right of dower. Mrs. Powell returned the value of that estate to the Commissioners at £40 a year; the truth-telling Milton returned it at £80, and paid the Royalist Composition fine on it in full. But he expected Mrs. Powell's third out of it to be taken into consideration. Mrs. Powell stated in her petition that Milton had been given allowance for her thirds — which was not the case, nor would the Commissioners grant it. In pleading extreme poverty, her children starving, etc., she deposed that " Mr Milton is a harsh and choleric man, and married Mrs Powell's daughter, who would be undone if any such course were taken against him by Mrs Powell, he having turned away his wife heretofore for a long space upon some other occasion ". It is to be feared that the lady was a liar.

Now in his blindness, having exhausted his eyes in the service of the state, Milton turned to the great epic which was the end and aim of his life. It is known that Book IV of *Paradise Lost* was, in part, first to be composed. And it is noticeable that here, of his later work, the visual element is at its strongest. Nor is it improbable to see depicted in

the portraits of Eve and Adam something of the relations
between Mary Powell and Milton. Certainly we recognise
Milton's sensuous delight in uxoriousness, his unbroken —
and unbreakable — self-esteem.

> So spake our general Mother, and with eyes
> Of conjugal attraction unreprov'd,
> And meek surrender, half embracing leaned
> On our first Father, half her swelling Breast
> Naked met his under the flowing Gold
> Of her loose tresses hid : he in delight
> Both of her Beauty and submissive Charms
> Smiled with superior Love, as Jupiter
> On Juno smiles, when he impregns the Clouds
> That shed May flowers. . . .

> To whom thus Eve replied : O thou for whom
> And from whom I was formed flesh of thy flesh,
> And without whom am to no end, my Guide
> And Head, what thou hast said is just and right.
> For we to him indeed all praises owe,
> And daily thanks, I chiefly who enjoy
> So far the happier Lot, enjoying thee
> Pre-eminent by so much odds, while thou
> Like consort to thyself canst nowhere find.

That certainly was true of Mr. Milton ; and of all the great
man's wonderful gifts there is no evidence that a sense of
humour was one of them. But a Puritan did not need a
sense of humour : perhaps with it, he would not have been
one. (Here is the greatest contrast of all between Milton
and Shakespeare, the two poles of our literature.) There
follows a hymn to wedded love : Hail, wedded Love,
mysterious Law — and all that. We find the landscape
more interesting.

It is indeed the landscape of Book IV that is so peculiarly
moving, so acutely visualised and with such nostalgia :
the delights of sight were not yet so far away from the
blind poet : they were just round the corner of the eye to
torment him.

Now to th' ascent of that steep savage Hill
Satan had journeyed on, pensive and slow;
But further way found none, so thick entwined,
As one continued brake, the undergrowth
Of shrubs and tangling bushes had perplext
All path of Man or Beast that passed that way . . .

It is the countryside of *Comus* : one can see him remembering
the extinguished landscape :

Watching where Shepherds pen their Flocks at eve
In hurdled Cotes amid the field secure.

Or there are such famous passages as :

Now came still Evening on, and Twilight gray
Had in her sober Livery all things clad;
Silence accompanied, for Beast and Bird,
They to their grassy Couch, these to their Nests
Were slunk, all but the wakeful Nightingale. . . .

Oxford men still go out in high summer to hear the night-
ingales in the coverts of Shotover.

Not far away, Mrs. Powell and her son had regained
possession at Forest Hill; they got the Wheatley property
back from Milton. With the Restoration his official employment ended — he was very lucky to escape with his life.
Indeed it is a mystery how Milton did escape punishment,
for he had been the official, the European, apologist for the
execution of the King. Several people had a hand in his
preservation, but he must have received protection in some
high quarter — tribute to the civilised ways of English life.
For his offence had been very grave : it was on a thin thread
that *Paradise Lost* depended. In the height of his prosperity,
he had protected Davenant and others; now they defended
him. His greatest admirer was Dryden, the laureate of the
Restoration, who was to become a Catholic. Such are the
amenities of civilisation. But he was poorer now and, blind,
could ill afford amanuenses. He taught his daughters to
read to him in the languages he needed, without bothering
to teach them the meaning of the words. Doubtless he was
right in thinking it would have been wasted on them. " One
tongue is enough for a woman ", he would say. But the

daughters were Powells and took after their grandmother — though she did nothing for them : " they made nothing of deserting him ; they did combine together and counsel the maid to cheat him in her marketings, and had made away with some of his books and would have sold the rest to the dunghill women ". In 1663 Milton married a third time : he was fifty-four, his wife twenty-four. When Mary, his second daughter, heard of it she said that " that was no news to hear of his wedding ; but if she could hear of his death, that *was* something". It was a Powell speaking, rather than a Milton.

Milton's third marriage was happy and successful. But when he came to die he remembered all that he had put up with at the hands of the Powells and in his will said : " The portion due to me from Mr. Powell, my former wife's father, I leave to the unkind children I had by her, having received no part of it ; but my meaning is they shall have no other benefit of my estate than the said portion and what I have besides done for them, they having been very undutiful to me ". Mrs. Powell backed her granddaughters in challenging the will ; but all was speedily arranged by the menfolk of the family, by Richard Powell on one side, Christopher Milton on the other, both of the Inner Temple.

There is the end of the story ; *terminus vitae sed non amoris.* It all goes back to Forest Hill ; and here we are, centuries after, walking on a summer afternoon to the village whose only significance is the memory of a long-dead poet. There is the little grey church, standing half-way up the shoulder of the hill, its bell-cote with three bells hanging in it looking down the steep slope to the road into Oxford. The big buttresses that shore it up were built — no doubt the squire aiding the work — in 1639 : it was all white and new when Milton came here in that early summer of 1642. Within the church, the roof has inscribed on its cross-beam : " C . 1630 . R." So that too was put up not long before — the Powells were active in the parish. In the church register are entered the baptisms of all the squire's numerous

children : among them, " Marie Powell, the daughter of
Richard Powell, baptized the XXIV day of January, 1625
[*i.e.* 1626] ". There are rushes of wind in the trees outside ;
a young thrush clamouring for attention on the tombs. The
sun goes in and comes out ; everywhere — so beautiful a
sound — is the summer buzzing of flies. Inside, the wind
rushes at the windows and the lines from the most wonderful
of Oxford poems come into mind :

> So have I heard the cuckoo's parting cry,
> > From the wet field, through the vext garden-trees,
> > Come with the volleying rain and tossing breeze :
> *The bloom is gone, and with the bloom go I.*

Just over the churchyard wall, on the north, is the manor-
house, with remains of the Caroline walling of its forecourt :
there is a beautiful decorative stone gate with curved pedi-
ment, just like the Laudian work then going up in Oxford.
It must have been built by Mary's father, the extravagant
Cavalier. I do not think the house so much changed, though
the interior and the fenestration have been altered. Its
situation anyway remains the same : on one side a little
breast of hill — I do not know why it should be so affecting —
leading the eye up to the blue spaces of sky ; on the other,
the slope down to the valley, with the ridge of Shotover
across the fields.

The road twists serpentine through the village to where
a line of young chestnuts marks the turning to Stanton
St. John. As Milton's grandfather, the under-ranger, went
along the road from Stanton to Forest Hill — it is a little
level plateau — there was on his left a long sweeping view
down the Buckinghamshire slopes towards the lower Thames
country where Horton lies. Ahead is the crest above Forest
Hill ; to the right the long and shapely ridge of Shotover.
Arrived now in Stanton, it is pleasant to see that the holder
of the ' George ' inn is a Jack Churchill, licensed to sell beer,
wine and spirits. Outside is the thick trunk of a pollarded
elm that may just go back to the time of the Miltons :
planted, I should say, about then. All the village is indeed
embowered in tall plumed elms, relics of the old forest. I

enter the churchyard, gay with its ramblers : so here is the church obstinate old Mr. Milton would not go to. The fabric is much unchanged : a beautiful arcade with Early English windows in the chancel, with some medieval glass ; I sit in the same medieval pews he would have sat in, with their curious two-headed tops, women's heads and animals. Up in the chancel a John Mather is buried ; a fine Georgian monument bespeaks his virtues. Laurence Squibb, a former Rector and Fellow of New College, has a decent tablet. In the church tower the clock ticks time away. Through the door I see the rambler roses that grow all round the churchyard, back to the belfry end where old Agnes Milton desired her body to be buried. The dust of the Miltons grows again in the ramblers and the tall cow-parsley.

Opposite the church-gate, on the road to Oxford, is an unchanged Elizabethan house in which John White was born in 1575, a chief founder of Massachusetts. It must have been the original rectory ; a tiny front garden brilliant with flowers against the warm stone, honey-coloured in the afternoon sun : hollyhocks, anchusa, snapdragon, phlox, and a small blue flower bright as birds' eyes. At the corner is the big buttressed barn of the large Elizabethan farmhouse, with sombre draped yews in the yard, holding all the stillness of an English summer in their plumes. Across the road the scent of sweet peas comes over with the cheeping of gregarious village birds. Now all the Mathers and the Squibbs, the Pembertons and the Whites are at rest. But not the Miltons. There are still Miltons in the village — one of them serving in the last war. Such is the continuity of English life.

I take the road to Oxford : along the verge, willow-herb, convolvulus, blue scabious and clumps of purple mallow. The sun comes out over these folded fields, the corn ripening, the larks high up. Away against the eastern gate the grey bell-cote of Forest Hill stands out very clear against the greenery of the crest ; there are the chimneys of Richard Powell's house, the thatched barns beyond. The air is full of the scent of hay, and across the valley the eye is led gently up the commanding green slopes of Shotover.

SWIFT AT LETCOMBE

THE first time that I went to Letcombe, in pursuit of Swift or his ghost or just his memory, it was a sullen lowering autumn day — like a mood of Swift's himself. I do not now remember the November roads, but only arriving at the house wedged into the side of the steep chalk hill, the lane up to the high Berkshire Downs greyish white. Gloom hung over the house; there was a touch of bitterness in the air. This was the house to which Swift had retreated in the great crisis of 1714, which settled his and his party's fortunes for good, those months in which the Queen was dying and the Tory Party — to which Swift had given his genius beyond recall — divided at the top, drifted to destruction. Sickened by these dissensions — which were also those of his closest friends — possessed by a sense of foreboding, of despair at the folly of it all, disquietened for some private reasons of his own, Swift left London and the Court for the quiet of this retreat, this rather inaccessible fastness on the northern lip of the Downs.

The house was not much changed: the centre of it the little gabled rectory of Queen Anne's time. Within, there was the stone-flagged hall, a small room on either side, parlour or study; beyond was a drawing-room, a later addition, giving on to the garden enclosed within eighteenth-century brick walls. From this garden one could see the amphitheatre of the Downs, a semicircle from Castle Hill to Hackpen Hill in the west, under the sullen ominous sky. The house had the sense of impending desertion upon it, the old lady, its occupant, about to leave it: perhaps she had died: I forget. The gardener, left over, said, pointing to a very old mulberry-tree: " They do say, sir, there was a gentleman that wrote a book under that tree long ago." It was, of course, Swift writing his *Free Thoughts on the Present State of Affairs* in the summer of 1714.

Now I have chosen to come again to Letcombe at the time of year he was here, walking up from Wantage, the way he came.

Outside the church I notice a house built in 1708 : it would have been new when Swift was last this way. I cross the road to the footpath over the fields to Letcombe Regis. Yes — who is this large lumbering figure, a powerful walker, with the hard and bright-blue eyes, but wearing a wig (that wig we hear so much about in the *Journal to Stella*), coming this way from Letcombe ? It is June again : there is the summer noise of the trees, the loud insistent susurration of the willows like a sea running in. Chaffinches pour out their little cascades of song in the green cages of the trees. All round are elms — old elms that may well have seen that redoubtable figure coming down from his retreat in the hills, to send something off to London — a pamphlet on affairs, a poem, a letter to Vanessa — by the post, or Robert Stone the Wantage carrier.

This is the cow-parsley and elder-blossom time of the year : the hedges and ditches are covered with white lace. The hay has been harvested in some fields, in others it is lying in swathes. The spired barley is lit by the scarlet lamps of poppies ; another field is bright yellow with charlock. Arrived in Letcombe Regis, I notice a timber-framed house on the corner : " H. K. M. 1698 ". The road to Letcombe Basset follows the curious formation from which the place has taken its name : a deep combe in the chalk formed by a leat, the stream that carries cress growing in its upper course. The combe is fringed by elms, and deep down is filled with withies, ash and dog-roses. From the depths of it come the fragrant summer scents : the acrid lime odour of stinging nettles, bloom of briars, the lemon scent of sap rising in the vegetation. Uphill to the village, a last lap, and here is a newly thatched barn as sleek as the flank of a well-groomed mare. The churchyard is embowered in tall limes with their fringed skirts ; beyond, there are elms again up towards the Downs. Enter now the church, a simple rustic interior not much changed, musty with the flapping of bats. Time in these silent places,

sacred to their country folk, rolls away. Within the Norman
arch, up in the narrow-chested chancel, one sees the two
bewigged clerics at their prayers : the younger, placid and
melancholy (he was Rector here for more than half a century,
1707–61) ; the other a man of forty-seven, a man filled with
disquiet, the tormented heart on the way to becoming the
conjured spirit : to both of them the duty of routine, the
formularies of the Establishment.

Follow them now out along the church-path — passing
the fine tomb-chests of Cotswold stone still there that were
new then — to the rectory across the road from the east end
of the churchyard. There is the house again, standing back
only a few feet from the lane to the Downs, the last in the
village. The figures disappear within, not a word between
them. It is June once more, as so many years before : June
of the year 1714.

For some time now Swift had meditated leaving London. The conflict between the two leaders of the Tory
Ministry, Robert Harley, Earl of Oxford, and the younger,
more brilliant Bolingbroke, was approaching a climax. The
country owed a great deal to this famous Ministry : the
Peace of Utrecht which brought to an end what seemed
the interminable war of Marlborough and the Whigs. The
country wanted peace : the Tories had given it them, not
without risks and difficulties. Now greater danger than
ever loomed before the Ministry and the party. What was
to happen on the Queen's death ? Could they safeguard
themselves on the accession of a foreign king, George of
Hanover ? Or should they try and make terms with the
Stuart Pretender, the Queen's half-brother, excluded from
the succession by his Catholicism ? Could they settle affairs
on such a firm foundation that the Tory Party — which was
representative of the great bulk of the English people —
could lay down terms upon which the succession should take
place ? Above all, was there time ? — for the Queen's health
was failing. In this critical state of affairs, the two Tory
leaders were locked in conflict ; and Swift judged that the
situation was irremediable.

What made it so torturing for him — in addition to the
fact that his nature was prone to self-torture — was that the
two great men were his close friends. To Harley, Swift was
deeply indebted : the Lord Treasurer had recognised his
genius, taken him up and made him his intimate, delivered
him during these last four brilliant years from the torment
of obscurity and non-recognition, made him a power in the
land.

> And now, the publick Inter'st to support,
> By Harley Swift invited comes to Court.
> In Favour grows with Ministers of State,
> Admitted private, when Superiors wait,
> And Harley, not asham'd his Choice to own,
> Takes him to Windsor in his Coach, alone.
> At Windsor Swift no sooner can appear,
> But, St. John comes and whispers in his Ear ;
> The Waiters stand in ranks ; the Yeomen cry
> Make room, as if a Duke were passing by.

Affection bound Swift even more strongly to Oxford than
to Bolingbroke. At the moment of his fall from power, dismissed from the Treasurership, Oxford wrote him, in a
famous phrase, " I believe in the mass of souls, ours were
placed near each other ".

But Swift could not disguise from himself that the Lord
Treasurer's powers were failing : he had advised him to
resign from office rather than be ignominiously dismissed.
But like all politicians he would not : when it was too late
he clung on tenaciously ; if only he had taken as much
trouble when he was in power as he did to hold on to it when
it was slipping from him. . . . A year before there had been
a rift between Oxford and Bolingbroke. Swift was then in
Ireland to be installed as Dean of St. Patrick's. Everybody
implored him to come back to heal the breach between his
friends. And on his return he had helped in doing so :
relations were outwardly patched up. But the leaders kept
the real split from him : however intimate he was with them
personally, he was still an outsider from the arcana of power
— a reminder that added bitterness to a mind that wanted

power more than anything, thought himself equal to it and had always been balked of it. His personal affections with Oxford, he was driven to side politically with Bolingbroke. What a situation for a man who saw with the clarity of genius — and of an outsider — that they were all drifting towards an abyss. Swift's constant plea was that the ministers should hold together, and all might yet be well. Instead, " I do not remember since you [the Earl of Peterborough] left us that we have continued above four days in the same view, or four minutes with any manner of concert. . . . The Queen is pretty well at present, but the least disorder she has puts all in alarm ; and when it is over we act as if she were immortal." And then, " people of my level must be content to have their opinion asked and to see it not followed ". That was what galled him ; he knew himself to be as able as any of them : what disqualified him was his genius — and perhaps rightly, such is the irony of human affairs.

Other considerations had contributed to his spleen. His remarkable services to the Ministry as their leading writer and prime propagandist had been ill-rewarded. The Queen, influenced by the Archbishop of York and the Duchess of Somerset, was determined to give him no preferment in England : the author of *A Tale of a Tub* had too infidel a mind. He could hope for nothing more than the deanery of St. Patrick's : he was to be confined to the Ireland he hated — a bound Prometheus, eating out his heart. " Since the Queen has been pleased that Ireland should be my home ", he would like to be Prolocutor of the Irish Convocation ; " but it would vex me to be proposed and not succeed ". It vexed him that he could always do something for others, nothing for himself.

Added to all this, there was a private anxiety : his relations with Vanessa, the impetuous young woman who had been rash enough to fall in love with him — a dean of forty-six — were reaching a climax. Away in Dublin was Stella, to whom he was committed by all the ties of a lifetime since they had been brought up together in Sir William Temple's household at Moor Park.

Everything counselled retreat, and fortunately there was a fastness at hand, a refuge in the Berkshire Downs. Here in this place, in those summer months of 1714, all the various sides of Swift's life were strangely brought together, and concentrated for us to watch as in a concave mirror, in miniature.

The living of Letcombe Basset was held by a young friend of Farnham days, son of the vicar there, who knew Stella and had some connection with the household at Moor Park — everything about that household is mysterious. We find Swift writing to Stella in 1712 : " Did I tell you that young Parson Geree is going to be married, and asked my advice when it was too late to break off ? " Swift, who had no intention of marrying himself, was hardly likely to approve of improvident marrying in others. But, as usual, he turned his hand to help and tackled Lord Harcourt, whose neighbourhood this was, for preferment : " Lord Keeper promised me yesterday the first convenient living to poor Mr. Geree, who is married and wants some addition to what he has ; he is a very worthy creature ".

At the end of April Swift sent down a present of wine, in preparation for his own coming. Geree writes wishing " you would give us leave to take it for an earnest that you intend yourself to follow in a little time and honour our poor habitation with your presence, where you will have a horse and garden and pretty good study of books, and the master and mistress entirely at your service ". In the meantime he hoped that Swift would help him by recommending some young gentlemen whom he might take to board as pupils : having married, he wanted the revenue. But he hoped Swift would not be frightened from making this the place of his residence whenever he thought fit to retire : the four or five boys he had were orderly and good.

On Monday, 1 June, Swift left London by coach for Oxford, where he stayed several days. Nothing is known of his movements, which he kept very close, except that on Thursday he set out for Letcombe with his servant and " a portmanteau big enough to contain his library as well as his

equipage ". To Ireland he wrote, " I was six weeks com-
passing the great work of leaving London and did it at last
abruptly enough. . . . I shall say no more but that I care
not to live in storms when I can no longer do service in the
ship and am able to get out of it." In fact, " as times are
like to be, I should be glad to have my money in another
place " : he even thought of putting it into the purchase of
some land in Ireland.

From Letcombe his first letter was to Vanessa : " You see
I am better than my word, and write to you before I have
been a week settled in the house where I am. . . . I am at a
clergyman's house, an old friend and acquaintance whom
I love very well ; but he is such a melancholy thoughtful
man, partly from nature and partly by a solitary life, that I
shall soon catch the spleen from him. . . . We dine exactly
between twelve and one, at eight we have some bread and
butter and a glass of ale, and at ten he goes to bed. . . . His
wife has been this month twenty miles off at her father's and
will not return these ten days. I never saw her, and perhaps
the house will be worse when she comes. I read all day, or
walk, and do not speak as many words, as I have now writ,
in three days. . . . This is the first syllable I have writ to
anybody since you saw me. I shall be glad to hear from you,
not as you are a Londoner, but a friend ; for I care not
threepence for news, nor have heard one syllable since I
came here. The Pretender, or Duke of Cambridge, may
both be landed, and I never the wiser. But if this place were
ten times worse, nothing shall make me return to town while
things are in the situation I left them. I give a guinea a
week for my board, and can eat anything. I hope you are
in good health and humour." One observes in this letter
Swift's concern to get his relations with Vanessa back to the
cooler level of friendship, which he had long observed with
Stella — a line altogether safer in the confusion and danger
of the time.

The news of Swift's retreat soon spread in London.
Barber, Printer to the City and of the *Examiner* — the government paper Swift directed and wrote for — sent him word :

I

" Everybody is in the greatest consternation at your retirement, and wonders at the cause. I tell them it is for your health's sake." The poet Gay, who owed his appointment as secretary to Lord Clarendon (now going Envoy Extraordinary to Hanover) to Swift's good offices, wrote to thank him. Swift replied in good humour, " I wonder how you could have the impudence to know where I am. . . . Take Mr. Lewis's advice in all things, and do not despise mine, and so God bless you, and make you able to make my fortunes." Dear Arbuthnot, the Queen's physician, the kindest heart among all these friends, wrote off : " I am glad your proud stomach is come down and that you submit to write to your friends ". To whom Swift replied : " My stomach is prouder than you imagine, and I scorned to write till I was writ to. I have already half lost the idea of Courts and Ministers. . . . I did not know till last night that the Princess Sophia was dead,[1] when my landlord and I chanced to pay a visit to a farmer in a neighbouring village [no doubt Letcombe Regis] and was told so over a mug of ale, by a brisk young fellow just come from London, who talked big and looked on us with great contempt." Then, with a change of mood and black resentment flooding into his mind : " You are a set of people drawn almost to the dregs ; you must try another game ; this is at an end. . . . The fashion of this world passeth away : however, I am angry at those who disperse us sooner than there was need. I have a mind to be very angry, and to let my anger break out in some manner that will not please them at the end of a pen."

So Swift was meditating, if he had not already begun, his *Free Thoughts on the Present State of Affairs* : one sees the spirit in which he would write it. Pope wrote him an elaborate letter : " At Button's it is reported you are gone to Hanover, and that Gay goes only on an embassy to you. Others apprehend some dangerous state treatise from your retirement, and a wit who affects to imitate Balzac, says that

---

[1] Electress of Hanover and heiress to the English Crown under the Act of Succession. She was granddaughter of James I.

the Ministry now are like those heathens of old who received their oracles from the woods." If Swift were too busied in state affairs to read Pope's letter, " yet you may find enter-tainment in folding it into divers figures, either doubling it into a pyramidical, or twisting it into a serpentine, form to light a pipe ". And more elaboration to the same effect — one does not like Pope's letters, so carefully composed and so artificial. Arbuthnot sent news from the centre of affairs : " I will plague you a little by telling you that the Dragon [*i.e.* Oxford] dies hard. He is now kicking and cuffing about him like the devil ; and you know parliamentary manage-ment is the *forte*, but no hopes of any settlement between the two champions."

On receiving news of the worsening of the situation and the hopelessness of Oxford's case, Swift sat down and com-posed a letter in the nature of a farewell and an apologia — perhaps to prepare him for the tone of his pamphlet when it should appear. It is a famous letter, and deservedly so for the loftiness of its sentiments and the magnificence of their expression. Hardly ever in our history has a falling minister been consoled with such majestic phrases, revealing — not concealing — warmth of affection. Impossible to quote it in full, but only a few sentences. " When I was with you, I have said more than once that I would never allow quality or station made any real difference between men. Being now absent and forgotten, I have changed my mind. You have a thousand people who can pretend they love you with as much appearance of sincerity as I, so that according to common justice I can have but a thousandth part in return of what I give. And this difference is wholly owing to your station. And the misfortune is still the greater because I always loved you just so much the worse for your station. For in your public capacity you have often angered me to the heart, but as a private man never once." And so the letter moves to its grand conclusion : " I will add one thing more, which is the highest compliment I can make, that I never was afraid of offending you, nor am now in any pain for the manner I write to you in. I have said enough ; and,

like one at your levee, having made my bow I shrink back
into the crowd."

Away in the country, but besieged by the solicitations
of his friends, the changing news from day to day, Swift
could not prevent his mind from churning politics and preferment over and over. If only the Dragon would stand in
with the rest, the Dragon and the Squire [*i.e.* Bolingbroke]
pull together. . . . To Arbuthnot, 3 July: " I find the
triumvirate of honest councillors is at an end ; I am gone,
Lewis [Under-Secretary of State] says he lives in ignorance
in his castle, and you meddle as little as you can ". It was
Arbuthnot's duty to advise Lady Masham, the Queen's
friend and confidante, at this juncture : there was no-one
else to give her sound advice and she needed it more than
ever. Questions of preferment teased his mind : " It is the
Ossorys that get the Derrys and the Chesters the Yorks ".
He could never be made a bishop. Better to think of the
crops and " retire to lament with my neighbours the want of
rain and dryness of hay. Farmer Tyler says the white mead
at Childrey has not been so bad in the memory of man and
the summer barley is quite dried up ; but we hope to have
a pretty good crop of wheat. . . . We cannot get a bit of
good butter for love or money. I could tell you more of
the state of our affairs, but doubt your taste is not refined
enough for it."

At this moment Swift's own business affairs in Ireland
rose up to tease him : his steward and tithe-collector, Parvisol, of whom we hear so much in the *Journal to Stella*, had
another spasm of incompetence   Swift wrote to thank Arch-
deacon Walls for " the pains you and Mr. Forbes are at
about my rotten affairs. I have made that Parvisol a rogue
by my own carelessness and trusting to his accounts ; and
have denied myself many a necessary thing, hoping to have
some money in bank against I wanted it. . . . He has
imposed upon my easiness, and that is what I never will
forgive." It reveals an interesting facet of Swift's complex
and provoking nature that he who was so careful and self-
denying on one side, where things were immediately under

his view and in his own control, should have a confiding and
rather careless attitude where others were concerned —
contrary, too, to his low view of human nature. Perhaps it
was a part of his immense confidence in himself. It is
precisely these contradictions that give his personality such
an endless fascination. Vanessa's mother had died, leaving
her affairs somewhat embarrassed, and Vanessa had been
bothered by a visit from a bailiff. At once Swift wrote off
telling her she was to raise any money she pleased from his
friends, John Barber and Ben Tooke — for whom Swift had
got the appointment as publisher of the *Gazette* — and she
might send the bond down for him to sign " and I will send
it back to you, and you may give it to Ben ". The warm
terms in which he wrote of his friends made Vanessa jealous.
" I have had now two letters of yours to answer. I am
pleased to see you piqued about my dearness to Ben and
John. They are worthy subjects ; there are some words I
never use to some people, let that satisfy. How many
gentlemen, says you, and fine young gentlemen truly, would
be proud to have you desire so much of them." One
observes the boring symptoms of her state : teasing her
provoked only the more the passion Swift then found intolerable and was determined not to satisfy.

Meanwhile, in London affairs were at a stand. William
Thomas, Oxford's secretary, wrote reproachfully : " I dare
not mention anything of politics to one that has purposely
withdrawn himself from the din of it. I shall only tell you
that your friends applaud your conduct with relation to your
own case ; but they think it hard you should abdicate at a
juncture your friendship seems to be of most use to them."
This thought must have given Swift a wry satisfaction as he
paced the garden or walked the lanes round Letcombe ; for
abnegation is itself a refinement of pride, a refusal of what
the heart most wants, the last exaction wrung by the conjured spirit. Only a duke knew how to deal with this state
of mind. Swift wrote, very grandly and politely, to Ormonde
to weigh in and hold the Ministry together — and to keep
his eye, by the way, on the disposal of the Irish bishoprics.

The Duke, equally politely, handed him a raspberry — or perhaps one should say, a strawberry — " I am very glad to hear from you. I thought you had hid yourself from the world, and given over all thoughts of your friends. I am very sorry for the reason of your retirement. . . . I send you some burgundy, which I hope you will like. It is very good to cure the spleen." Only such ducal mortals could afford to take such a lofty line : the disaster, which the mere man of genius had been the first to apprehend, was none the less approaching.

For the moment, it held off and things even appeared to be a little better. It seemed that the Ministry could not, after all, get rid of the Lord Treasurer or get on without him. Swift's friend, Lewis, wrote *à propos* of Bolingbroke as an alternative : " the man of Mercury's bottom is too narrow, his faults of the first magnitude ; and we cannot find that there is any scheme in the world how to proceed. Mercurialis complains that the Dragon has used him barbarously ; that he is in with the democraticals and never conferred a single obligation upon him since he had the wand. *Le temps nous éclaircira.*"

To this *éclaircissement* Swift now had his pamphlet ready to contribute, which he had written in the quiet of Letcombe. Anything but quiet in tone, it reveals the temper in which he had viewed the haymaking in those fields and talked rural politics with his host or a neighbouring farmer : there is the edge on the irony, the resentment at the folly in high places, the sweep of mind to universalise out of particular political circumstances. Though only a few pages, they are by the author of *Gulliver*. " I have been frequently assured by great ministers that politics were nothing but common sense; which, as it was the only true thing they spoke, so it was the only thing they could have wished I should not believe. God hath given the bulk of mankind a capacity to understand reason when it is fairly offered ; and by reason they would easily be governed, if it were left to their choice." But governments will not be candid and sincere with their peoples, and come to disaster in consequence. " Nor are examples less frequent of ministers famed for men of great intrigue, whose politics have produced little more than murmurings, factions and discontents, which usually terminated in the disgrace and ruin of the authors." Swift could not see any reason for mystifying the public or confusing the issues by over-manœuvring when there was a clear majority of the country for a clear Tory policy. [Harley was never candid or clear; he was an artful and disingenuous party-manager, not a statesman; with his canting Nonconformist background, he had much in common with the late Lord Baldwin. For the rest, like him, at his best in personal relations.] Swift was a sceptic as to the greatness of ministers : " I could produce innumerable instances from my own memory and observation, of events imputed to the profound skill and address of a minister, which in reality were either the mere effects of negligence, weakness, humour, passion, or pride, or at best but the natural course of things left to themselves ". People are apt in searching for the causes of political events to be mistaken by searching too deep. " And as I have known this to be the frequent error of many others, so I am sure it hath been perpetually mine, whenever I have attempted to discover the causes of political events by refinement and conjecture; which, I must acknowledge, hath very much abated my veneration for what they call *arcana imperii*; whereof I dare pronounce that the fewer there are in any administration, it is just so much the better."

Experience had brought disillusionment : we are halfway between the exhilaration of the years of triumph, depicted in the *Journal to Stella*, and the contempt and despair of *Gulliver*.

On the other hand, nothing he said was intended to detract from " the qualities requisite in those who are trusted with the administration of public affairs; on the contrary, I know no station of life where great abilities and virtues of all kinds are so highly necessary, and where the want of any is so quickly or universally felt. A great minister hath no virtue for which the public may not be the better, nor any defect by which the public is not certainly a sufferer." Both

Oxford and Bolingbroke are directly criticised : " on one side very great reserve, and certainly very great resentment on the other . . . have inflamed animosities to such a height as to make all reconcilement impracticable. Supposing this to be true, it may serve for a great lesson of humiliation to mankind, to behold the habits and passions of men otherwise highly accomplished, triumphing over interest, friendship, honour and their own personal safety, as well as that of their country, and probably of a most gracious princess, who hath entrusted it to them." What a condemnation of human foolery it was, in the most gifted and trusted specimens of the genus ! It may be seen that there was a curious rationalism at the bottom of Swift's mind : he really expected human beings to behave according to reason : it was their unreason that shocked him. He had yet a long way to go along the road, great progress in disillusionment to make, before he arrived at the Houyhnhnms. But events were helping him.

" It may seem impertinent in one of my level ", he went on with bitterness, " to point out to those who sit at the helm, what course they ought to steer. I know enough of courts to be sensible how mean an opinion great ministers have of most men's understanding ; to a degree that in any other science would be called the grossest pedantry." Nevertheless he proceeded (for Swift was never afraid of anybody) to give advice. What it came to was — unity of the Tory Party on a forward policy. Why stay on the defensive when you have a majority in Parliament and the country with you ? Why mystify and confound your own supporters for the *beaux yeux* of your opponents — the Whig faction ? [The fact was that Harley was such a past-master of intrigue that he could not play a straight game.] Make the Church of England secure in her rights and privileges ; keep the dissenters out of power ; and so secure the future for the Protestant succession on terms agreeable to the majority of the nation. Then " for the future it shall not be in the power of the Crown, although in conjunction with any rich and factious body of men, to choose an ill majority in the House of Commons ".

This was common-sense advice and a coherent policy for

the Tory Party. But the rift within the leadership reduced them to incoherence : a most dangerous situation to be caught in if the Queen should die with the conflict still unresolved. Which was, in effect, what happened ; the party as such was broken irretrievably. The Whigs, though a small minority of the nation, ruled the high eighteenth century and made it theirs.

What the upshot of the pamphlet came to was support for Bolingbroke's hand in remodelling the Ministry and proceeding upon a more Tory basis, a coherent plan. Swift can never have had any suspicion that Bolingbroke was guilty of an even more dangerous incoherence than Oxford, was playing about with the idea of a Stuart restoration, was even now in touch with the Pretender at St. Germains. If Swift had known what subsequent historians know, it would have fed all the more his misanthropy and despair. His greatest friends were not only keeping the essential facts from him, they were betraying him. But what did that signify ? He was not a person of their level ; he was a mere pamphleteer and wit to whom a deanery — an Irish deanery — had been thrown for his services.

But his services were not yet at an end. The pamphlet was sent up for his friend Charles Ford to see through the press. Ford was a good scholar, a man of taste, a devotee of opera, with whom Swift had been to see the tombs in Westminster Abbey ; moreover, as usual, Swift's good offices had got him a job, as Gazetteer. Ford wrote, giving his opinion of the work : " There is so great a tenderness and regard shown all along to the Queen that I could have wished this expression had been out — ' the uncertain timorous nature of the Queen '. But there was no striking it out without quite spoiling the beauty of the passage ; and, as if I had been the author myself, I preferred beauty to discretion. I really think it is at least equal to anything you have writ ; and I dare say it will do great services as matters stand at present." To preserve its anonymity Ford sent the tract to Barber under an assumed name. The printer probably suspected it was Swift's : he spotted that it was well written,

saw the passages that galled and submitted it to Bolingbroke
to be vetted. Bolingbroke kept it for weeks and made alterations in it. Ford wrote : " there is something very mean in
his desiring to make alterations, when I am sure he has no
reason to complain and is at least as fairly dealt with as his
competitor ". He asked for another copy to be sent up and
Swift complied. But before it could appear, all their hopes
and projects were reduced to dust by the Queen's death. It
was not printed until almost all those concerned in it had
left the scene for ever. The version of it that we have is
that altered by Bolingbroke, with the offending passages
cut out.

On Sunday, 4 July, Swift received a visit from Pope and
Parnell, who had ridden over from Binfield. They were
fellow members of the Scriblerus Club, which Arbuthnot,
Swift, Gay and they had constituted the preceding winter.
Out of its burlesque proceedings sprang various poems and
papers, many jokes and ultimately, in some sort, *Gulliver's
Travels* itself. Since this is Parnell's one appearance, we may
say that Swift had praised his verses and introduced him to
Oxford and Bolingbroke, from whose patronage he got his
Irish archdeaconry. (It seems that under this Ministry
Irish church preferment was thought proper for poets. They
might do worse.) Parnell and Pope reported their visit as
Scriblerus Envoys in a mock news-letter. It gives us a
pleasing glimpse — and the only one apart from Swift's first
letters — into the Letcombe interior.

" This day the envoys deputed to Dean S[wift] on the
part of his late confederates, arrived here during the time of
Divine Service. They were received at the back-door, and
having paid the usual compliments on their part, and received
the usual chidings on that of the Dean, were introduced to
his landlady, and entertained with a pint of the Lord
Bolingbroke's Florence. The health of that great Minister
was drank in this pint, together with the Lord Treasurer's
whose wine we also wished for ; after which were com-
memorated Dr. Arbuthnot, and Mr. Lewis, in a sort of cider,
plentiful in those parts, and not altogether unknown in the

taverns of London. There was likewise a sideboard of coffee, which the Dean roasted with his own hands in an engine for the purpose, his landlady attending all the while that office was performing. He talked of politics over coffee, with the air and style of an old statesman, who had known something formerly, but was shamefully ignorant of the last three weeks. When we mentioned the welfare of England he laughed at us, and said Muscovy would become a flourishing empire very shortly. He seems to have wrong notions of the British Court, but gave us a hint as if he had a correspondence with the King of Sweden. As for the methods of passing his time, I must tell you one which constantly employs an hour about noon. He has in his windows an orbicular glass, which by contraction of the solar beams into a proper focus, doth burn, singe, or speckle white or printed paper, in curious little holes or various figures. We chanced to find some experiments of this nature upon the votes of the House of Commons. The name of Thomas Hanmer, Speaker, was much singed, and that of John Barber entirely burnt out. There was a large gap at the edge of the Bill of Schism, and several specks upon the proclamation for the Pretender. I doubt not but these marks of his are mystical, and that the figures he makes this way are a significant cypher to those who have the skill to explain them."

At Westminster Tory prospects were improving. The government had come off victorious in the Lords from an awkward investigation into the dropping of certain duties imposed under the Treaty of Utrecht. It was alleged that this was prejudicial to our commercial interests and obtained by bribery. The responsibility was Bolingbroke's. The attack was made by the Whigs, but Oxford had instigated it. The Commissioners of Trade had been examined at the bar of the House of Lords. " They are prodigiously pleased with what has been done." But these economic matters were beyond the cultivated Under-Secretary of State : " I do not understand it well enough to give you an account of it ; for the rapture they are in hinders them from explaining themselves clearly. I can only gather from their manner

of discourse that they are come off without censure." Bolingbroke was in high spirits. John Barber had met him the
minute he had Swift's letter. " I attacked him for some
wine, and he immediately ordered you two dozen of red
French wine, and one dozen of strong Anziana white wine.
The hamper will be sent tomorrow by Robert Stone the
Wantage carrier, and will be there on Friday. . . . My
Lord bid me tell you that he will write to you, and let you
know that as great a philosopher as you are, you have had
the pip, that the public affairs are carried on with the same
zeal and dispatch as when you was here ; nay, that they are
improved in several particulars ; that the same good understanding continues ; that he hopes the world will be the
better for your retirement ; that your inimitable pen was
never more wanted than now ; and more, which I cannot
remember. I believe he expects you should write to him.
He spoke many affectionate and handsome things in your
favour." From which one sees that complacency is the
besetting sin of politicians.

Swift must have replied to Bolingbroke's message, for
down came a letter from the coming great man, with all the
style and jaunty humour characteristic of him. " I never
laughed, my dear Dean, at your leaving the town : on the
contrary, I thought the resolution of doing so, at the time
when you took it, a very wise one. But I confess I laughed,
and very heartily too, when I heard that you affected to find
within the village of Letcombe all your heart desired. . . .
If my grooms did not live a happier life than I have done
this great while, I am sure they would quit my service. Be
pleased to apply this reflection. Indeed I wish I had been
with you, with Pope and Parnell, *quibus neque animi candidiores*.
In a little time, perhaps, I may have leisure to be happy.
I continue in the same opinions and resolutions as you left
me in ; I will stand or fall by them. Adieu. No alteration
in my fortune or circumstances can ever alter that sincere
friendship with which I am, dear Dean, yours." Here, too,
with this politician there was a seductive charm in the
private man.

The office of Historiographer Royal was at this time vacant. Surely he who had written so much for the Ministry, and had it in mind to write its history, or even that of the Queen's reign, might hope to be considered for it? Before leaving London, Swift had written a memorial for the Queen, asking to be considered a candidate, " not from any view of the profit (which is so inconsiderable that it will hardly serve to pay the expense of searching offices), but from an earnest desire to serve his Queen and country ". Lady Masham was sympathetic about it : she told Arbuthnot that " she has it very much at heart and would gladly do it for her own sake and that of her friends ; but thinks it not a fit season to speak about it ". A week later Lewis was in despair of Swift's getting it and " thinks it quite over since a certain affair ". Arbuthnot gave a copy of the memorial to Bolingbroke, who said it would be to the eternal scandal of the government to suffer someone of Swift's standing, who had deserved so well of them, to be uneasy about such a matter.

A few days later Ford wrote that the office had been already disposed of : to one Madox — none of them knew who he was. " It would be impudence in them to send for you ; but I hope you will come. A reconcilement is impossible and I can guess no reason why matters are delayed." When Swift heard, he wrote to Arbuthnot : " I wonder Lord Bolingbroke knew nothing of it. So there is an end of that, and of twenty reflections one might make upon it. If the Queen is indifferent in those matters, I may well be so too." And to Vanessa, without any reserve : " I am not of your opinion about Lord Bolingbroke ; perhaps he may get the staff, but I cannot rely on his love to me. He knew I had a mind to be Historiographer, though I valued it not but for the public service, yet it is gone to a worthless rogue that nobody knows. I am writ to earnestly by somebody to come to town and join with these people now in power, but I will not do it."

Actually Madox was a great scholar, who had already published a masterpiece of historical research on the Antiquities of the Exchequer. In the curious English way, the right man had been appointed. No doubt Swift, if he had known who he was, would have considered him fit for a professorship in the island of Laputa. But it was no less galling to be overlooked for such a person.

In London pamphlets were already circulating about the absent, the absconding, Dean ; and very amusing, and cruel, they were. Swift, who did not spare his enemies, could not but expect to be lacerated by them. His was a personality that excited either devotion or detestation ; on one side (especially with those who knew him well) friendship and affection, on the other (particularly with those who did not) envy and dislike. He was a marked man, and some of the attacks on him searched the sensitive spots : his pathetic desire for recognition, his naïf liking for the company of the great, his change of party, the doubt that existed over his religious convictions. The *Hue and Cry after Dr. Swift* particularly went home. It was written in the manner of the *Journal to Stella* — which was still in manuscript — and therefore probably by some kind friend who knew him well enough and wished him no good. " Thursday. Waked with the headache. Said no prayers that morning. Dressed immediately. Looked confounded rakish. Repeated verses whilst I was washing my hands. Resolved (whilst I was putting on my gown) to ridicule the orders of bishop, priest and deacon after dinner at my Lord Bolingbroke's. . . . Resolved to write an ode upon changing one's mind, in imitation of Horace's *Justum et tenacem* etc. . . . *Mem.* To write a paper when I am in the country to bring with me to town and to publish at my first appearance, called ' Dr. Swift's Reasons ' : viz. for Ingratitude, for Irreligion, for Turning, for Returning and to serve any turn ; to be bound up with the *Tale of a Tub*."

All this only helped to make him, a naturally affectionate man, hate humans the more. Nor had he much for which to be grateful to his grand friends. Then there was the Queen, who vetoed any preferment for him in the Church this side the Irish Channel ; she was advised by the stupid Archbishop Sharp and the Duchess of Somerset, who had had

an awkward passage when young and her first husband had
been murdered by her lover, Count Königsmarck. On her,
Swift had written a terrible lampoon, "The Windsor
Prophecy". Now at Letcombe, his mind free to play on
these resentments, he wrote a poem on himself:

> By an old redhair'd, murd'ring Hag pursued,
> A crazy Prelate, and a Royal Prude.
> By dull Divines, who look with envious Eyes
> On ev'ry Genius that attempts to rise;
> And pausing o'er a Pipe, with doubtful Nod,
> Give Hints, that Poets ne'er believe in God.
> So, Clowns on Scholars as on Wizards look,
> And take a Folio for a conj'ring Book.

> Swift had the Sin of Wit, no venial Crime;
> Nay, 'twas affirm'd, he sometimes dealt in Rhime:
> Humour, and Mirth, had Place in all he writ:
> He reconcil'd Divinity and Wit.
> He mov'd, and bow'd, and talk't with too much Grace;
> Nor shew'd the Parson in his Gait or Face;
> Despis'd luxurious Wines, and costly Meat;
> Yet, still was at the tables of the Great.
> Frequented Lords; *saw those that saw the Queen*;
> At *Child's* or *Truby's* never once had been;
> Where Town and Country Vicars flock in Tribes,
> Secur'd by Numbers from the Lay-men's Gibes;
> And deal in Vices of the graver Sort,
> Tobacco, Censure, Coffee, Pride and Port.

From all which we may read Swift's complexes as in a book.
And so, on to the conclusion:

> By Faction tir'd, with Grief he waits a while,
> His great contending Friends to reconcile.
> Performs what Friendship, Justice, Truth require:
> What could he more, but decently retire?

The pleasures of retirement and the desire for independence are celebrated in another poem, in a gentler mood,
written at Letcombe: an *Imitation of a Satire of Horace*:

> I often wish'd, that I had clear
> For Life, six hundred Pounds a Year,

> A handsome House to lodge a Friend,
> A River at my Garden's End,
> A Terras walk, and half a Rood
> Of Land set out to plant a Wood.

After an amusing description of his life in London, he concludes :

> Thus in a Sea of Folly tost,
> My choicest Hours of Life are lost :
> Yet always wishing to retreat ;
> Oh, could I see my Country Seat.
> There leaning near a gentle Brook,
> Sleep, or peruse some antient Book ;
> And there in sweet Oblivion drown
> Those Cares that haunt the Court and Town.

But those cares were becoming more pressing than ever. Lady Masham, who had the confidence of the Queen, had broken openly with Oxford : she told him, " You never did the Queen any service, nor are you capable of doing her any ". Arbuthnot wrote that the circle round the Queen had bidden him defiance " without any scheme, or likeness of it in any form or shape, as far as I can see ". At this juncture Swift went into Oxford to stay at Christ Church for a few days with Lord Harley, the Lord Treasurer's son and heir, who was staying with his old tutor. Swift wrote urgently to Arbuthnot to advise Lady Masham, " who in my opinion is going on upon a very dangerous adventure without one creature to direct her. . . . What she said to the Dragon a week ago is of so desperate a strain that I cannot think her in a temper to be at the head or the bottom of a change ; nor do I believe a change accompanied with such fusions can ever succeed. . . . If I were to be of necessity always at Court like you, I could never let people run mad without telling and warning them sufficiently." Lord Harley left Swift at Oxford " horribly in the dumps ". When he got back to London his father had at last fallen from power.

Lewis wrote from Whitehall to tell Swift the news : " The triumph of the enemy makes me mad. I feel a strange tenderness within myself, and scarce bear the thoughts of dating letters from this place, when my old friend is out, whose fortune I have shared for so many years. . . . The moment I turned this page, I had intelligence that the Dragon has broke out in a fiery passion with my Lord Chancellor, sworn a thousand oaths that he would be revenged etc. This impotent, womanish behaviour vexes me more than his being out. This last stroke shows *quantula sint hominum corpuscula.*"

The fact is that it was the Queen herself in the end who was resolved to be rid of the Treasurer. She may have had an uncertain, timorous nature, as Swift said ; but she was also very obstinate and — as Swift wrote before leaving Letcombe — " upon some occasions positive to a great degree ". Arbuthnot wrote from Court, " the fall of the Dragon does not proceed altogether from his old friend, but from the great person, whom I perceive to be highly offended, by little hints that I have received ". According to Lewis, the Queen told all the Lords the reasons for her parting with him, " viz. that he neglected all business ; that he was seldom to be understood ; that when he did explain himself she could not depend upon the truth of what he said ; that he never came to her at the time she appointed ; that he often came drunk ; that lastly, to crown all, he behaved himself toward her with ill manner, indecency and disrespect ". Kindly Lewis had long been of the opinion that the Dragon's parts were decayed ; it was not his going, but the manner of it, that enraged Lewis. " They would not give the Dragon the least quarter, excepting only a pension, if he will work journey-work by the quarter." Such is the in- gratitude of politics, the heartlessness of people in high place.

Whoever else was heartless and ungrateful, Swift was not : he wrote at once to Oxford offering to accompany him in his retirement. Oxford replied like the man of good heart he was : " If I tell my dear friend the value I put upon his undeserved friendship, it will look like suspecting you or myself. . . . If I have not tired you *tête à tête*, fling away so

K

much time upon one who loves you." Oxford intended to
retire to his country seat, Brampton Castle, in Herefordshire.
Swift had fixed his journey to Ireland for 2 August, for his
licence of absence from his deanery had almost expired.
" My trunk with all my clothes and linen was sent last week
to Chester, and I am almost in rags." But he at once
consented to go with Lord Oxford into Herefordshire for
company, when news from London disrupted all their plans.

Swift expected that his following the fallen Treasurer
into retreat would " lose him all favour with those now in
power. . . . I am hitherto very fair with them, but that
will be at an end." This was never put to the test. On
29 July Lady Masham addressed Swift the strongest possible
appeal not to go to Ireland, but to remain and help the
Queen and the reconstructed Ministry. " I was resolved to
stay till I could tell you the Queen had got so far the better
of the Dragon as to take her power out of his hands. . . .
I cannot have so much time now to write all my mind,
because my dear mistress is not well, and I think I may lay
her illness to the charge of the Treasurer, who for three
weeks together was teasing her and vexing her without
intermission, and she could not get rid of him till Tuesday
last." Lady Masham went on to a direct personal appeal
for Swift's help. " I must put you in mind of one passage in
your letter to me, which is : ' I pray God send you wise
and faithful friends to advise you at this time, when there
are so great difficulties to struggle with '. That is very plain
and true ; therefore will you, who have gone through so
much, and taken more than anybody pains, and given wise
advice, if that wretched man had had sense enough and
honesty to have taken it, I say, will you leave us and go into
Ireland ? No, it is impossible ; your goodness is still the
same, your charity and compassion for this poor lady, who
has been barbarously used, would not let you do it. I know
you take delight to help the distressed ; and there cannot be
a greater object than this good lady, who deserves pity.
Pray, dear friend, stay here ; and do not believe us all alike
to throw away good advice, and despise everybody's under-

standing but their own. I could say a great deal upon the subject, but I must go to her, for she is not well."

What a turmoil this must have set going in Swift's mind, as he paced his cage at Letcombe: to be within a hand's reach of real power at last. But, like everything in his life, it was too late. In fact, the Queen was dying. The struggle had been too much for her. At her last Council the debate as to who should take Oxford's place raged until two o'clock in the morning and the Queen remained throughout until the end. It brought on a stroke. On 31 July Barber informed Swift: " I am heartily sorry I should be the messenger of so ill news as to tell you the Queen is dead, or dying: if alive, it is said she cannot live till morning. . . . I had set out yesterday to wait on you, but for this sad accident, and should have brought letters from Lord Bolingbroke and Lady Masham to have prevented your going." Lewis was writing simultaneously: " At the time I am writing, the breath is said to be in the Queen's nostrils; but that is all. No hope of her recovery. Lord Oxford is in Council; so are the Whigs. We expect the demise tonight. There is a prospect that the Elector [George I] will meet with no opposition." Ford wrote Swift an account of the last crisis and the Queen's illness: " She was not prayed for, even at her own chapel at St. James's, and what is more infamous, stocks arose three per cent upon it in the City ". The Whigs were romping home on the Hanoverian Succession. Next day the Vicar of Wantage sent a hurried note up to Letcombe: " At twelve o'clock Lord Bolingbroke's man rid through Wantage to call Mr. Packer to London, the Queen being dead. I am confounded at the melancholy news; yet could not forbear sending it to you."

All that Swift feared had come to pass with that one stroke. The Tories had lost control of the situation by their divisions, and now they were to be its victims — for the best part of the century. No use now to think of John Barber's consolations: " Lord Bolingbroke told me last Friday that he would reconcile you to Lady Somerset, and then it would be easy to set you right with the Queen, and that you should be easy here, and not go over. He said twenty things in your favour, and commanded me to bring you up, whatever was the consequence. But all vanished in a minute." It was all the more bitter to hear from Ford that Bolingbroke " could have done anything. No minister was ever in that height of favour ; and Lady Masham was at least in as much credit as she had been in any time of her life. But these are melancholy reflections. Pray send me your poem : *Hoc erat* etc." Bolingbroke himself summed it all up in a famous letter : " The Earl of Oxford was removed on Tuesday ; the Queen died on Sunday. What a world is this, and how does Fortune banter us." Then came the tell-tale postscript, revealing the truth : " I have lost all by the death of the Queen, but my spirit ; and I protest to you, I feel that increase upon me. The Whigs are a pack of Jacobites ; that shall be the cry in a month, if you please." It was the cry of a gambler. The truth of the situation was expressed by one of the smaller men outside, who saw more clearly : " Stocks never rose so much in so few days ".

Only one of all these expressed any human feeling for the poor woman upon whom the weight of these events had fallen, and that was her own physician, dear Dr. Arbuthnot : " My mistress's days were numbered even in my imagination, and could not exceed such certain limits ; but of that small number a great deal was cut off by the last troublesome scene of this contention among her servants. I believe sleep was never more welcome to a weary traveller than death was to her." Since the circle of friends was not to be broken, and some of them to be in danger and put on trial for treason, Arbuthnot concluded with a tribute to Swift which enables us to see what the real character of his friendship was and what so many people valued in him : " Dear friend, the last sentence of your letter quite kills me. Never repeat that melancholy tender word, that you will endeavour to forget me. I am sure I never can forget you, till I meet with — what is impossible — another whose conversation I can delight so much in as Dr. Swift's, and yet that is the smallest thing I ought to value you for. That hearty sincere friendship, that plain and open ingenuity in all your commerce, is what I am sure I never can find in another man. . . . God knows I write this with tears in my eyes."

Arbuthnot wanted Swift to come up at once. Lewis gave him better advice : to go to Ireland and take the oaths to the new king, and so qualify himself to hold his deanery : there would be danger enough for the members of the High Tory circle. It remained for Swift to tie up a few loose ends before going. He wrote to thank Lady Masham — now as completely *écartée* as her patron, Sarah, Duchess of Marlborough, had been before her — for her favourable intentions, " written at a time when you were at the height of favour and power ". Swift drew the moral of the disaster in a remarkable long analytic letter to Bolingbroke, which that statesman found it impossible to answer — it was, indeed, unanswerable. In it Swift acquitted him of the major responsibility for the disaster. " I never left pressing my Lord Oxford with the utmost earnestness, and perhaps more than became me, that we might be put in such a condition as not to lie at mercy on this great event ; and I am your lordship's witness that you have nothing to answer for in that matter." This was too generous an acquittal : Swift could not have known that his great friends — Oxford, Bolingbroke and Ormonde — had all been in treasonable communication with St. Germains.

On 9 August Swift set pen to paper on a new pamphlet, *Some Considerations upon the Consequences to be hoped and feared from the Death of the Queen.* He had not written more than a few pages when he was interrupted by the most dangerous visitor he could imagine — Vanessa, in full heat, coming openly by Wantage. The pamphlet was never finished. Instead, he wrote her a letter — alarmed, angry, apprehensive — which sets the tone for their subsequent intercourse in Ireland that came to so grievous an end. There are those who think that on this occasion Vanessa got underneath the Dean's defences. In any case, there is no doubting the tone of the letter that followed her back to London : " I think, since I have known you, I have drawn an old

house upon my head. You should not have come by
Wantage for a thousand pounds. You used to brag you
were very discreet : where is it gone ? " He goes on to lay
down conditions for their future communication : when he
is in Ireland he will write " as soon as I can conveniently,
but it shall always be under a cover ; and if you write to me,
let some other direct it ; and I beg you will write nothing
that is particular, but what may be seen ; for I apprehend
letters may be opened and inconveniences will happen. If
you are in Ireland while I am there, I shall see you very
seldom. It is not a place for any freedom, but where everything is known in a week, and magnified a hundred degrees.
These are rigorous laws that must be passed through ; but it
is probable that we may meet in London in winter, or, if
not, leave all to fate, that seldom cares to humour our
inclinations. I say all this out of the perfect esteem and
friendship I have for you. These public misfortunes have
altered all my measures and broke my spirits. I shall, I
hope, be on horseback in a day after this comes to your hand.
I would not answer your questions for a million, nor can I
think of them with any ease of mind. Adieu."

It is easy enough to see what had happened : that she
had declared her passion and that this was his farewell to
Vanessa, in spite of her coming to Ireland after him and
her attempts to force herself upon him. It seems that
the Monday following, 16 August, Swift left Letcombe for
Ireland : of the circumstances attending his journey nothing
whatsoever is known.

No wonder there is such a tradition of Swift's residence
at Letcombe. Up till quite lately the country folk would
tell you that the great man used to ride into Oxford every
day — it is the way that country memories magnify the
event. The Reverend John Geree lived there in the rectory
all his life : he got no preferment from Lord Harcourt,
" trimmer Harcourt " as Swift called him. Only a canonry
at Hereford came his way, in 1734. For the rest, he lived on

at Letcombe, the chief events in his life the births and deaths of his children. There they are noted in the little musty brown Register, that once was lost and was found again as long ago as 1791. My thoughts wander as I turn over the faded pages with their rustic entries, more moving to me than anything in life — for these are lives, folded and put away for ever. Outside, the noise of the summer wind in the trees has sunk to a whisper. A cow is lowing loudly in the village — as it might be Parson Geree's. Through the church-door I see the jackdaws chattering round the rick. Turning over the pages I note that the Rector's wife, Elizabeth, usually presents him with a child every other year : John is baptized in 1713, Stephen in 1715, Thomas in 1717, William in 1719; then Elizabeth in 1720, Mary in 1721, Hester in 1722. Next year, after a life of child-bearing, the Rector's wife dies.

The Rector himself pops up a head in 1736 with a letter to Swift. From its terms there seems to have been no communication between them since they parted, twenty-two years before. " Mr. Dean, If you have not quite forgot an old acquaintance, living in a little obscure corner of the world called Letcombe near Wantage in Berks, I beg leave to recommend to you the bearer, a gentleman belonging to the Army, son to the Lady Scroggs who is my parishioner." The Rector sends some translations of Horace, " which I beg you would look over, and give me your impartial opinion ". At some time the melancholy, thoughtful clergyman married again; for, three years after Swift died — in the year 1748 we find a child baptized Deborah, daughter of the Rev. Mr. John Geree and Deborah his wife. The Rector was at that time seventy-six years old. Thirteen years later : " John Geree, S.T.B. and Rector of this parish was buried 29 August 1761. Rector of this parish 54 years, aged 89." They brought him from that rectory thronging with memories of one crowded summer, across the white road that goes up and over the Downs to Hungerford, past the old black-and-white timber-framed cottages that are still there, along the churchyard path and in through the porch, to bury him in the chancel under the communion-table where he lies. It is strange to think that this old clergyman, who had known Swift and Stella in their earlier days at Moor Park and whose rectory had received Vanessa, knew the secrets of Swift's enigmatic life as few others. But, if so, nothing ever escaped his lips.

AFTERNOON AT HAWORTH
PARSONAGE

It is an October day, and all the way up the valley of the
Aire from Keighley in the bus I can hardly restrain my
excitement. What *will* it be like? — this place that I know
so intimately, that I have known about since my childhood
(a tattered copy of *Jane Eyre* was the only book in the house,
beside the family Bible and the *Home Preacher*) and yet have
never set eyes on until now in middle age. It is not often
that I have this specific excitement about what a place will
be like and what new experience awaits me there, though
it happens more often as I grow older. I dreamed of Venice
before I went there, and very remote and wonderful it was,
like a Turner water-colour — though I saw it all in terms
of the bay at home, a starry Gribbin in a haze farther out to
sea. I remember the same feeling on my first visit to Stratford, which I postponed long enough — the heightening expectancy as the car went through the Cotswold countryside
and drew near the town; and once before, when younger,
on going to tea with the Prime Minister at Chequers. Today
one might have been going to tea with the Queen.

There was all the sharpened sensitivity with which one
kept a look-out on the unfamiliar country — that was yet
familiar and recognisable as in a dream. There were the
factories strung out along the valley — the smoke from them
could already be seen from Haworth when the Brontës were
children. Occasionally one passed the substantial house of
a mill-owner in its own grounds — the kind of place at which
the girls expected to be governesses, at which they tried
their hands and were such dismal failures. The country was
grey, gaunt and raw: it had something of the look of the
Cornish uplands about it, the china-clay area behind St.
Austell — a Nonconformist countryside: I recognised the
stigmata — the honesty, the independent spirit, the rough

goodness of heart, the rawness. Sometimes the bus showed the steep overhanging side of the valley; the wind raged in the trees; the trees became more infrequent; the valley narrowed; the bus stopped at the foot of a steep hill. This was Haworth: what should I find when I got to the top of the hill?

The sky was now leaden and lowering, the pull up from the Aire to the village at the top, clinging around the church to the side of the hill, completely exposed and bare. At the entrance to the village proper, the old cobbled street skirting the escarpment, I noticed a small Tudor manor-house: very small but with wide mullioned window on the first floor looking out over the valley and down to Bingley and Keighley. Now the view is obstructed by a large classical chapel — ' strict Baptist ' — erected in 1824 on the Hall Green. This can have given no pleasure to the Rev. Patrick Brontë, incumbent of Haworth. The extraordinary old man to have outlived them all: he must have been tough: he certainly wore out his wife — or perhaps she introduced a delicate strain, a consumptive tendency from the Branwells? These cogitations, the picture of Mount's Bay and Penzance along its blue rim just round the corner of my eye, occupied my mind up the last corkscrew turn, the clogs clattering past me on the fierce hard-bitten stones. Now it is raining and the wind howling. I look across the street to the ' Black Bull ' at the church-gate that was frequented by Branwell. The creeper on the wall blows disconsolately about, the rain pours down. A Yorkshire voice passing: " Proper Haworth weather. What do y' expect ? "

All round the church the October wind rages, in the few trees in front of the parsonage sheltered a little behind the church. The leaves silt up outside the church-gate. The church itself was rebuilt in 1879 — an idiotic thing to have done: it has no interest, or very little Brontë interest. This is not the church that the Rev. Patrick ministered in, the formidable Grimshaw thundered in, the family attended Sunday by Sunday until life — too bright a flame in them — burnt itself out. True, in a vault beneath the south pillar of the chancel they are buried — there are Charlotte and Emily; a bunch of withered heather hangs above them. At the back of the church is a mural tablet to all the family extinguished here; the Cornish mother blown out by these winds and too much child-bearing, at the same age — one notes — as Charlotte. " In memory of Maria, wife of the Rev. Patrick Brontë, A.B., Minister of Haworth. She died Sep. 15th 1821 in the 39th year of her age. Also of Maria their daughter who died May 6th 1825 in the 12th year of her age. Also of Elizabeth their daughter who died June 15th 1825 in the 11th year of her age. Also of Patrick Branwell their son who died September 24th 1848, aged 31 years. Also of Emily Jane their daughter who died December 19th 1848, aged 30 years. Also of Anne their daughter who died May 28th 1849, aged 29 years. She was buried at the old church, Scarborough. Also of Charlotte their daughter, wife of the Rev. A. B. Nicholls, B.A. She died Mar. 31st 1855 in the 39th year of her age. Also of the afore-named Rev. Patrick Brontë, A.B., who died June 7th 1861 in the 85th year of his age, having been incumbent of Haworth for upwards of 41 years. ' The sting of death is sin, and the strength of sin is the law, but thanks be to God, which giveth us the victory through our Lord Jesus Christ.' 1 Cor. xv, 56, 57."

Now what can that possibly mean, I wonder, sitting there in the pew beneath; what consolation can anyone suppose it to have for such a story? The wind in the parsonage trees rages like the sea — like the noise of the sea in Mount's Bay. The church is so dark I can hardly see. Sometimes a pallid glimmer of wintry light comes through, enabling me to descry the names and dates inscribed on the tablet. The door-handle rattles like someone wanting to get in — like the ghost-child at the window-pane in *Wuthering Heights*. Rap! Rap! — there it goes again.

I leave the church to its ghosts.

What a day! In the few steps up the lane to the parsonage I have to take shelter in the porch of the Church School, where I can imagine Emily, or at least Charlotte, sheltering before me. Sheets of rain sweep across the churchyard forested with headstones. I see a thing I have never seen before — the large minute-hand of the church clock shaking and dipping in the wind. The sea rages overhead. Talk about ' Wild Decembers ', if this is what it is like in October — how infinitely glad they must have been to see the harebells of summer that Emily wrote about with such feeling.

One last step or two across the lane and I am in at the gate ; the little square of garden that had currant-bushes in their days now has evening primroses, marigolds, June daisies (how late ! but this is the North) blowing their heads off. Now I am on the threshold ; the door opens and I am inside, out of the rain and wind — glad of the welcoming shelter of the little house, as they must often have felt, coming in from the moors behind or struggling up that hill on the way back from Keighley and civilisation.

The house is just what I expected it to be ; I know my way round it at once. There on the right is the door to Mr. Brontë's study, where he spent all his days and took his meals alone ; whence he emerged one fine day to cross the passage and look in on the girls in the dining-room opposite, where they lived and planned and discussed and wrote their books : " Girls, do you know Charlotte has been writing a book, and it is much better than likely ? " (This was *Jane Eyre*.) There on the left was their living-room, hive of so much activity, buzzing with plans and projects, the very walls witness of so much intensity of experience, of suffering and grief for these children of genius, and — what we have only recently come to understand — the spot to which the dream-world they created and inhabited from their early days was tethered. Straight ahead are the stairs, where Emily thrashed her great mastiff, Keeper, into obedience. On the right, behind their study, would be the kitchen, where Tabitha reigned supreme and where Emily liked to be about the baking. Upstairs, over the study, Mr. Brontë's bedroom, which he shared with Branwell ; over the dining-room, Aunt Branwell's room, where she lived for twenty

years after she came up from Penzance to take charge of her
sister's motherless family; between these rooms, the little
passage room where the girls slept, which Charlotte has
described in words that are famous, though their significance
has only lately come to be understood: "Pen cannot portray
the deep interest of the scenes, of the continued train of
events, I have witnessed in that little room with the low
narrow bed and bare white-washed walls. . . . Remembrance yields up many fragments of twilight hours spent in
that little unfurnished room. There have I sat on the low
bedstead, my eyes fixed on the window, through which
appeared no other landscape than a monotonous stretch of
moorland and a grey church tower rising from the centre
of a churchyard so filled with graves that the rank weeds
and coarse grass scarce had room to shoot up amid the
monuments. Over these hangs in the eye of memory a sky
of such grey clouds as often veil the chill close of an October
day." But it was not the sky of Haworth that Charlotte
saw with her eyes fixed on the window, nor the moorland,
nor the grey church tower. Her mind was away: "it had
launched on a distant voyage, and haply it was nearing the
shores of some far and unknown island under whose cliffs no
bark had ever before cast anchor ".

In short, her mind was away in the kingdom of Angria,
which all her childhood and right up into womanhood she
shared and inhabited with her brother.

It all sprang from the box of wooden soldiers that Mr.
Brontë brought back one day from Leeds for Branwell.
Next morning he was at his sister's door — the little passage
room; Charlotte selected the tallest and handsomest, with
" This is the Duke of Wellington ! This shall be the Duke ! "
The others selected their favourites and gave them names.
So started the series of games for which they now had
characters. One night the game took a new turn. The
scene is described by Charlotte, while still a child of only
thirteen, with that incomparable gift of realisation of the
actual, which she shared with Emily, already fully developed.
" The play of the *Islanders* was formed in December 1827,

in the following manner. One night, about the time when the cold sleet and stormy fogs of November are succeeded by the snowstorms and high piercing night-winds of confirmed winter, we were all sitting round the warm blazing kitchen fire, having just concluded a quarrel with Tabby concerning the propriety of lighting a candle, from which she came off victorious, no candle having been produced. A long pause succeeded, which at last was broken by Branwell saying, in a lazy manner, ' I don't know what to do.' This was echoed by Emily and Anne.

Tabby : ' Wha ya may go t'bed.'

Branwell : ' I'd rather do anything than that.'

Charlotte : ' Why are you so glum tonight, Tabby ? Oh ! suppose we had each an island of our own.'

Branwell : ' If we had I would choose the Island of Man.'

Charlotte : ' And I would choose the Isle of Wight.'

Emily : ' The Isle of Arran for me.'

Anne : ' And mine should be Guernsey.' "

One can already see something of their characters revealed in their choices ; any Freudian would have something to go on for his fancies. The children proceeded to populate their islands with their favourites, Charlotte's being, as usual, the Duke of Wellington and his two sons, Lord Arthur and Lord Charles Wellesley. These under various guises are central figures in the events of the islands, which began to form a saga that accompanied Charlotte secretly into womanhood and fame. Even *Shirley*, twenty years later, she concludes with a paean in praise of Wellington — not a whit different in temper from what she was writing at thirteen : time had only taught her to be defensive about her dreams.

So those tiny miniature books began, recounting the adventures of these characters as they developed and changed habitation, from the Islands to the Glasstown Confederacy and so to the kingdom of Angria. Already by the time she was fourteen Charlotte had written twenty-two of them, for in 1830 she compiled a " Catalogue of my Books ". There remain over a hundred of these, written by Charlotte and

Branwell, equalling altogether the published works of the Brontës : all in tiny printed script, which it often needs a magnifying-glass to read — no wonder that Charlotte became so short-sighted : one sees her characteristic pose, reading or writing with nose close to book or paper. In her *History of the Year 1829* Charlotte again records the scene for us with her acute realisation of her surroundings : " While I write this I am in the kitchen of the Parsonage, Haworth ; Tabby, the servant, is washing up the breakfast-things and Anne, my youngest sister (Maria was my eldest), is kneeling on a chair, looking at some cakes which Tabby has been baking for us. Emily is in the parlour, brushing the carpet. Papa and Branwell are gone to Keighley. Aunt is upstairs in her room, and I am sitting by the table writing this in the kitchen. Keighley is a small town four miles from here. . . . Our plays were established ; *Young Men*, June 1826 ; *Our Fellows*, July 1827 ; *Islanders*, December 1827. These are our three great plays that are not kept secret. Emily's and my best plays were established the 1st of December, 1827 ; the others March, 1828. Best plays mean secret plays ; they are very nice ones. All our plays are very strange ones. Their nature I need not write on paper, for I think I shall always remember them."

There was indeed no danger of her forgetting. Away from home now, a few years later, engaged in the discouraging struggle to become a young woman earning her living as a schoolmistress with Miss Wooler at Roe Head, she describes the evening scene : " E. C——k on one side of me ; E. L——r on the other ; and Miss W——r in the background, stupidity the atmosphere, school-books the employment, asses the society ! What in all this is there to remind me of the divine silent unseen land of thought, dim now and indefinite as the dream of a dream, the shadow of a shade ? . . . That wind, pouring in impetuous current through the air, sounding wildly, unremittingly from hour to hour, deepening in tone as the night advances, coming not in gusts, but with a rapid, gathering stormy swell — that wind I know is heard at this moment far away on the moors of

Haworth. Branwell and Emily hear it, and as it sweeps
over our house, down the churchyard and round the old
church, they think, perhaps, of me and Anne ! " The
storm reminded her of Northangerland. Before her eyes
was Quashia, one of its heroes, who had penetrated to the
Queen of Angria's sanctuary for his solitary drunken revel —
there he was, lying full length on the disordered couch. At
this moment, " while this apparition was before me, the
dining-room door opened, and Miss Wooler came in with a
plate of butter in her hand. ' A stormy night, my dear ! '
said she."

Charlotte has a wonderful evocation of the Yorkshire
scene. It is an August morning and she goes to the window
of her prison, the school-room, to look out : " The dew was
not yet dried off the field, the early shadows were stretching
cool and dim from the haystacks and the roots of the grand
old oaks and thorns scattered along the sunk fence. . . . I
flung up the sash. An uncertain sound of inexpressible
sweetness came on a dying gale from the south. I looked in
that direction. Huddersfield and the hills beyond it were
all veiled in blue mist. The woods of Hopton and Heaton
Lodge were clouding the water's edge, the Calder, silent but
bright, was shooting among them like a silver arrow. I
listened — the sound sailed full and liquid down the descent ;
it was the bells of Huddersfield Parish Church. I shut the
window and went back to my seat. Then came on me,
rushing impetuously, all the mighty phantasm that this had
conjured up from nothing — from nothing to a system
strange as some religious creed. I felt as if I could have
written gloriously — I longed to write. The spirit of all
Verdopolis — of all the mountainous North — of all the
woodland West — of all the river-watered East, came crowd-
ing into my mind. If I had had time to indulge it I felt
that the vague sensations of that moment would have settled
down into some narrative better at least than anything I
ever produced before. But just then a dolt came up with a
lesson."

From which one sees that Charlotte was not made for a

schoolmistress, or a governess — for all that her fame was made by a book whose title, in its French dress, was *Jane Eyre: Mémoires d'une gouvernante*. How much else one sees from this passage, too : the nostalgia for the present, the realisation of the passing moment as a moment of eternity, this insatiable torment of the imagination that only writing can alleviate, not satisfy — they are all the stigmata of the born writer, for it is out of nostalgia that all art springs. Then, too, there is the suggestion of the passions that swept the hearts of the inhabitants of these imagined countries : the wars and conquests, murder and sudden death, the debauchery, the hopeless passions and illicit loves. No wonder Charlotte found society insipid compared with the secret world she shared with Branwell, the characters and creations of their dream : " Far from home I cannot write of them ; except in total solitude, I scarce dare think of them ". We see also the incipient struggle Charlotte was beginning to put up against the domination of the dream, for her sense of the external world was as acute as her nostalgia for the other. Branwell was never to come to terms with actuality. A phrase in one of his Verdopolis stories reveals his " instinctive fear of ending his pleasure by approaching reality ". He fell a victim to the dream-world, his own life its first casualty. But Charlotte was tougher : she carried through her determination to subordinate the dream to the real world ; out of the two she made a fusion, from which came her novels. But the significant characters in them have their prototypes in Angrian characters and situations. No wonder the Victorian world was surprised by their passion : " They tell me *Jane Eyre* has been written by Mr. Thackeray's mistress ", said Mrs. Carlyle.

It is not extraordinary that these children should have created a saga, or even a series of them ; other children have done so. And the conditions at Haworth were surely very propitious : there was the extreme isolation of the place, the loneliness of life there (" They kept themselves very close ", said a neighbour who remembered their coming there) ; Mr. Brontë and Aunt Branwell were both addicts

L

of privacy; the children were left to their own resources. ("You would not have known there was a child in the house, they were such still, noiseless, good little creatures.") They had something better to do than to make a noise. In short, Haworth Parsonage was a forcing-house of their genius, and their adult works were continuous with the creations of their childhood.

What is extraordinary is the completeness of the hold their imaginary world had on them, the tenacity with which they held to it, the gifts that went into it and that developed from it. Here are Emily and Anne, only a year before the writing of *Wuthering Heights*: "Anne and I went our first long journey by ourselves together, leaving home on the 30th of June, Monday, sleeping at York, returning to Keighley, Tuesday evening, sleeping there and walking home on Wednesday morning. . . . During our excursion we were, Ronald Macalgin, Henry Angora, Juliet Augusteena, Rosabella Esmaldan, Ella and Julian Egremont, Catherine Navarre and Cordelia Fitzaphnold, escaping from the palaces of instruction to join the Royalists who are hard driven at present by the victorious Republicans. The Gondals still flourish bright as ever. I am at present writing a book on the first wars. Anne has been writing some articles on this, and a book by Henry Sophona. We intend sticking firm by the rascals as long as they delight us, which I am glad to say they do at present." This is Emily at twenty-seven — she had already written some of her finest poems; she was dead at thirty. Years ago she and Anne had broken away from Charlotte and Branwell's game and set up a kingdom of their own — Gondal, to which all her best known poems relate : this is the explanation of their mystery.

Much nonsense has been written about Emily: whether she was not in love with her brother, whether he did not write *Wuthering Heights*, whether she had not a demon-lover, who can have been her nocturnal visitant :

He comes with western winds, with evening's wandering airs,
With that clear dusk of heaven that brings the thickest stars;

Winds take a pensive tone, and stars a tender fire,
And visions rise and change which kill me with desire . . .

Or again :

Cold in the earth, and the deep snow piled above thee !
Far, far removed, cold in the dreary grave !
Have I forgot, my only love, to love thee,
Severed at last by Time's all-wearing wave ?

Such poems, and many others, are utterances of characters
in the Gondal saga, and are to be understood in relation to
that context. But they express herself all the same within
that imagined world. The mystery is gone, but its place is
taken by a richer subtlety. The words may be placed in the
mouth of Gondal figures, but it is Emily that is speaking,
who reveals herself through them.

Vain are the thousand creeds
That move men's hearts, unutterably vain,
Worthless as withered weeds
Or idlest froth amid the boundless main

To waken doubt in one
Holding so fast by thy infinity
So surely anchored on
The steadfast rock of Immortality.

The realm may be Gondal, but the scene is Haworth :

Silent is the house — all are laid asleep ;
One, alone, looks out o'er the snow wreaths deep ;
Watching every cloud, dreading every breeze
That whirls the wildering drifts and bends the groaning trees.

Cheerful is the hearth, soft the matted floor ;
Not one shivering gust creeps through pane or door ;
The little lamp burns straight, its rays shoot strong and far ;
I trim it well to be the Wanderer's guiding-star.

Our knowledge of all this has cleared up several mysteries
about the Brontës and their work. For one thing, it has disposed of the Branwell legend : there is no question of his
having part in *Wuthering Heights*. All of him was in col-
laboration with Charlotte over Angria. And that was the

family grouping : Charlotte and Branwell; Emily and Anne.
Branwell's part turns out odder and more pathetic even than
one had thought : his own work inferior and without any
touch of genius, it was left for him to fertilise the imagination
of his sister. But if it solves these old literary questions, it
opens up a still greater mystery; for the story of these little
books provides a unique example of the development of
literary genius — there is nothing else like it, so far as I
know, in European literature. And genius, whatever form
it takes, is the ultimate human mystery; for it is life rendered
conscious of itself and achieving expression.

Emily's power of evoking the actual was, from early
years, as acute as Charlotte's and her attachment to Haworth
even more intense. Here she is at sixteen : " Tabby said
just now, ' Come Anne, pilloputate (*i.e.* pill a potato).' Aunt
has come into the kitchen just now and said, ' Where are
your feet, Anne ? ' Anne answered, ' On the floor, Aunt.'
Papa opened the parlour door and gave Branwell a letter
saying, ' Here, Branwell, read this and show it to your Aunt
and Charlotte.' The Gondals are discovering the interior
of Gaaldine. Sally Mosely is washing in the back kitchen."
Seven years later, " It is Friday evening, near 9 o'clock —
wild rainy weather. I am seated in the dining-room, after
having just concluded tidying our desk boxes, writing this
document. Papa is in the parlour — aunt upstairs in her
room. She has been reading *Blackwood's Magazine* to Papa.
Victoria and Adelaide are ensconced in the peat-house.
Keeper is in the kitchen — Hero in his cage. We are all
stout and hearty, as I hope is the case with Charlotte,
Branwell and Anne, of whom the first is at John White,
Esqr's, Upperwood House, Rawdon; the second is at Lud-
denden Foot; and the third is, I believe, at Scarborough
inditing perhaps a paper corresponding to this." More
usually her evocations of Haworth are in her poetry :

> There is a spot mid barren hills
> Where winter howls and driving rain,
> But if the dreary tempest chills
> There is a light that warms again.

> The house is old, the trees are bare
> And moonless bends the misty dome,
> But what on earth is half so dear —
> So longed for as the hearth of home ? . . .

> A little and a lone green lane
> That opened on a common wide,
> A distant, dreamy, dim blue chain
> Of mountains circling every side . . .

Actually, Emily could not support absence from Haworth : to be away made her ill. She had to be taken away from school at Roe Head. Charlotte wrote, " My sister Emily loved the moors. Flowers brighter than the rose bloomed in the blackest of the heath for her — out of a sullen hollow in a livid hill-side, her mind could make an Eden. She found in the bleak hill-side many and dear delights ; and not the least and best-loved was liberty. Liberty was the breath oi Emily's nostrils ; without it she perished. . . . Every morning, when she woke, the vision of home and the moors rushed on her, and darkened and saddened the day that lay before her. . . . In this struggle her health was quickly broken : her white face, attenuated form and failing strength, threatened rapid decline. I felt in my heart she would die, if she did not go home." It was no ordinary homesickness. " Nobody knew what ailed her but me ", Charlotte wrote. " I knew only too well."

Well, now Emily and Charlotte, and all of them, are at Haworth for ever. It is not their ghosts, nor the spirit of their dream-world that lingers in the Parsonage ; one has the sense that it is theirs as much as when they were alive, that they inhabit it still.

I enter the parlour. There is the horsehair sofa on which Emily died — refusing to go to bed, refusing to admit even that she was ill, " torn quivering ", Charlotte says, " from the midst of life ". " Never in all her life had she lingered over any task that lay before her, and she did not linger now. She sank rapidly. She made haste to leave us. Yet, while physically she perished, mentally she grew stronger than we had yet known her. Day by day, when I saw with what a front she met suffering, I looked on her with an anguish of wonder and love. I have seen nothing like it; but, indeed, I have never seen her parallel in anything. Stronger than a man, simpler than a child's, her nature stood alone." Here is the small upright piano, made by John Green, on which the sisters played; on the wall a print of their favourite John Martin's " Belshazzar's Feast " and pretty silk-work flower pictures worked by the family. There is a little water-colour of Mrs. Brontë — auburn curls peeping out from her Regency lace cap, with " Portrait of my dear wife " written on the back. There is a photograph of the old man with high choker, large nose and big hands — evidently it was no sinecure to be his wife. One day, when he and Charlotte were left alone of all the family, " a little incident happened which curiously touched me ", she wrote. " Papa put into my hands a little packet of letters and papers — telling me that they were mamma's, and that I might read them. I did read them, in a frame of mind I cannot describe. The papers were yellow with time, all having been written before I was born : it was strange now to peruse, for the first time, the records of a mind whence my own sprang; and most strange, and at once sad and sweet, to find that mind of a truly fine, pure and elevated order. They were written to papa before they were married. . . . I wish that she had lived, and that I had known her."

I cross the passage, as Mr. Brontë used to do to look in on the girls at work in the dining-room. It looks out on the little patch of garden and away across to the other side of the valley. It is here that one gets the sense of the innumerable occupations that kept them so busy, the picture of Victorian home-life — so different from ours — where the family created its own interests and enjoyments, here at its most concentrated. Somewhere, in a fragment of diary, one of the children, perhaps Charlotte, remarks of their games and their writings that there is so much to be done. One has the same sense from fragments of diary written by Emily as a child and preserved here : " It is past twelve o'clock. Anne and I have not tided ourselves, done our bed work, or done our lessons and we want to go out to play. We are going to have for dinner Boiled Beef, Turnips, potatoes and apple pudding. The kitchin is in a very untidy state. Anne and I have not done our music exercise which consists of b major. Taby said on my putting a pen in her face, Ya pither pottering there instead of pilling a potate. I answered, O Dear, O Dear, O Dear, I will derectly. With that I get up, take a knife and begin pilling. Finished pilling the potatoes. Papa going to walk. Mr. Sunderland expected."

Here all round are the evidences of their activities, particularly of the dream-world that occupied so much of their childhood. Here are some of the miniature magazines written by Charlotte, with her fixation on Wellington well in evidence : " An Extraordinary Dream by Lord Charles Wellesley ", " The Strange Incident in the Duke of Wellington's Life ", " Napoleon and the Ghost Story " and more of her miniature script-books written about twelve and thirteen. There are some remarkable pencil drawings by Branwell of characters in the kingdom of Angria, full of fire and energy ; and beautiful water-colours of scenes in that imaginary land, done by Charlotte, influenced very much by John Martin — there is one of Glasstown touched similarly by his architectural megalomania. Other rare writings date from a little later — Horace's Odes translated by Branwell, and music which he copied out for his flute. From the transition period in Brussels, so fateful for the girls (for from that dates the novel-writing), there is a French exercise by Emily, in her firm masculine hand, on " L'Amour filial ", and an essay by Charlotte on " La Justice humaine ", corrected by the Professor, *her* Professor, M. Héger, and marked, one is glad to see, *Bon*.

Perhaps the later evidences are more moving, for one associates this room with the planning of the novels, those ardours and expectations and disappointments, under the generalship of Charlotte. Without that, indeed, — her drive and determination, — they could have come to nothing, or we should have heard nothing of them. One sees to what point her childhood fixation on the Duke led and what it indicated. Mrs. Gaskell describes those evenings in this room just a hundred years ago. " It was the household custom among these girls to sew till nine o'clock at night. At that hour, Miss Branwell generally went to bed, and her nieces' duties for the day were accounted done. They put away their work, and began to pace the room backwards and forwards, up and down — as often with the candles extinguished for economy's sake, as not — their figures glancing into the firelight, and out into the shadow, perpetually. At this time they talked over past cares and troubles ; they planned for the future and consulted each other as to their plans. In after years this was the time for discussing together the plots of their novels."

One piece of furniture that played its part in the novels has come to rest here at last : the large painted Apostles' cupboard that belonged to the Eyres of Moorseats near Rothersage. It is interesting that Charlotte should have given her most famous character their name. And here is the cupboard as it appears in *Jane Eyre* ; Jane, it will be remembered, is watching beside the injured body of Mr. Rochester's brother-in-law, who has been savaged by Rochester's mad wife, up in the sinister attics of the Hall : " I must see the light of the unsnuffed candle wane on my employment ; the shadows darken on the wrought, antique tapestry round me, and grow black under the hangings of the vast old bed, and quiver strangely over the doors of a great cabinet opposite — whose front, divided into twelve panels, bore in grim design, the heads of the twelve apostles, each enclosed in its separate panel as in a frame ; while above them at the top rose an ebon crucifix and a dying Christ. According as the shifting obscurity and flickering gleam hovered here or glanced there, it was now the bearded physician, Luke, that bent his brow ; now St. John's long hair that waved ; and anon the devilish face of Judas, that grew out of the panel, and seemed gathering life and threatening a revelation of the arch-traitor — of Satan himself — in his subordinate's form."

Here is Emily's small rosewood writing-desk, into which Charlotte pried one day and discovered the poems. We remember the story — Emily's intense resentment, how it took Charlotte several days to persuade her to allow them to be published, and only then on an appeal that it would enable the other sisters to publish their poems too. " By dint of entreaty and reason I at last wrung out a reluctant consent to have the ' rhymes ', as they were contemptuously called, published. The author never alludes to them ; or, when she does, it is with scorn. But I know no other woman that ever lived ever wrote such poetry before." Charlotte, of course, was right : *how* right she was about her family and what we owe to her practical sense and ambition ! Without her, we might never have had *Wuthering Heights* — Emily would not have cared, might even have destroyed it, as she destroyed whatever it was she was working on when she died. The little desk now has a letter from the publisher to Ellis Bell, giving advice about the next work, hoping it will be an improvement on the first. Really, what unutterable fools humans are ! As if it were possible to improve on *Wuthering Heights* : there is nothing like it in the whole of our literature — such imagination, such intensity and passion, such tragic nobility (in that like *Lear*), such power and strangeness that is yet familiar for it re-echoes the deepest reverberations of the human heart.

Somehow this room has as much of her spirit and presence — silent and unspeaking as she was — as it has of Charlotte's. (Anne is a frail ghost beside them.) There is Emily's favourite post, on the hearth-rug in front of the fire ; she used to read there in the firelight with her arms round Keeper's neck. One sees her sometimes smiling, but never a word. A friend sends her a present — " she smiled when I gave the collar to her as your present, with an expression at once well-pleased and slightly surprised ". Once, in one of their discussions, she put in a couple of words. Charlotte's friend, Mary Taylor, who was staying with them, said that someone had asked her what her religion was and she had replied that this was between God and herself. At this Emily looked up from the firelight and said, " That's right ".

That was her sole contribution to the subject; but it was enough. Someone who knew her said, " She never showed regard to any human creature; all her love was reserved for animals ". She would come back from the moors with helpless wounded creatures, a fledgling or a young rabbit, holding them so softly that they were no longer afraid, and telling them stories which she was sure they understood.

No wonder Charlotte felt on returning to Haworth, her dream achieved and now a famous writer, but Emily and Anne dead : " The dogs seemed in strange ecstasy. I am certain they regarded me as the harbinger of others. The dumb creatures thought that as I was returned, those who had been so long absent were not far behind. I left Papa soon, and went into the dining-room : I shut the door — I tried to be glad that I was come home. I have always been glad before — except once — even then I was cheered. But this time joy was not to be the sensation. I felt that the house was all silent — the rooms were all empty. I remembered where the three were laid — in what narrow dark dwellings — never more to reappear on earth. . . . The great trial is when evening closes and night approaches. At that hour, we used to assemble in the dining-room — we used to talk. Now I sit by myself — necessarily I am silent."

The room is as silent now; I have it to myself and am glad for that : I can inhabit it alone with my thoughts of them. Nothing but the noise of rain all round the house, the runnels gurgling, the window-panes pattering, the trees outside shivering, all the world dripping — one cannot imagine that the clouds will ever roll away, that behind them somewhere is clear bright sunlight. Rain has its usual curious effect on me : it gives me strangely mingled sensations : on one side a cold feeling of desolation, on the other a heightened sense of intimacy within the house, cut off and sheltered from it all. Charlotte describes it once and again, though not those sensations ; in *Shirley* : " This is an autumn evening, wet and wild. There is only one cloud in the sky ; but it curtains it from pole to pole. The wind cannot rest ; it hurries sobbing over hills of sullen outline, colourless with twilight and mist. Rain has beat all day on that church tower : it rises from the stony enclosure of its graveyard : the nettles, the long grass, and the tombs all dripping with wet." And then, the domestic interior, from a letter : " Papa and I have just had tea ; he is sitting quietly in his room, and I in mine ; ' storms of rain ' are sweeping over the garden and churchyard : as to the moors, they are hidden in thick fog ".

I prowl about the darkened, rustling house, into Tabby's kitchen and upstairs, lingering in the rooms. Here, above Mr. Brontë's study, is his bedroom, which he shared with Branwell. It has a couple of Branwell's portraits : rightly for him, one of W. Thomas, of Thomas the wine and spirit merchants of Haworth; another of John Brown, sexton and drinking crony. They have a certain power, but the pigment is so dark one can hardly tell. There are a couple of landscapes and a water-colour copied from John Martin — a great influence in the family. Here is a saddle-bag Branwell gave to Nancy Craggs, a flame of his, and bits and pieces from *his* room at the ' Black Bull '. The only portrait of him is a silhouette of a singularly clerical figure : good profile like his father, thick wavy hair, spectacles on aquiline nose, high stock. Branwell's was a wasted life : one has little or no sympathy for him, after all the anguish he caused his sisters, the bitterness of the disappointment he was to Charlotte, the wastrel's life he led after such expectations formed of him. His death was the one thing that redeemed him : the tradition is that he insisted on dying on his feet. This room was the witness of that last scene.

Next is the little passage room, described by Charlotte, the girls' bedroom. In it there is a charming Paisley shawl of red and blue that belonged to Mrs. Brontë, and the silk shawls of her famous daughter. More remarkable, there are still faint traces on the wallpaper of the drawings that illustrated their childhood imaginings. Outside in the passage I stumble upon an adult symbol — the actual trunk bought by Charlotte in Brussels.

Here is Charlotte's bedroom after her marriage — that

above the dining-room, occupied by Aunt Branwell for so many years. It has a mass of pretty objects in it now : beads worn by the girls, strands of their hair as children — how fond the Victorians were of taking these mementoes. Anne's hair was so flaxen as to be almost white ; Charlotte's was fair as a child, later it darkened. There is a pink frock and cape worn by her, and black satin shoes a little worn at the toe of the right foot. A grander dress is that she wore at the Thackeray dinner in Kensington in 1850. Here are all her needlework implements, the under-bodices she made and wore, a pair of white stockings, the tea-cosy she worked. Against the wall stands a case of their household crockery : the pretty, inexpensive tea-cups they used, the black glaze tea-pot with " Wm. Grimshaw, Haworth " on it, the big family tea-pot with spout broken. It all makes a convincing picture of their domestic interior ; again one has this sensation of Victorian life as endlessly active and busy and self-occupied, employing, entertaining, amusing themselves — like the picture one has of it in *Shirley*. (Now the gale is blowing itself out, but the light is failing. It will rain again.) By the window, on a stand, is the lavender silk dress Charlotte wore on her wedding tour. Someone comes in behind me at the door, treads on a loose board : the silk dress trembles and shudders a little, giving it a faint evanescent impression of life.

I pass out of the room, leaving it to another occupant, and go downstairs, passing Emily's water-colour drawing of Keeper's head. It is right that he should be here on the stairs where he was once thrashed. He followed her coffin faithfully to church. Charlotte put him in at the end of her first novel, *The Professor*, and she brings him in again, rightly, into *Shirley* as the companion of Shirley Keeldar, for as Charlotte has told us — Emily was her original.

Wherever one looks out of the windows of this house one looks on tombstones — it is a house besieged by the dead. So thinking, I go into the little museum, the one addition to the house. There is a silhouette of Aunt Branwell facing me — pug-faced and Methodistical, in her high collar and mob-cap. Here are the foreign translations of the works :

Wutheringshöhe and the *Mémoires d'une gouvernante* — it is interesting to see how famous they became quite early — *Jane Eyre* in Russian and Turkish. But here, too, are Keeper's big metal collar and the tiny glass lamp of Emily's poem.

Pursued, I make for the last room in the house, the one with no associations, the gloomy little passage at the back of the dining-room that became Mr. Nicholls's study, after he married Charlotte. There is his portrait : he looks a potent type — dark thick hair, wide winged nostrils, lively eyes as a young man. In later life, with white hair and beard — muffled in hair — he looks mellowed and resigned. He was a Puseyite, we remember. Here is an engraving of the Reverend and horrid Mr. Carus-Wilson, of whom Charlotte gave such a scarifying portrait as Mr. Brocklehurst, and of his school as Lowood, in *Jane Eyre*. He has lofty, bony, aristocratic features ; a lithograph of his lady reveals her reclining in silk shawls reading a letter. Now they are only remembered for their connection with these girls. Here are Charlotte's eye-glass and her reading-glass ; another of her miniature magazines in microscopic print, her work-case and a lock of her hair — light brown. The wind blows a gale in the trees and rattles the window of the Rev. Mr. Nicholls's study that looks out on the churchyard.

I do not know why it should be that this dank little room, of no associations, should have affected my imagination all unawares so strangely that I should remember its strange atmosphere long after. It may have been due to the light, the queer western light coming refractedly in from the afternoon now quietening from the storm ; or it may be due to something out of my own childhood, in the light, or the atmosphere, or the smell of the place — something out of the wells of the unconscious. There are these strange, inexpressible sensations by which I date life, weigh it and feel it — the sense of waiting for something, of expectancy mingled with the " old " smell of flour in a bin, cheese on a shelf, mice in a corner cupboard : these intimations of the illimitable, of occult ecstasy shot with insatisfaction, joy mingled with the sense of being alone, that come upon one in childhood. This dark passage-like interior yet has a comforting intimacy for all its gloom — like the lonely sitting-room of my childhood in remote Cornwall — it is so bound up with such sensations, the excitement of rain, storm patter-ing on the pane, torrenting along the runnel outside; the gleam of pallid late-afternoon light in October, announcing the hour of tea — already the cups tinkle in the dining-room, there are steps outside along the passage from the kitchen, old and lame and shuffling; the door of the study opens; the subdued voices have an Irish burr; or after tea, in the dark here, there is the sense of a tingling vacuity, of nothing to do — just like that evening that started the dream-world of the Islands. How to express these esoteric sensations of childhood? — esoteric, in spite of being common to us all (I suspect), for no-one can ever express them: the smell of the moment, the look of the light, the feel of time.

I passed out of that thronging, haunted house into clear blue autumn sunlight. The wind had blown the rain com-pletely away; the afternoon, what was left of it, was clear with rain-washed water-colours. But what a bitter place! — coming out into the street I see that people have to hold on to their hats. I take the path along the church-way through the stile at the back of the Parsonage into the glebe — Emily's way to the moors. There is a high wind and now bright afternoon sun; an immense view opens out across the valley to high moors in every direction, and, in the west, I do not know what magnificent ridges of the Pennines. I understand Emily's passion for the moors, that breathes in all her poetry and palpitates through and through *Wuthering Heights*. I understand her longing, when dying, for the moors in August: " every breath from the hills so full of life, that it seemed, whoever respired it, though dying, might revive " ; her invocation for the moorland graves of Catherine and Heathcliff: " I lingered round them, under that benign sky ; watched the moths fluttering among the heath and harebells, listened to the soft wind breathing through the grass, and wondered how any one could ever imagine unquiet slumbers for the sleepers in that quiet earth ".

THOMAS HARDY AND MAX GATE

I WAS on my way to see Thomas Hardy. For that is how I think of it when going to see the place where a great man lived, one of the elect spirits of the past, or even some ordinary soul about whose course in life I know something now that it is finished. Some impress of personality remains on the place, all the stronger the more you know about the man, or perhaps the more subtly you are in tune with something in his personality or something that befell him in life. The scenes that surrounded him, the places that his eyes looked upon as a child, where he grew up, that were woven by a thousand threads, visible and invisible, into his work and life, where he lived and walked, the roads and lanes, field and hedge and woodland, where he was sometimes happy and sometimes suffered, where he is buried at last : all this retains some impress of him, a peculiar poignancy.

In fact Hardy was long dead. But not to me. For me he was more alive than anyone living there today : the whole place spoke to me of him — the bare dry roads, the scraggy pines about the house, the rustle of dead beech-leaves, the defensive privet hedge, the path worn along the bank by so many admiring feet.

We were in the railway carriage approaching Dorchester. In the opposite corner an elderly business man who had been born there and lived there all his boyhood, his sister a companion to the first Mrs. Hardy. (Little did he know how much that meant to me, or how well I knew her — that difficult, unsympathetic woman — from the Life, the poems, from what Q. had told me and Arthur McDowell and others who knew her.) In the other corners two sailors, one of them sunk in silence and reserve, the other gay, alert, vivacious, all on the surface — as it might be Bob, the Trumpet-Major's sailor brother.

Dorchester people did not care for Thomas Hardy, I

learned. But that much I knew already; and how characteristic of the idiot reaction of ordinary human beings to the man of genius who had made their town famous, I thought, my mind half-swerving with the motion of the train to another western county, not so far away now, I suddenly realised, with the familiar throb in the left temple. But I restrained my anger, showed no reaction at all: there was evidently so much to learn. I was fascinated.

"But why did they feel like that about him?" I asked innocently.

"Well, he was a *grouchy* old man," was the answer.

I felt myself in the presence of one of those words so full of character as to be hardly definable in any other words, that come straight out of the heart's life of the country people of England in the places where they live. I felt something of what it meant, but if I knew precisely I should know what it was that Dorchester people had against Hardy.

"What does that mean exactly?" I said. But, alas, he could not find another word to tell me; I was left to infer its sense from its sound — something between 'grudging' and 'grousing'. And that is about it, I gather from the Dictionary.

I remember that Dorchester people held his silence and solitariness against him, that he did not greet people as he walked about the streets. How could they know what went on in his mind? — that the place was peopled for him by shadows of half a century or a century before, the figures of his imagination, by Michael Henchard and Elizabeth Jane, by malicious old Uncle Silas and the melancholy hussar and a hundred others, all of them ghosts, children of his fancy; his mind occupied with colloquies over the past, the friends of his youth, William Barnes the poet who kept school next door to the architect to whom Hardy was articled, the other pupils with whom he read the Greek Testament and discussed the nicer points of Paedo-Baptism when young; or recalling the faces of the bell-ringers at Stinsford, or his father and uncle whom he had often accompanied with their fiddles to Christmas parties and carol-singing, barn-dance

and harvest-home? As if, absorbed in his dream, he did
not see, he who used to notice such things, had so mar-
vellously reported the talk of the gaffers at the bridge in
The Mayor of Casterbridge or round the heath-fires in *The
Return of the Native*. How *could* they know? (Yet they might
read his books.)

It appeared that Hardy was thought mean, not open-
handed: he never did anything for the town. (Except
make its name known all over the world, and to all posterity,
I reflected.) Once, when there was a reception or something
at the Town Hall and they wanted Hardy to come, he
wouldn't come unless they sent a car to fetch him. (The
usual petty grievances and small talk of a small town, I
registered.)

My informant grew more interesting. As a boy he had
frequently to take messages to his sister at Max Gate. One
winter evening — it was a November evening in the dusk —
going up the drive, he saw a head appear above the bushes
without a body to it. In the dark it gave him an awful
start. It was Thomas Hardy out looking for his cat.

Another winter's evening, when the choir had been singing carols outside the house, a window was thrown up and
Thomas Hardy put his head out and threw out sixpence to
them. " What do you think of that? " one said. " Well,
what did you expect? " said the others.

Evidently Hardy had kept the careful habits of his early
life, when he was poor and had nothing to spare, had only
himself to rely on, into his later years of security and ease.

Then came the most interesting thing, such as only someone in touch with the interior life of the house could have
known: Hardy was very careful to tear up all pieces of
paper he had written on into little bits, so that nobody
should get hold of his writing or make anything out of it.
I remembered a reminiscence of Desmond MacCarthy, who
had met the little old great man at a big country-house
party, crowded with the important and the distinguished.
Hardy, who was shy and diffident, seeing another literary
man, made for him and took refuge. He found all that

M

impressive and formidable, but he felt out of it. They were all so clever and talked so much. "All the same," said he to his fellow writer, with a countryman's shrewdness, "do you tell them your ideas? Because I don't." There is a certain charm in that, and also an instinctive rightness: his ideas were not those they would be most likely to appreciate.

In the little County Museum that belongs to the Dorset Field and Antiquarian Society, of which Hardy was their ' most distinguished member ', there is a delightful feature, one that is more interesting than anything I remember in any of the grander galleries in the country. Behind a window is a complete reconstruction of Hardy's study as it was about the turn of the century. It gives you a speaking picture, as hardly anything else could, of the surroundings of his daily life and of its progress from such simple beginnings to success and world fame. For there in the middle is the plain deal table on which many of the earlier works were written, with, on top, the little writing-box he bought as a lad. And then at the window there is the big Georgian writing-desk, with its elegant decorative brass rim, at which he wrote his later works. There are the very pens with which he wrote *Tess* and *Jude* and *The Dynasts*. All the paraphernalia of the writing man are here: the ivory paper-knife, blotter, inkstands and pen-wiper, the little roller-calendar, magnifying-glasses and, most affecting of all, his pince-nez laid down, just as he might have laid them down for the last time.

His favourite walking-stick is by the chair; by the door the grandfather clock, and the barometer that had belonged to William Barnes. The fireplace has tiles depicting scenes from Tennyson's poems; beside it, bellows — an old-fashioned West Country touch — and a stand for the kettle. Above the mantelpiece is a print of the young Tennyson — handsome as Apollo. It is interesting, and rather curious, to note the place Tennyson had in Hardy's mind: one would hardly have expected it from the Poems, in a way:

one would have thought, rather, Browning. Alongside are
two rows of old prints, arranged vertically; underneath, on
the mantelpiece, a small pair of scales and a wise old earthen-
ware owl, full of character — it might be Hardy himself, I
thought, looking out of those alert, intent eyes. In the corner,
the bass-viol that Hardy's father loved so well — too well
for the prosperity of his business as builder — which he used
to take round with him to Christmas parties and carol-
singing, and which he played for years in the gallery of
Stinsford church; standing there along with Hardy's violin.
I thought how full the Poems are, from one end to the other,
of the old-fashioned music they made together and the
forgotten tunes they played:

> Through snowy woods and shady
>   We went to play a tune
> To the lonely manor-lady
>   By the light of the Christmas moon.

or

> On afternoons of drowsy calm
>   We stood in the panelled pew,
> Singing one-voiced a Tate-and-Brady psalm
>   To the tune of " Cambridge New ".

Or there is the poem Hardy addressed to his father's violin:

> And, too, what merry tunes
> He would bow at nights or noons
> That chanced to find him bent to lute a measure,
>   When he made you speak his heart
>   As in dream.
> Without book or music-chart,
>   On some theme
> Elusive as a jack-o'-lanthorn's gleam,
> And the psalm of duty shelved for trill of pleasure.

Against the opposite wall is the big Georgian bookcase
with the books on the Napoleonic war which he used in
writing *The Dynasts*. Above the door a print of Napoleon;
on the wall a painting of Shakespeare — one thinks of that
enduring influence upon all the older English writers. There

is the formal chair in which Hardy sat to receive visitors, his Cambridge gown as Doctor of Letters thrown over the arm.

The ante-room has a small and shapely wash-stand from the cottage at Higher Bockhampton, which the young Hardy used as his writing-table and on which some of the earliest works were written. In the bureau I notice a pretty mug he had as a child, a jug with a cartoon of John Bull defying Bonaparte and another with portraits of Nelson and Captain Hardy. All these objects, like so much else that surrounded his childhood, the memories of his grandfather who had been a volunteer waiting with his company at Weymouth for Bonaparte, the very associations of the places and the tales they told him — all fed his imagination as a child, out of which there came *The Trumpet-Major*, the short stories and at last *The Dynasts*. No wonder — as T. E. Lawrence found, when he visited him, an old man of eighty, after the 1914–18 war — that the Great War to him was the war against Bonaparte, with its threats of a descent upon the Dorset coast, the great sailing-ships lying in Weymouth Bay, Nelson in the *Victory* passing down-Channel off Portland Bill to the campaign that ended with Trafalgar.

In a case by the wall is Hardy's christening-robe, and by it — a telling juxtaposition — the map he drew of Wessex with all the place-names he invented for the novels : the world of his imagination, the province he added to English literature, going back in direct descent — as it does, along with William Barnes — to the language of the Anglo-Saxon Chronicle. There is the manuscript of the earliest of his authentic books, *Under the Greenwood Tree*, with its original title, *The Mellstock Quire*, crossed out : written 1871. *The Mayor of Casterbridge* lies open at the scene of the banquet in the 'King's Arms' — that pretty bow-window of the Regency looking up and down the High Street — written 1884–5 : the handwriting clear, fluent, scholarly, a beautiful hand, stylish though simple : that of the don Hardy might have been, if the Vicar of Fordington had been a little more encouraging and the Fates a little less kind.

Beside them lies a much later manuscript, one of the last — the handwriting hardly at all changed — *The Famous Tragedy of Iseult, Queen of Cornwall*. I notice, what I had not observed before, that Hardy's sub-title describes it as " A Poetical Version of the Old Mummers' Play ". In the next case, along with his watch, is a fibula taken from the forehead of a skull exhumed at Max Gate, inscribed ' Romano-British' in Hardy's hand. Here is Hardy the antiquarian, the loyal member of the Dorset Field and Antiquarian Society — a side of him that people know little of, though it was a genuine interest of his mind. A curious consecration of his chosen place it seems ; but all around are the tracks and remains of the Romano-Britons, the barrows, the Roman plan of Dorchester itself, the camp, and but a few miles away, Maiden Hill.

Above, there is a drawing of an old shepherd, a great favourite with Hardy : it hung always by his bedside ; below, his orders and honours, the gold medal of the Royal Society of Literature, the ribbon and badge of the Order of Merit. The whole gives a speaking picture of the man and his life : the simple country origins and attachments, the world of poetry and of the imagination, the attraction to scholarship ; an utter simplicity and integrity ; in the end, success, recognition, renown.

Near by is a fine collection of photographs, of the family and places connected with them, scenes made famous in the novels. The series begins with his father and mother. There is one of his grandfather, a master-mason or local builder, whose chief interest, like his son's after him, was music : it was he that built the cottage at Bockhampton and settled there in 1801. The son's portrait, Hardy's father, shows an old countryman's face, humorous, whimsical, with remarkable grey eyes, the eyes that he handed on to his son, so animated as to have something " touched " — as a countryman would say — about them. Touched with what ? one might ask. The fire of latent genius, is the only possible reply. Then there is Hardy's mother, very alert and bird-like and on the qui vive, ready to pounce. It was from his mother that Hardy got his intelligence and his tenacity; from his father that he got his temperament, his quiet reflective nature, his love of music. Out of some incalculable magic in the combination of the two came his genius.

Actually the Hardy stock was coming to an end, when — as sometimes happens with genius — there was this sudden inexplicable illumination before extinction. As Hardy himself says of his family in a remarkable phrase: "They had all the characteristics of an old family of spent social energies". They had come of old country stock, of yeoman standing, and perhaps something more, to which Nelson's Hardy belonged, and the Elizabethan burgess who endowed Dorchester Grammar School, whose monument you will see inside the porch-door of St. Peter's, Dorchester. But they were coming down in the world; they had not yet become peasants or mere labourers: they were small landholders existing on a life-tenure of their property: a class becoming extinguished, when the family threw up a son through whom it will not be forgotten.

Hardy's mother once described his father to him as he was when she first set eyes on him in the gallery of Stinsford church, one Sunday about the year 1836: he appeared to her, who had known Weymouth and London, "rather amusingly old-fashioned, in spite of being decidedly good-looking — wearing the blue swallow-tailed coat with gilt embossed buttons then customary, a red and black flowered waistcoat, Wellington boots, and French-blue trousers". She had evidently taken a good look at him. That memory bore fruit in the son's sonnet, "A Church Romance":

> She turned in the high pew, until her sight
> Swept the west gallery, and caught its row
> Of music-men with viol, book, and bow
> Against the sinking, sad tower-window light.
> She turned again; and in her pride's despite
> One strenuous viol's inspirer seemed to throw
> A message from his string to her below,
> Which said: "I claim thee as my own forthright!"

Thus their hearts' bond began, in due time signed,
And long years thence, when Age had scared Romance,
At some old attitude of his or glance
That gallery-scene would break upon her mind,
With him as minstrel, ardent, young, and trim,
Bowing " New Sabbath " or " Mount Ephraim ".

Next day being Sunday, we decided — my American
friend and I — to go out to Stinsford and see the church
before morning service. We walked down the bare deserted
High Street and out along the main road to the bridge. A
soldier stood leaning against it with a map in hand. We
looked into the clear water of the Frome and across the
November meadows. " How far is Stinsford ? " I said.

" It isn't far, is Stinsford," he replied. The inversion
revealed the North Countryman.

" How is the North Country ? " I said. " Been there
lately ? "

He started. " How did you know I was North Country ? "
He was a fellow of some education, without any marked
accent, just a flavour in his intonation.

I said I was interested in regional differences and loved
local variations. That did not appease him.

" But how did you know ? "

He was insistent.

I looked at him : a strong, tall, dark Yorkshireman, with
black eyes blazing. He had been a choirboy in York Minster.

So interested and gay we were in the fresh Sunday-
morning air that I forgot to look at the map, and so, after
leaving our companion, we overshot the turning for Stinsford. We went straight on, the other side of a fine park,
into an enchanted lonely world with not a house in view :
nothing but November browns and greens, hips and haws
red on the hedges, and everywhere fine spiders' webs and
stillness. No-one. No-one to be seen. No-one to ask.

Going downhill I got more and more alarmed : time
was passing : we were in a hurry : we should run into the
service.

I kept my ears open for the sound of church bells. There were no church bells to be heard. The park was brown and dun; there were signs of its having been occupied lately by the military. At the bottom of the dip, within the pale, were vast galvanised iron huts, left wide open, gaping, sepulchral. There was barbed wire all round the park. But *where* was Stinsford church? One should be able to see it: we must be within half a mile of it. How provoking! I rushed on ahead frantically, scanning the skyline, the fields and pastures for sign of a church tower. Don ambled peacefully along, getting left further and further behind among the brambles and bushes edging the park.

Suddenly in a clearing appeared a wing of a large eighteenth-century house with classical windows and tall Georgian chimneys, very stately and deserted on the top of the slope. No time to give much thought to the Squire and Lady Susan — though they too appeared round the corner of my thoroughly vexed mind — I wondered now whether to break through the barbed wire and across the park. Everything seemed deserted, forlorn, empty, as if some grey hand had stopped its life. Nobody about; no sign of church or village.

"This is the way places in England hide themselves away," I said to my American friend. "We must be within half a mile of it, and we can neither see the church nor hear the bells."

By this time I was thoroughly vexed with myself and quite frantic at time passing when it would soon be impossible to get into the church — our one chance: we were leaving Dorchester that afternoon. We turned back up the hill and met a daft-looking local-preacher man with a facial growth (The Distracted Preacher? I thought) who was also deaf. However, he pointed out the way.

As we turned into the lane we heard the bells at last, three of them in varying rotation. A buxom farmer's wife, in full spread of sail, was making her way to church. We tore along. There was the farm — then up the little slope and down to the churchyard — the manor-house, not the large one in the park, almost touching the church.

And the Squire, and Lady Susan, lie in Mellstock churchyard now.

Yes, indeed, I noted — and all the Hardys too. There they were in a row under the yew-tree by the path.

Down we rushed to get into church in time. Already the Sunday-school children were in their place, agape as I moved about hurriedly trying to memorise the monuments. Here was a fine one in the aisle to George Pitt, of Strathfield-say, with a portrait bust of him above the monument in the Kingston Maurward aisle. So that was the great house with the tall façade I had seen looking down the park. Apparently he built it, or re-built it in stone, to please the whim of George III on his way to Weymouth. He must have married a Grey heiress, who brought him the estate; for further down the aisle was another eighteenth-century tablet, to the Greys, and upon it the name of Angel Grey. So that was where Angel Clare's name came from.

There was not more than a moment to make it all out. The church bells came to an end; the service began : we were marooned.

We sat down in the Kingston Maurward pew under the monument. No-one from the great house to disturb us — only the shadows. The church had been well enough re-stored — but O for the old pews and the clear glass through which the young Hardy looked at the trees in the churchyard :

> We watched the elms, we watched the rooks,
> The clouds upon the breeze,
> Between the whiles of glancing at our books,
> And swaying like the trees.

There, half-way up the aisle, immediately under the Angel Grey monument, had been the pew in which Hardy worshipped Sunday by Sunday for years as child, boy and young man.

> When I weekly knew
> An ancient pew,
> And murmured there
> The forms of prayer
> And thanks and praise
> In the ancient ways. . . .

The congregation consisted almost entirely of women and children, the menfolk still away at the war. Treble voices sang the familiar responses that I had not heard for years, the Te Deum and Jubilate, recited the Our Father and the Creed. In a dream, I hardly took in what was going on; the old accustomed phrases and cadences passed over me like the waves over someone under the sea. I only knew that I was here at last and that I was very near to tears, not so much for myself as for him who had belonged here, whose life had been so bound up with this place, from that moment when his mother turned and saw his father in that vanished gallery. I wept inwardly, silently, for all the unknown mystery that surrounds our lives, that makes us what we are and that bears us onward to our deaths. The spell of the old ways and prayers upon me, even as it had been upon him — though neither of us could subscribe to the old beliefs any more, my heart was full of tears at the pathos of life, at the thought of such genius ripening here in country simplicity Sunday by Sunday in this quiet place; the very spirit of the English Church formed and moulded him, made him what he was, was in his veins like the beat of his heart — and yet he could no more believe what it said, as once when a child, innocent and unquestioning :

> So mindless were those outpourings ! —
>   Though I am not aware
> That I have gained by subtle thought on things
>   Since we stood psalming there.

And now it was all over, all stilled for ever : only a memory, like the shadows of the trees through the windows of a century ago, out there in the churchyard where they all lie. In that moment, it was as if my mind touched his in that well-loved spot.

The parson mounted the pulpit and announced his text in a thin throaty voice. The spell was broken. I sat up : my astonished ears heard :

" Whosoever committeth sin doeth lawlessness : for sin is the transgression of the law.

" And ye know that he was manifested to take away our
sins ; and in him is no sin.

" He that committeth sin is of the devil ; for the devil
sinneth from the beginning."

And more to the same purpose. It was to be a sermon on
Sin. The preacher began by saying that it was unfashion-
able nowadays to preach on sin ; few people cared or
recognised their actions for what they were or considered
that it mattered. The thin, high, strained voice went on :
I ceased to listen : I gave myself up again to my inner dream.

At the Communion we went out into the quiet of the
churchyard ; in the sudden silence the cheeping of the
smaller birds sounded loud in that enclosed space. A light
mist lay over the meadows and fields ; the presence of
the neighbouring house — so near as to be almost touching
the church — made itself felt. I looked over the wall into the
peaceful green court, with the great plane-tree at the angle,
a few leaves caught lemon-yellow in the pale sunlight : a
fine Georgian upper storey with a long unbroken line of
windows looking upon the lawn ; underneath an earlier
stone range going back perhaps to the monks of Shaston
who had had their grange here. A house Hardy must have
often visited : a house full of memories and with its own
stories to tell.

> —The Lady Gertrude, proud, high-bred,
>   Sir or Madam,
> Am I — this laurel that shades your head ;
> Into its veins I have stilly sped,
> And made them of me ; and my leaves now shine,
> As did my satins superfine,
>   All day cheerily,
>   All night eerily !

And so up the path to the Hardy graves under the big
yew-tree. There is a Sunday silence over everything, while
the Communion service is going on inside the church ; the
hard unfeeling voice is but a faint murmur out here against
the chatter of birds. There is no other sound save the cheeping of sparrows, the cawing of rooks. The churchyard slopes

down to the valley, the trees stripped. A small boy released
from church runs up the path ; the rest of the Sunday-school
dribbles out. Silence returns and settles down again with
the pallid sun.

Here they all are : Hardy's grandfather, the first Thomas,
of Puddletown and Bockhampton, born 26 October 1778,
died 1 August 1837. Next comes his grandmother, who
came, I note, from Fawley in Berkshire : hence Jude's
name, Jude Fawley. On either side of the old couple are
their children, Hardy's uncle, then going up the path, his
father and mother. Next to them, the heart of their famous
son, whose ashes lie in Westminster Abbey ; in the same
grave his two wives, the first, Emma Lavinia, born at
Plymouth 24 November 1840, lived at St. Juliot, Cornwall,
1868–73, where Hardy found her.

> I found her out there
> On a slope few see,
> That falls westwardly
> To the salt-edged air,
> Where the ocean breaks
> On the purple strand,
> Or the hurricane shakes
> The solid land.
> I brought her here,
> And have laid her to rest
> In a noiseless nest
> No sea breaks near.
> She will never be stirred
> In her loamy cell
> By the waves long heard
> And loved so well.

Inscribed on the stone are the words : " This for remembrance ".

In the last grave are Henry, Mary and Katherine, Hardy's
brother and sisters : all unmarried, I think ; like himself,
childless : the end of a family, all complete and rounded-off
there. We lingered long and lovingly over the graves, reading and noting the inscriptions. How beautifully Hardy
had arranged it all. I thought of the Wordsworth graves at

Grasmere, looking up to the high fells and with the sound of the mountain stream running by on its way to the lake. That spot even richer in its memories and gifts, for along with Wordsworth are Dorothy, and Dora and Edward Quillinan, and Hartley Coleridge. This was the nearest parallel to that, and no less touching in this quiet, altogether less exciting spot, so exquisite and true to the man who lived here all his days. Important to choose where you are buried, I thought, as the congregation began to come out of church; the thought of Chateaubriand's grave in the island off St. Malo came into my mind, and, with it, Luxulyan.

But how to get to Max Gate? I wanted to walk back across the fields and water-meadows by the Frome, the way Hardy used to come. But there was no time. A lady gave us a lift round by the road and dropped us at the gate.

Arrived at Max Gate, we hesitated; and then, after a preliminary scanning, stole up the drive. How familiar it all looked, though I had only seen it once before for a few minutes and then from the road. It was as if I had known the house all my life — as if I belonged there. I could not feel a stranger about a house I knew so intimately and so much of what went on in it. If I thought about it, it would have felt altogether more unnatural to me to be regarded as a stranger in that place that was so familiar to me: infinitely more so than to the people who now lived there, to whom it belonged.

There was no-one about. It was all still and quiet and melancholy, as if waiting for a visit. Everything was as I expected it to be, more than autumnal, wintry and forlorn. The trees and shrubs and evergreens made it dark and gloomy: they had all grown up since Hardy came here in the eighteen-eighties: he had planted them all, and now the house seemed to be in the dark depths of a wood. When he came here — buying his plot of land from the Duchy of Cornwall, to which all the land hereabout belongs — the new, raw red-brick house caught the sun's first rays and the last sunset glow across the open down. Now it might be a house in a wood out of Hans Andersen or Grimm, in which everyone was asleep. The wind sang in the tops of the trees and in the telephone wires, and across the flats to the ridge looking down on Weymouth.

Suddenly a car turned in at the gate and drove up to the door : the family returning from church. There were the voices of children in that melancholy, childless spot that had never known any children. An old lady came towards us on a stick. I said we hoped we might be forgiven for trespassing, that we only wanted to *look* at the outside of the house, and would touch nothing and do no damage. The old lady was quite welcoming and very ready to talk.

There was first some preliminary skirmishing about where we came from, our respective universities, our relations and hers in various parts of America.

Then we got down to business.

" You admire Thomas Hardy ? " she said.

" We're not only admirers, we worship him," I said.

Silence.

It amused me that I had at once made a mistake.

I didn't care : I went on looking at the house, while Don carried on polite conversation. Yes, there was the turret on which Hardy planned all his life to fix a sun-dial — at the time of his death it was being made in Dorchester. There was the drawing-room on the right, in which the Hardys had received so many distinguished visitors — the thought of T. E. Lawrence sitting in that room and his wonderful description of it, passed through my mind, and the Prince of Wales and one and the other of them — the Balliol Players playing the *Oresteia* and *Hippolytus* on the lawn. And then the most congenial shade of all coming up the drive, that of Robert Louis Stevenson, one of the first visitors to the house : he had a great admiration for Hardy, and wanted to dramatise *The Woodlanders*.

There above the drawing-room was Hardy's first study, in which *The Woodlanders* was written. Later he moved away from the front of the house — always this desire for

greater privacy and solitariness — to a room at the back
looking west, where *Tess* was written. Later, he moved to a
room looking east out over the enclosed lawn I could see
from where I stood. Here *The Dynasts* and the later poems
were composed. The moon rising over the tops of the pines
looked in at his window :

> " What have you looked at, Moon,
>   In your time,
> Now long past your prime ? "
> " O, I have looked at, often looked at
>   Sweet, sublime,
> Sore things, shudderful, night and noon
>   In my time."
>
> " What have you mused on, Moon,
>   In your day,
> So aloof, so far away ? "
> " O, I have mused on, often mused on
>   Growth, decay,
> Nations alive, dead, mad, aswoon,
>   In my day ! "

The conversation had come back from America to Hardy.

" So you like Thomas Hardy ? " The old lady couldn't
resist telling us what she thought on the subject. " *I* don't
like Thomas Hardy. *Miserable* old man, I call him. I like
cheerful people."

I said propitiatingly that I hoped we were cheerful
people — looking at Don, who corroborated this with an
irresistible smile.

The old lady would not be pacified : " A *horrid* old
pessimist," she said, emphasising the point by jabbing her
stick into the ground, as if she would fix him there. " I
can't bear pessimists. Can you ? " turning to me.

" Perhaps he felt it that he was the end of his family," I
said.

" But why should that make you melancholy ? " she
replied, looking at her grandchildren as if with some disfavour. " That's no reason."

" Oh, well, people do feel like that when they're the end of their stock."

" Well, I like cheerful people," she said conclusively, shooing away her small grandson with her stick. It was evidently a cliché of hers.

" Have you ever read any of his novels ? " I asked.

" Oh, no ; I wouldn't read any of them."

" *Jude the Obscure* ? " I said.

" Oh, JUDE THE OBSCURE ! " she repeated with impatience and some disgust. Then with animation and enthusiasm : " I will tell you a book you ought to read — it's all about life in Dorchester — a wonderful book : *Sarah Tuldon* it's called." (With emphasis) " *Far truer* than any of Hardy's."

Then feeling that she had gone a little too far and that she ought to say something in his favour, or perhaps it was that she had caught the amusement on our faces :

" There was one that I did read. I think it *was Jude the Obscure*. I must say I was rather surprised by that. Rather different to what I expected." (Consciously making a concession) " That was not too bad."

It added to our inner amusement to find *Jude*, of all the novels, given an accolade, or half a one — and with that stick. But we were surprised by nothing now.

Then relenting a little further :

" But still they do say that a prophet is not without honour . . ."

" Save in his own country," I completed. (A mouse nibbled at the skirtings of my mind, turning westward.)

" I always understood that it was a sore trial to him that he never had a university education."

" Did he plant the trees ? " I asked, to turn the conversation into another channel.

" Oh, I think so. He was one that didn't like to be overlooked."

" No. Just like Kipling — he was determined to keep his own privacy too."

This made no impression. " Oh, I think they were just terrified," she said easily. Somehow the phrase gave one a curious feeling of the life they lived. Of course, they would be terrified of intruders. (I thought of the horrid woman from Liverpool marching all over my house in my absence.)

" Well, you must have a lot of people coming to see the place," I said, taking leave. " Forgive our trespassing."

" Not at all. No : very few people come here on the whole," she said, determined that Thomas Hardy should not have the last word. " And don't forget : *Sarah Tuldon* is the name of the book you should read."

We went down the drive, and, once outside the gate, laughed like a couple of schoolboys all the way to Dorchester.

(*1944*)

N

JOHN BUCHAN AT ELSFIELD

WHEN John Buchan died, the editor of *The Times* told me that never had they received so many tributes to a public figure, sheaves of them pouring in from men of all walks and conditions of life — only a tithe of which could be published. That already gives us some indication of the man himself; it tells us two things. It is testimony to the extraordinary range and variety of his contacts and friendships with people. But it also shows that these contacts were not merely formal : John Buchan belonged to the rare class of public figure who comes across to people as a friend, with whom they feel a personal bond, and in whom they feel a reciprocal care for them and their concerns.

To a degree that was remarkable and that singled him out among the public men of his time : I suppose there was no-one in his generation — and few at any time — who made a real contact, not merely a nodding acquaintance, with so many people.

I can testify from my own experience. When he was on his last leave from Canada and already desperately ill — within a year of his death — I was ill in London of the same duodenal complaint of which he was in the end a victim, and he found time amid all the innumerable claims on him and in his own illness to write me encouraging letters in his own hand. Hundreds of people have had similar experiences of his kindness and thought of them. I appreciated it much then ; how much more now : perhaps only a busy author, with writing of all kinds on his hands, knows so well what it means.

No doubt he suffered something, paid some price in energy and concentration of achievement for his readiness and willingness, his constant services to all and sundry. What he gained in stature was unmistakable ; what others gained from him immeasurable. He gave himself away, right and left, with no thought for his own strength, with an inner generosity of spirit that was more than generosity, like the man in the fable, *L'Homme à la cervelle d'or.*

With that there went — and perhaps from it came — the extraordinary catholicism of his sympathy. A strong Tory himself, his instinctive conservatism rooted in his sense of history — though that did not mean that he was not a progressive — his sympathies and, indeed, affections were readily extended in every direction politically. In fact I believe it was a special recommendation with him that you were on the other side. I remember well the particular affection and regard in which he held, and always spoke of, James Maxton, then much in the public eye as leader of the I.L.P. and a notable figure in Parliament. With one young neophyte of the Left, ardent, impatient, fanatical, touchy, he was patience and courtesy itself.

Alas, with what can one reward his kindness now? Nothing — except to cherish the memory of the man he was : that quick, spare, gallant figure, with the grave face and frosty northern eyes that could yet sparkle with liveliness and good-humour, with his old-fashioned Scots courtesy and bird-like quickness of movement, walking cap in hand and in loose-fitting tweeds, along the lanes and up the hill from Marston to his home on the brow of Elsfield overlooking Oxford ; or walking on the terrace in the green shades of a summer evening, looking down upon Otmoor and, in the gathered blue of distance, his beloved Cotswolds ; or again, sitting on a low chair in a corner of the library at Elsfield, the firelight leaping up and gleaming in the ranks of books, himself the heart and soul of the talk.

The foundation of his life, I realise now, was the principle of Christian love. He really loved people. And everything, apart from his gifts — though they derived strength from it — sprang from that. There was the secret spring of the two qualities that were so marked in him : the limitless, the un-sleeping sense of duty, the breadth and catholicism of his sympathy. As to duty, his devotion to it was obvious in every sphere of his life. He was very stern with himself in his work : always beforehand with his engagements (like Trollope), never failing to perform what he had promised — in that so unlike the ways of authors in general. He was a good deal of a stoic — except that, to balance that strain in him, no-one had a greater natural gift for the enjoyment of life. But only someone who knows the physical anguish and pain that goes along with that illness from which he suffered, knows what such devotion to work and duty must have cost. He himself once said to his wife, towards the end : " I think I have become a perfect Red Indian as regards pain ".

Perhaps I may say something of him as a writer, though it is a great disadvantage not to know the Scottish background, the society, the tradition out of which he sprang and against which his work must be regarded. But I appreciate all the more the importance of that background, what he owed to it in his work, the very inspiration that came from his native region, the memories and associations that went back to his childhood there, since a writer, to be any good, must have roots. His were vigorous and idiosyncratic, at once hardy and nourishing to the life of the imagination : there were the beginnings in the manse in Fife looking out upon the Forth ; the long summer holidays in the Border country that was Sir Walter Scott's own country too, the beloved Tweedside. The memory of those hills and streams is never far away in his writings, and it may be said that his best books are either inspired by them or somewhere carry their authentic signature. When he came to sum up his own work in *Memory-Hold-the-Door*, he wrote : " The woods and beaches [of Fife] were always foreign places, in which I was at best a sojourner. But the Border hills were my own possession, a countryside in which my roots went deep. . . . The dying shepherd asked not for the conventional Heaven, but for ' Bourhope at a reasonable rent ', and, if Paradise be a renewal of what was happy and innocent in our earthly days, mine will be some such golden afternoon within sight and sound of Tweed."

One can see something of what he owed to that distinctive background and the life of its people. For a writer, it was a great advantage to have been born a son of the manse : he knew what it was to be poor, to work hard, to share the life of the people ; at the same time, the standards that he imbibed from childhood were the educated standards of ministry and gentle-folk. It meant, as with Kilvert or Crabbe — to take writers from different English environments — that all doors were open to him, the ways of life of all classes. There was, too, the very freshness and vividness of the Border country itself, the sense of the soil and its life, the love of its solitary spaces, above all for him the historic memories with which it is crowded ; nor should one forget the importance attached to intellect and the things of the mind — in a way that Scots are apt to feel more keenly than English people — to appreciate learning, scholarship, intellect as such. There you have a further strain in him, the tradition of Adam Smith and of so many generations of Scots coming up to Balliol. He once told me that he should have come up to Balliol in the usual way, if it had not been for his intense admiration, in his undergraduate days at Glasgow, for Walter Pater as a writer. And it was out of that romantic devotion that he chose to come up to Brasenose. (By the time he came up Pater had died.)

But how right the young John Buchan was to follow his instinct ! There is a tendency today, in letters as well as in life, to make a cult of what is intrinsically uninteresting, to disclaim admiration for what is exceptional or remarkable, to cultivate the colourless and squalid. It is really a form of inverted snobbery ; for, of course, the uninteresting is less worthy of attention than the interesting, the standardised than the exceptional. Not to see that is, quite simply, a denial of quality, or even, in a way, of virtue.

John Buchan had no such inclination. He was a romantic and he had the simplicity of heart of the countryman : two qualities insufficiently regarded in the literary fashions of our time. But they are both important in his make-up as a writer.

I conceive that he started very much as a follower of,

and inspired by, Robert Louis Stevenson. There could be
no better school for a beginner. For Stevenson was a
wonderful craftsman and Buchan had a mastery of words —
an initial gift which greater writers have sometimes been
without and which some writers who make a noise nevertheless never achieve. His romantic temperament, a spirit
naturally gallant and courageous, his preference for the life
of action, admiring the heroic and stirring deeds, responded
to Stevenson and one sees the influence on his early stories
— among his best. John Buchan has told us how potent that
influence was over the young men of his generation, especially at the universities in Scotland. R. L. S. was "at once
Scottish and cosmopolitan, artist and adventurer, scholar
and gipsy. Above all he was a true companion. He took
us by the hand and shared in all our avocations. It was a
profound and over-mastering influence."

But it was one that Buchan himself grew out of. In time
"Stevenson seemed to me to have altogether too much
artifice about him, and I felt a suspicion of pose behind his
optimism and masculinity". And that helps to define a
point for us about Buchan's own work : he was an admirable
stylist. His own style was the reverse of artificial or affected :
it was vigorous and natural, athletic and spare, running
beautifully clear like one of his own Border streams, with an
occasional rare and coloured pebble in it to arrest the
attention, some infrequent word that was yet authentic,
coming out of the life of the land and the language of its
people. He had a most discriminating use of words,
deliberate, sensitive, scholarly. He was, by nature and
inclination, a scholarly writer, having both a classical education, with its accompanying training in the use of words,
and a strong and imaginative historical feeling. In consequence he wrote — to use an old-fashioned phrase, which
he would not reject — like a scholar and a gentleman :
would that more people did today. Since style is one of the
most preservative elements in literature, his best books will
continue to be read, so long as we care for good standards
in letters.

Of his novels I am not really qualified to speak; but it is obvious that to his gifts we must add — what again is something not very common — the sheer faculty of telling a story. John Buchan was a Tusitala in his own right. He loved the story for its own sake — an accent perhaps insufficiently regarded at the moment, which is yet a lasting thing and will see out the more temporary moods of literary fashion. He certainly understood suspense, the art of excitement, the thrilling quality of his master, Stevenson, in such stories as *The Thirty-Nine Steps*; that he was a master of atmosphere may be seen from a story like " The Grove of Ashtaroth " (one of his best) in *The Moon Endureth*. In his autobiography he tells us how from early days he told himself stories, or, rather, stories told themselves in his head : in that one sees the born story-teller — it reminds one of what Trollope says of himself in his *Autobiography*.

I think John Buchan kept a clear distinction in his mind — such as the literary public has not sufficiently appreciated, hence some mis-estimate of his work — between his lighter efforts, his thrillers and tales of adventure, and his more serious permanent work, whether in fiction, *belles lettres* or in the field which came to weigh most in his ultimate output, historical biography. I remember him telling me one day that he wrote his novels at dictation speed; but that he never could write more than fifteen hundred words a day at serious history. That from one of the quickest of workers, tells us something : that he took biography as serious history, devoted himself to it with all the energy and application of his mind, working hard at his sources, making himself into a professional historian — but a professional who could write : there is the difference. And here in this field, in my opinion, is to be found his most lasting work.

That coincides with his own judgment; and usually an author knows best about his own books. He tells us in his autobiography, of his *Montrose, Sir Walter Scott, Cromwell* and *Augustus* : " All these four books were, indeed, in a sense a confession of faith, for they enabled me to define my own creed on many matters of doctrine and practice, and thereby cleared my mind. They were laborious affairs compared to my facile novels, but they were also a relaxation, for they gave me a background into which I could escape from contemporary futilities, a watch-tower from which I had a long prospect, and could see modern problems in juster proportions. That is the supreme value of history."

Above all, there is the Life of Scott. Good judges have held that this is the best of all Buchan's books. There he had a magnificent subject, to which all his impulses, his very heart-strings, responded. " It is a book which I was bound one day or other to write, for I have had the fortune to be born and bred under the shadow of that great tradition." There was the noble background of Scott's country, Edinburgh — the most striking, the most sharply-etched, the most idiosyncratic town in this island, with its fugitive and mingled sharpness and sweetness, like the cold showers and rare lights of a northern spring; there were the shared experiences of beloved Tweedside: " Above all Scott had that kindest bequest of the good fairies at his cradle, a tradition, bone of his bone, a free life lived among clear waters and green hills as in the innocency of the world. . . . The world opened to him as a wide wind-blown country, with a prospect of twenty miles past the triple peaks of Eildon to the line of Cheviot, the homely fragrance and bustle of a moorland farm, the old keep of Smailholm as a background, and a motley of figures out of an earlier age. . . . He had mingled intimately with every class and condition of men, he had enough education to broaden his outlook but not enough to dim it; he was familiar alike with city and moorland, with the sown and the desert, and he escaped the pedantry of both the class-room and the drawing-room; above all he had the good fortune to stand at the meeting-place of two worlds, and to have it in him to be their chief interpreter." From the country that gave him birth to the man himself: there was the poetry, the peopled imagination, the human nobility of Sir Walter, one of the grandest and most magnanimous men that ever lived — besides being a great genius. John Buchan devoted to him a Life worthy of the greatest, the most Shakespearian, of Scots. It is a splendid biography, a noble book.

Of his historical biographies, *Montrose* and *Cromwell* have special claims. *Montrose* because Buchan had a lifelong devotion to that gallant and romantic figure out of the Scottish past, and, more, because he had an inner sympathy with him and his point of view. It is true, and perhaps unavoidable, that he sees the history of that time with all its unhappy confusion and inextricable politics, through the eyes of Montrose. But he gives a just estimate of the character of Montrose's great opponent, Argyll, and, as in all these books, he has a firm hold of the personalities of the historical figures, whether his sympathies are with them or not. This book must be regarded as his chief contribution to historical research, in the strict sense of the term ; it is written wholly from original sources and he had various additions and corrections of his own to offer in writing it. Here, too, he had a wonderful subject which he had made very much his own. He had an intimate knowledge of the countryside over which Montrose fought, all those astonishing marches and counter-marches in and out the Highlands, the Homeric battles — the whole story has a Greek flavour, as of an early heroic age. He had an intimate knowledge of the literature, and even of the pamphlet literature, of the seventeenth century ; he collected the traditions and stories, what there was of verbal tradition. It all goes to make a masterly historical biography.

The Life of Cromwell is not less, though it necessarily covers a less original track, a more well-trodden field. It is an even more splendid subject, a large canvas crowded with fascinating figures, and Buchan made of it a very fine book. It sprang out of his deep and abiding interest in the seventeenth century, which he had made his own chosen period of history, where he was most at home. He read, conscientiously and critically, all the sources and authorities ; he visited, as an historian should, the places and studied the battlefields. He had a very good understanding of military history. (An historian friend of mine, who fought in the last war, told me that Buchan's account of trench warfare, in his *History of the Great War*, was both vivid and very true to the fact.) But he brought something more to his study of Cromwell — his own gifts of mind.

Here we see the breadth of his sympathies at their most advantageous, enabling him to thread his way with fairness and understanding through the maze of sects and sectaries, the parties and factions and cliques. There is an essential justice of mind — the proper attribute of the historian, though not all possess it — in his treatment of the men on both sides, Cromwell and Charles, Laud and Strafford, Ireton and Vane, of those men whose fate it was in life to bring each other down. With Cromwell himself, that extraordinary man, Buchan had an inner sympathy that makes him at last clear to one. I believe that his view of Cromwell — that character so open to controversy, the subject of so much debate — is essentially right. Then there is the firm composition of the book, so well conceived and built up, the sense of scene, the practised rendering of action, the unsleeping gift of phrase. Of Cromwell's religion, for example : " He has been called a religious genius, but on his genius it is not easy to be dogmatic ; like Bunyan's Muchafraid, when he went through the River none could understand what he said ". On the constitutional dilemma of the great Protector's government, its inner contradiction : " He was to be a prince, but a prince who must remain standing, since he had no throne ".

I remember meeting Buchan on his way back to Elsfield the afternoon he came down into Oxford to send off the manuscript of *Cromwell*. (He did all his writing in his own hand : hence the high standard he always maintained.) It was early summer, June over the Oxfordshire countryside, the long grass lush in the water-meadows, the elms of Marston in their full panoply of foliage. He was feeling a little sad, he said, at parting with someone with whom he had lived for two years now. Not a word about the immense labour and effort that had gone into it : he took all that for granted : it was very like him.

The truth is that he lived most willingly in the realm of the historical imagination. How naturally it came to him may be seen in a delightful essay, " Thoughts on a Distant Prospect of Oxford ", full of feeling for the place and its thronging memories : it is printed in that very agreeable volume of essays, in which the sense of history illumines the study of literature, *Homilies and Recreations.*

Of his classical biographies, *Julius Caesar* and *Augustus* — the latter his last big work — I am not able to speak. But they have this quality of authenticity, that they go back for their inspiration to his youthful interest in Roman history, to the ambition of his undergraduate days to paint a portrait of Augustus. " I had already done a good deal of work on the subject," he wrote lightly — amid all the distractions and the calls on his time of being a Governor-General — " and my first two winters in Canada gave me leisure to re-read the Latin and Greek texts." " I have rarely found more enjoyment in a task," he adds, " for I was going over again carefully the ground which I had scampered across in my youth." What spirit, what boyishness, what verve ! — and this from a man in highest office and often in pain.

It testifies, too, to the extraordinary width of his reading and culture : a man of a type all too rare in public life today. For he was a great reading man. " Reading has always filled so large a part of my life ", he says disarmingly — as if there were not a score of other interests and avocations : fishing, bird-watching, walking ; the Empire — first South Africa, then Canada ; publishing, Reuter's, serving on the University Chest at Oxford and on the Preservation Trust ; being a member of Parliament, Governor-General of Canada. And this in addition to being one of the most prolific authors of his time. Yet — reading filled a large part of his life all the same. You will get some idea of his powers in this direction — and there went along with it a most retentive and concrete memory — from an essay on Scott in *Homilies and Recreations.* He tells of how during his serious illness after an operation in 1917 he read through a dozen of the Waverley Novels, the Valois and d'Artagnan cycles of Dumas, then

Victor Hugo's *Notre-Dame* and the immense *Les Misérables*, almost a library in itself, ending up with half a dozen of Balzac ; and this in order to consider how Scott stood the test. He quite clearly had a good deal of Sir Walter's amazing powers of work. How he contrived to get through all the reading and writing he did, let alone everything else he accomplished, beats me ; though I do not forget the ceaseless watchfulness and care, the aid and help, direct and indirect, of his wife : a rare comradeship in life, in work and public service.

When in those days one went up to Elsfield, when he was there, one always found him abreast of contemporary reading as of affairs, interested in all that was being written and thought. Alas, being young, one took so much for granted ! It is only now that one knows how remarkable that was, the gift of such vivid sympathies, the passionate enjoyment of everything good life has to offer. There was such generosity of spirit in it : he was by nature an admirer, an encourager of others' work ; he had nothing of the denigrator about him : I never heard him utter depreciatory words of anyone — a rare attitude in literary circles. But then he did not move in literary circles : he was by nature a man of action, who happened to have the gifts of a writer. I well remember how he won me by his warm appreciation of Q's novels and stories — then, as now, under-estimated ; and, for a young Labour man, his friendly admiration for the ability (and industry) of some of the leading writers of the Left, even though he did not agree with them.

And now, when one thinks of Elsfield, something rare has gone from the familiar landscape. Everything there reminds one of him : the way up the hill, the little bridge and culvert at the foot, the road winding between the elms and ash-trees, the elder I once saw in blossom-time gleaming like a ball of snow in the frozen moonlight, while a great parachute-flare slowly descended over Otmoor, lighting up its spaces with the strange light of another world. There is the little church, hipped up on its platform, with its bell-cote at the west end overlooking the road ; then around the bend to the tall house with its eighteenth-century core, and something Scottish about its rigid vertical lines — that ever-hospitable house with its friendly welcome for the young. On Sunday afternoons in those days there was always a crowd and much good talk. Out of a kindly thought for my shyness, I used to be asked on quieter occasions, when there was just the inner circle of the family, a few guests, and all the gracious domesticity and firelit charm which those two, John and Susan Buchan, gathered naturally around them. Evening wore on; the firelight leaped on the hearth and made a comfortable glow in that square shelved room with its cargo of books. Now it is autumn and the trees outside are turning lemon and gold and brown; the mellow evening light comes across the green spaces of Otmoor and in at the western windows. Or it is winter and there is a winter stillness outside — darkness in the trees, a little snow light upon the slopes, the village street moonlit as in Arnold's poem. At the door one takes leave of that friendly house, which will not soon be forgotten in English letters; it is time to go downhill once more, back to the spires and colleges waiting down there in the night. As one recalls that so familiar routine, the village on the brow, that well-loved house, time slips away and one is there again, the circle, that is now broken, rounded and complete once more.

NOTTINGHAM: A MIDLANDS
CAPITAL

I

IN these years when it has been impossible to travel abroad
— at least if one is an ordinary civilian — I have found it a
good idea to take the opportunity to discover one's own
country. And for someone whose life is lived wholly between
Oxford and Cornwall, with an occasional excursion to
London, it is very much a matter of discovery. Though at
Oxford I am on the threshold of the Midlands, to venture
into them is a venture indeed. Armed with a guide-book,
fortified by railway and bus time-tables, accompanied by a
companion to keep me on the rails, moving into the Midlands
with as much trepidation as if I were going into a foreign
country, I arrive at Nottingham to discover a magnificent
town, full of improbable splendours.

Why had no-one told me about it? Why had I never
heard of it before, I felt — like George Moore when someone
first drew his attention, in late middle-age, to *Lycidas*. On
my return to Oxford I realise the answer. I find that I am
not alone in my ignorance : of half a dozen friends I meet —
all of them historians too — only one of them has ever been
there, or has any idea of what an astonishing town it is.
Like myself, they had all passed by a dimly-realised, smoke-
clouded landscape in the train on their way to York, Durham,
Edinburgh. They had never got out and looked. They
would have been very much surprised if they had — as surprised, and impressed, as I was myself.

It was no mere archaeological quirk that led me to pay
my visit. I am content to remain unsure what the original
name — apparently Snottingaham — means or who the
Snottings were ; nor do I wish to follow up the fantasies of

John Rowse, Canon of Osney, who, according to Thoroton, had some very far-fetched notions as to the early British inhabitants. But I confess it intrigued me to be going to one of the Five Towns of the Danelaw, and the moment I arrived I was electrified by the extraordinary accent of the (lady) station-announcer. " So that is how Mercian sounds ", I registered, as I stepped out into a strange, a foreign, town.

It was not long before it made its impression on me. For one thing, it has the finest situation of any big town in the Midlands, almost of any English town.   One thinks of Edinburgh, when looking up at the Castle upon its great limestone rock rising sheer out of that industrial plain.   Or one sees the shape of the old town more clearly as a Tudor galleon, high in the prow and stern, low in the waist : at one end the Castle on its rock, at the other St. Mary's church on its hill, the line of the old ramparts (alas, vanished) sinking down to Low Pavement whence the road issues out to bridge the Trent.

The oval shape of the old town can be followed very clearly along that line and round to Parliament Street and Upper and Lower Parliament Streets, which take the place of the town walls.   Nearly everything that is interesting can be found within this circuit, for outside, my guide-book tells me, up to 1845 it was surrounded by the Lammas Fields, " which, belonging to the community from August till February, were divided between private owners during the rest of the year, and so formed a belt of open space which, while enclosing the town, led to the growth of a number of surrounding villages, now part of the city ".   Outside, all is industrialism, factories, workshops, sheds, endless railway lines, all smouldering and smoking in the mirk and gloom. But within — what riches !

I had never expected to see such a wealth of Queen Anne, Georgian, early-nineteenth-century houses.   It was easy to see that Nottingham had long been a provincial capital, inhabited by people of style and taste and distinction in those days.   But what is extraordinary is that it should have preserved so much — may it continue to do so in the horrible age of further ravages and disfigurements which will descend upon us with the end of the war!

All along the half-mile or more from the Castle to St. Mary's there are these beautiful old houses. Going down Castle-gate there is Newdigate House, a fine Queen Anne house, rather *délabré* now and occupied by a Canine Beauty Parlour. There Marshal Tallard, who was captured by Marlborough at Blenheim, lived during the years from 1705 to 1711. It must have been very new and up-to-date then, tattered and down-at-heel as it looks now : the Marshal was given about the best house in the town. I dare say he had a very agreeable time of it, if he did not too much miss the splendours, and the intrigues, of Versailles. For he had for company half a dozen high-ranking officers, his compatriots captured in the war. And he left a benevolent mark of his stay in the town : he got the inhabitants interested in gardening — a mark, it is said, which has continued in a tradition of much allotment gardening among the workmen, a feature of the modern town.

But there must be altogether a score of fine Georgian houses in Castle-gate, now occupied mostly as offices — may they be for ever preserved! — along with one appalling Victorian excrescence, I think a vicarage, which should be removed, or allowed to moulder quietly away. Set back from the street is the church of St. Nicholas, which has all the interest of a church built in 1682 — a rare time for churches, outside of London. My guide-book, of 1910, tells me that it " presents the usual lack of interest which attaches to brick churches ". Actually, it is enchanting ; melancholy, forlorn and lovely, it cries out to be painted by John Piper.

The original church was destroyed during the Civil War. That Nottinghamshire classic, Lucy Hutchinson's *Memoirs of the Life of Colonel Hutchinson,* tells us how the Cavaliers fired into the Castle-yard from the steeple of St. Nicholas, and how Colonel Hutchinson trained his ordnance on it and demolished it. Now the church stands, a little neglected and sad, the tide of life having moved away from this old quarter of the city; inside, a touching monument of more prosperous Georgian days, with admirable wainscot and woodwork. For a moment, in the straggling winter sunshine and the silence, one could half-shut one's eyes and picture it painted in black and gold, see once more the pompous bewigged aldermen, their ladies and their household marching up the aisle.

And so down Castle-gate and up Low Pavement, passing the splendid town-house of the Willoughbys of Wollaton — regular, formal, dignified, like the external forms of the society in which they lived — standing back somewhat from the street, behind its own fore-court, for the Willoughbys were the great people of hereabouts, from medieval times to our own declining days, the brave — and deplorably uninteresting — new social order and all that.

I confess that I went to Nottingham to see Wollaton Hall just outside, a very notable Elizabethan house. It seems that John Thorpe had a hand in the design; and certainly it is a complete expression of the soaring fantasy, the boundless audacity of the Elizabethans. The great hall, around which it is built, goes up to twice the height of the house around it, and then there is a high, unapproachable ballroom on top of that; the whole tricked out with pepper-pot turrets, so that when you see it across the park in the mingled sunshine and mist of a December morning, it achieves that quality of fantasy and dream that the Elizabethans pursued. There it is as it was finished in the year 1588, with its Renaissance niches and busts of Plato, Aristoteles, Virgil, the presiding deities of the time. Sir Francis Willoughby impoverished himself to build it: it cost £80,000 — multiply by ten or fifteen to get a contemporary idea of its cost. In our time bought by the Nottingham Corporation for £200,000 — which, being good business men, they have already recovered from housing development over part of the park.

The house itself they have turned into a Natural History Museum, full of young people studying and drawing the animals that morning. What better way is there of preserv-

ing and turning to account these great houses that are themselves like some extinct creatures of an earlier epoch stranded
upon the shores of this ? Nottingham has set a good example
for all such towns to follow ; instead of allowing this Elizabethan palace to decay, or ordering it to be pulled down,
they have preserved it and its gardens, and made the park
an open space for ever. And I am glad that they have
proved it good business to do so.

It is evident everywhere in Nottingham that there is a
remarkable civic spirit guiding and inspiring the town. The
group of university buildings designed upon a hill outside
the city, with its terraces overlooking a lake, are beyond
question the finest of modern university buildings anywhere
in the country. In them Morley Horder made a first-class
contribution to modern architecture. In the city, the new
Council House, at the end of the historic Market Place, is
not in the same class ; but it has a good dome, which presides
well over the city and makes a satisfying focal point for the
whole town, old as well as new.

Indeed the town has been fortunate in its modern buildings, as in the earlier nineteenth-century factories, simple
and not without distinction as many of them are. At least
two modern buildings of distinction I observed, both the
work of government departments. The Post Office, which
is beyond praise in its sense of duty to the country, has put
up a new sorting-station in the modern style, simple and
streamlined, like a great ship, and with the most graceful
curves. Then, immediately under the Castle, the Ministry
of Labour has put up an Employment Exchange, red brick
and traditional Queen Anne : a building of elegance and
perfection of proportion. I do not know who their architects
were ; but when I think of what has been done by laurelled and
beknighted architects in modern Oxford, I feel that Oxford
should go on its knees to Nottingham to learn how it is done.

One dreadful exception is not the town's fault. In every
town in England the multiple shops, Marks & Spencer,
Woolworth, the Fifty Shilling Tailors, worst of all, Montague

Burton, and the rest, are doing their best to disfigure and destroy. Nottingham is no exception, but, like hundreds of other towns, is the victim of plans ordered by the foot, like so much elastic, somewhere in London. Cannot these great concerns, and others like them, which are going to be much more important in the future, be persuaded that they have a greater responsibility in consequence to the country, than they had in the past? If it can be done by the Post Office and Ministry of Labour — and so admirably and beautifully — it can be done by them.

What does one take away with one, then, from Nottingham? A sense of inspiration, an impression of marked public spirit, a feeling of pride in the past, of some hope in the future. For this town proves a lesson that needs to be learned all over the country : that the past and the future are not enemies, but mutually complementary ; that the proper, and the simple, way to behave about our heritage from the past, so creative and full as it has been, is to cherish and preserve all that is best in it, and in our time to add to it all the best that we are capable of. Nothing short of the best is ever good enough.

And then one carries away, too, fragmentary and loving memories of things seen and heard : the superb great dappled greys of Shipstone's breweries — they breed them themselves — pulling their red-painted drays over the cobbles ; the medieval alabaster panel in St. Mary's depicting Thomas Becket's presentation to the Pope, a work of grave, unforgettable beauty, full of a speaking, poignant solemnity ; the chapel where Coleridge once preached, and Byron once worshipped, where Bonington was baptized ; the Castle where Charles hoisted his standard in the breeze and where Colonel Hutchinson held out ; the sound of those bells, male and powerful, yet sweet-toned and resonant upon the busy Market Place ; the agreeable book-shops that indicate a cultivated, reading public ; the politeness and courtesy of the police, and everywhere the kindliness of the Midlands people — no sign of the strain of the war.

All towns have their characters. How would one describe that of Nottingham? I should say a character essentially masculine, self-possessed and assured, confident, having pride in the past, a generous spirit and no fear of the future.

(1945)

II

So much I had discovered on a first visit in the last winter of the war, while all was still muffled and darkened, life stretched and taut, the town — like everything else in England at that time — bare and under a sense of strain.

Now I have been again, to see things that were closed or put away then, and to extend my acquaintance with its streets as far as a short stay can contrive. My idea was not exhaustion, either of myself or of the town. For one of the pleasures of inhabiting an old country, full of the accumulated riches of earlier and better times, is that there are always new objects of interest and beauty to see, for the eye to delight in and the mind to draw satisfaction and profit from.

The first object of my return was to see the Castle and the collection of Nottingham alabasters in its Museum, inaccessible and stowed away during the war. There it was, that heavy, imposing, Italianate palace of the late seventeenth century, built, after its Cavendish fashion, high up on a precipice, like Bolsover or Hardwick, looking ducally down upon the world at the foot. The Castle was bought by the Duke of Newcastle in 1674, the site cleared of the medieval buildings that survived the Civil War, and the present classical pile built 1674–9. The builders were the son and grandson of the builder of Bolsover ; and the Castle originally had a grand staircase in the middle of its façade like that in the centre of the long gallery front at Bolsover. It was pouring with rain. What better way of spending a morning than inspecting the treasures of an interior ?

My first surprise was the Flawford figures, discovered in 1779 : from the time of Richard II, half life-size and in

beautiful preservation, among the finest surviving examples
of English medieval sculpture. I suppose they were buried
at the Reformation — imagine what destruction there must
have been! I suppose no time can have approached that
for destruction of things of beauty, until we come to the
twentieth century, which must surely hold the record in
that line. There are three figures : the middle one a bishop
in full pontificals giving his blessing, the whole thing full of
suavity and tenderness, coming out of a world that could
receive such blessings easily and gratefully as part of the
order of nature, or rather of the divine order. The smaller
figure is of St. Peter as Pope, gay and appealing, with slightly
curved stance. This is still more marked in the Virgin and
Child, the child carried gaily on the hip, the delightful imp
pressing milk from her exposed breast. The Middle Ages
took all that very naturally — like their religion. It gave
them joy as well as consolation : it expressed the whole of
life as no version of Christianity or sect has done since. But
that was because the medieval Church itself was an expression of the whole society. The Peter has a figure of an
ecclesiastic — the donor — praying at his feet on a couple
of cushions : all with that naturalness which was the genius
of the Middle Ages, that childlike naturalness which runs
through their literature, through Chaucer, their religious
poems, their politics, their behaviour — life uninhibited,
irrepressed, the life of children.

Beside these most moving figures there are small alabaster
panels in relief of the more usual kind. One is of the common
motif of Christ rising from the tomb, stepping blithely out
on a sleeping soldier, others astonished, abashed. Another
is a pietà of beautiful sentiment and workmanship, the cloth
round the Virgin's head, held in one hand, forming a lovely,
mournful, shadowy oval — the body of the Son across her
knees. A third shows the head of St. John the Baptist on a
charger, supported by St. Peter and St. William of York.
All the colour is left — from which one can see how it was
done : the background green with white spots, the effect of
a flowery meadow ; the angels' wings are red, with black and

white feathers; the beard and hair of the saint are gilt, the robes just outlined with colour, leaving most of the space the natural ivory colour of the stone.

Alabaster seems to have been used for sculpture from the twelfth century; but the trade in plaques and altar-pieces did not start till the fourteenth. Nottingham, with the alabaster quarries of the county near at hand, became the chief centre of the craft. It was at its height of perfection from 1340 to 1420, the period of carving in low relief with a shallow edge to the plaque. Out of this, carving in high relief developed with elaborate, overgrown canopies. Gradually there evolved, from plaques like this St. John, composite altar-pieces built up from separate panels, like the very elaborate altar-piece from Spain now in the Victoria and Albert Museum. A large trade in Nottingham alabasters grew up that reached as far as Spain, Southern Italy, Iceland. Some three or four thousand plaques from this second period survive; immense numbers must have disappeared. As the trade grew, more and more mass production led to artistic collapse, worthlessness of the product. What would one expect?

I like provincial galleries and museums to have their own proper local inflection, as they so often have in France — at Arles, for example, or at Nantes. In this respect Nottingham pleases and engages me. Here are portraits of their local figures: a Hoppner of Kirke White, the pathetic young poet: attractively good-looking, with fashionably disarranged hair of the Regency and fine eyes. I do not suppose he was much of a poet; but Byron admired him and paid him a tribute when he died. The poor young man's first book was savagely criticised, and he wilted under it: " it affects my respectability ", he said. Four years later Byron's first book was published from Newark and he also was savaged by the critics. They got *English Bards and Scotch Reviewers* for their impertinence, and they have not been forgotten.

But here is something more arresting: a self-portrait of Bonington; an extraordinarily aristocratic head, a mop of dark hair like a woman's — and indeed there is something feminine about the face, except for the aquiline, prominent nose. Thin cheeks, alas, and piercing blue eyes, the face turned away on the high pillar of green stock, narrow shoulders in a brown coat. Here he is, surrounded by sketches on the French coast, water-colours of Italy — the Piazza of St. Mark and an enchanting coloured view of the Gesù from the Callete di Sant' Agnese. There is a big picture of Fisher Folk on the coast of Normandy : not a masterpiece, but beautifully fresh, with the bright-red cloaks of fisherwomen, blue sea and sky — the heat of a vanished day a century ago through the eyes of that boy of genius.

There is another coast scene with exquisite sky — a character study of figures in fancy dress, called " Meditation ". (So he, too, liked old days and ways — like Lamb or me!) On the staircase there is a portrait of him by Thomas Phillips : face tilted upward and eyes looking up reveal how fine they were, hair light brown, flushed cheeks of the consumptive, chin resting on hand, a signet ring, light-blue coat. Here, in the eyes of a fellow painter, he is the artist rather than the gentleman he saw himself. It is interesting to note how often artists, and not painters only, depict themselves as aristocrats — and quite right too, in a way. Actually Bonington's grandfather was the gaoler at Nottingham. The Town Records preserve many gruesome bills of his for the executions of criminals, payments to him for the whipping and transportation of prisoners. There are bills for their diets, for branding them in the hand, for their medical treatment — purging powders, cataplasms, boluses, emulsions, juleps — for straw for the felons. One thinks of those condemned cells deep down beneath the Shire Hall on St. Mary's Hill. What a transformation from the grandfather and the scenes of his life to the sensibility and sunny spirit of the grandson, the thirst for sky and sea and air, the joy in the visual glory of life!

I do not notice a portrait of Byron, much of whose Newstead life was associated with Nottingham, from the time when in 1799, aged about eleven, he was sent into the town under the care of the incompetent Lavender, who treated his foot by twisting it in a machine. In all the discussion as to what was wrong with Byron, the Nottingham bootmaker's evidence seems most reliable. He said that Byron's feet were perfectly formed, but weakness of the ankle necessitated that the foot should be supported ; he did *not* have club foot, but the calf of the left leg was weaker than the other and he was made to wear a piece of iron with a joint at the ankle when he was a boy. He walked in such a way as to disguise his infirmity. While he was at Harrow, Newstead was let and his mother lived here in Pelham Street, where Byron came in the holidays. The holidays of 1804 and 1806 he spent at Southwell — in that charming Georgian house on the green. In 1808–9 he lived at Newstead, engaging in the Medmenham frolics that won him the notoriety he both sought and fled from. Next year he sold the house, cutting the names " Byron " and " Augusta " on a tree in the park. In 1824 Nottingham saw the last scene enacted in that extraordinary career : the famous body, back from Missolonghi, was brought back once more to Pelham Street, where he lay in state in the Blackmoor's Head. Immense crowds received him and filed by the coffin with its lighted candles, before the funeral procession set out for Hucknall. In 1852 Ada joined him in the vault.

There is a portrait of Captain Albert Ball, V.C., hero of the Royal Flying Corps in the first war — portrayed with ribbons, D.S.O. 2 bars, M.C., Légion d'Honneur — just a dark, handsome boy, shot down in 1917 ; his torn pennant hanging now beneath him. But no Byron, no D. H. Lawrence. Nottingham should hurry up and get a portrait of their greatest man of genius since Byron.

An interesting collection of clothes of different periods comes from Wollaton, lent by Lord Middleton. There is the beautiful eighteenth-century court dress of the men, flowered silk waistcoats, silver-buttoned coats of plum and rusty black, exquisitely cut. Here are women's coifs of Elizabethan needlework, silk on linen, mostly black flowers and leaves on white ground, every sort of stitch, buttonhole, back, chain-stitch and raised knots. It is specially interesting to me — since this is my period — to see the nightcaps Elizabethan men wore (one sees them occasionally in their portraits, that of Drummond of Hawthornden for example) : worked with silver gilt and gilt thread, with raised work and braid. The lady's bodices of the same time have silver spangles and couched work. One imagines these lovely coloured clothes lighting up like a parterre the grey deserted corridors and galleries of Wollaton, deserted — or filled with natural history exhibits gaped on by uncomprehending school children.

It gives one a melancholy pleasure, too, to look at fragments brought together here from which one can see how beautiful the town once was — as almost all English towns were before the Industrial Revolution undermined the beauty of England, a process that has overwhelmed us in our time with fifteen million people too many in the island. Here is a group of columns and arches from a house in Long Row — pulled down for ' improvements ' in 1896 — last portion of the colonnade of the Elizabethan houses that surrounded the Market Place : three fine classical arches with pendant ball from the centre and columns of oak from Sherwood Forest. A coloured engraving of 1824 shows how beautiful the Market Place was, with its great uninterrupted space and late Georgian guildhall at the end. There is all the charm of the life of the time : covered carts, horsemen on horses, dogs at heel, a coach and four goes by, a great log of timber is being dragged along, here is a porter with pack on back, a woman pushing a wheelbarrow, gaffers chaffering : all the delightful *va-et-vient* of the Georgian age, when life was personal, idiosyncratic and still manageable, before we came to be overwhelmed in the mass.

Even Leland, matter-of-fact as he was, grew eloquent about Nottingham Market Place : " both for the buildings on the site of it and for the very great wideness of the street and the clean paving of it, it is the fairest without exception of all England ". This was in Henry VIII's reign. Nearly two centuries later Thoroton writes : " this dance of building

new fronts hath been of late very well followed, as I hope it
will be still, because many people of good quality from several
parts make choice of habitations here, where they find good
accomodation ". They could take pride in what they built,
for what they put up was even better than what they pulled
down. Not so with us : the sense of spaciousness of the great
Market Place has been diminished by a trivial lay-out, seats
for the people, beds, stone wastepaper-baskets. The people,
of course, would not notice it ; but then they see nothing.
" Eyes have they, and see not ", says the Psalmist. " They
have ears, and hear not : noses have they, and smell not."
And more to the same effect.

Let us go down Castle-gate once more and peer in
through the fine ironwork of Newdigate House to see what
we can see. It is the year 1705 : Marshal Tallard with a
dozen other French aristocrats have arrived in Nottingham
from the field at Blenheim via Market Harborough, where
they lodged, of course, at the ' Swan '. At once the amenities
of an aristocratic civilisation are set in motion ; the neighbourhood buzzes. There are polite exchanges between
Thomas Coke of Melbourne, Vice-Chamberlain of the
Household at St. James's, and the distinguished enemy.
Coke sends him fifty bottles of champagne and fifty of volne,
with his apologies, " knowing how much they fail to be so
good as those which one drinks in France ". He lends the
Marshal books and exerts himself to get the Queen to allow
Tallard's own wine to pass the Customs. The Marshal visits
in the country houses round about, at Bretby and at Melbourne, where Coke's sister was afraid " I must make a
simple figure, where I could not speak nor understand
perfectly ". The Duke of Rutland invites the Marshal and
the rest of the French officers to Belvoir, where they are
entertained at a banquet in the Long Gallery. During his
residence at Newdigate House Tallard laid out a garden,
which became one of the chief sights of the town, for it was in
the formal French fashion unknown to English provincial
towns. In 1711, as part of their peace offensive, the Tories
freed him without ransom. He must have been missed in

Nottingham, a figure familiar with the resplendent glories of Versailles. Now the house has gone to the dogs.

Walking down Castle-gate you come to No. 44, which has an extraordinary Norman porch with primitive animals on the capitals — it is said to have come from Lenton priory. George King has a magnificent house with fine late Georgian door-case; Castle-gate Chambers is a smaller, pretty George I house. Best of all is the house occupied by Barber, Solicitors, which has a beautiful entrance-hall: I trespass inside to look at the pretty cornice: all nicely painted and kept, good doors. The portico has columns with feathered capitals, repeated within. The bottom of this noble street is rendered hideous by a contribution of the twentieth century — a shop front in chewing gum (polished).

Here we cross over and follow Low Pavement, the waistline of the galleon to which I have likened the town, and mount the street past several noble houses such as Willoughby House — the town-house of the Wollaton family in old days — to arrive at St. Mary's church on its hill dominating all this part of the town. Around this great parish church the burgess life of the town revolved as against the military stronghold, a royal fortress, on the opposite hill. Here were the close-packed streets, the shops and booths, the crowded tradesmen and artificers, the parish life of which St. Mary's was the hive: one sees those long-dead citizens as so many bees passing in and out the church through the days, the years, the centuries. But they have left evidences of their trades and occupations in the charming names of the streets: Pilcher-gate, Fletcher-gate, Goose-gate — so I suppose the flocks of geese used to come this way to the Goose Fair in the Market Place — Hounds-gate, Bridlesmith-gate, Warser-gate, Blowbladder Street, Byard Lane. The churchyard is quiet enough now, surrounded mostly by offices, with the fine shallow curve of High Pavement bounding it on the south, along the cliff edge.

Let us enter the church and read the monuments: the book of past Nottingham life is open before us. Here is a tablet to George Coldham, Town Clerk, killed by the overturn of a carriage at Brighton in 1815 : erected by the Mayor and Common Council " publicly to express their warmest commendation of his meritorious exertions in the preservation of the peace of this populous town during the late threatening period ". The Luddites ! — it means, I suppose, that they left him to it. Next to him is the honourable Lady Mary Brabazon, " a devout and constant attendant on God's public worship here ". She died in 1738 and " lies here interred near her father the Right Honourable Chamber, Earl of Meath ". The Rt. Hon. Chamber makes rather a figure in the Town Records : we find the Mayor and Common Council waiting on him in 1709 to congratulate him on his new accession to honour and to present him with the " usual presents to persons of like quality ".

Nottingham was a favourite residence with such persons in the eighteenth century. Besides the enforced residence of the Marshal, there was the voluntary accession of the Marquis of Dorchester, the Earl of Clare, the Pierrepont Earls of Kingston, whose house makes such a fine figure in the town engravings of the time. Next to the Lady Mary reposes the perpetual curate of Tong and first domestic chaplain to the Rt. Hon. the Earl Manvers. O what a vanished world these tablets recall ! Not all of these personages were of a like domestic sobriety. In 1774 we find a bastardy order made out against the Hon. George Byron of Nottingham, younger brother of the wicked Lord, the poet's great-uncle. This was on the complaint of the churchwardens and overseers of the poor that Mary Goddard had had a child ever since chargeable to the parish. Mr. Byron was to pay 20s. expenses and half a crown a week — cheap enough. In 1789 he died and in 1796 his widow received 30s. per annum in lieu of her burgess part — " late of the widow of John Oldknow, framework knitter." So Byron must have married her. This is the generation before the poet succeeded to Newstead. One sees something of the heritage of the ' bad blood of the Byrons ', and also how intimately they were associated with the life of Nottingham.

But here is a memorial of an earlier world, far earlier

and more touching than these buoyant Georgian relics.
This fragment of a Nottingham alabaster is a work of art
worlds removed from the bad Byrons and the Rt. Hon.
Chamber. It is a panel from a reredos, depicting a scene
in the life of St. Thomas of Canterbury, from an age when
saints could still be created — for it is an attitude of mind
that creates them. The scene is depicted in low relief: St
Thomas advancing up the steps to the Pope on his throne;
a cardinal is in attendance, a monk holds St. Thomas's cross
behind him: all rendered with majesty and yet with that
speaking simplicity, the fidelity of a vanished world of faith.
The panel was found buried face downwards under the floor
of the chancel.

Out into the streets, out into Broadway: a fascinating
Victorian street with a double curve in it very well managed:
the round-headed windows make a nice rhythm. It is good
Crimean War architecture. As one rounds the bend one
sees what a fine composition the street is as a whole and
reflects what a mess a contemporary architect would make
of it compared with this Victorian. Who *was* he, one
wonders? There seems to be a lot of his work about,
factories too, to judge from his characteristic rhythm of
classical Italianate fenestration. It can hardly have been
S. S. Rawlinson — he must have been earlier — whose almshouses in front of the General Cemetery are described with
some satisfaction as exhibiting, " from their finished style of
classical architecture, which is Grecian, with an Italian
finish, a peculiar sweetness and beauty ". Today no-one
would notice.

Old Nottingham testified to considerable public spirit
in the number of its almshouses. Those of Abel Collins,
mercer, begun and finished in 1709, exist unchanged: a
little red-bricked court with baroque-decorated entrance —
" in his life he was of an extensive charity to the poor of all
societies. At his death he left a competent estate for erecting
these almshouses." On the south side there is a good sun-
dial, a little garden, and two pretty Queen Anne houses on
either side of the gate. Next door stood the Baptist chapel

in which William Carey preached his memorable missionary sermon on 30 May 1792 — so the tablet on the wall informs us. From that Carey went on to become the first Baptist missionary in India, to a lifetime of devoted labour, in the course of which — as a side-line — he made himself a remarkable Orientalist, pouring out grammars of numerous Indian languages and preparing one of all those derived from Sanskrit, in which he became a great scholar. From these grey skies to the burning sun of Bengal : what energy these early nineteenth-century missionaries had — he was a Henry Martyn of the Midlands — what energy of faith driving them on, until, worn out with work and fever, they lay down their bleached bones under those alien skies, themselves consumed, burnt up by the ardour within them.

But here we are back in the Castle area — that part of the town over which broods the spirit of the most ardent of them all, the most fever-haunted and possessed, the brightest luminary in these skies, the only one who can be compared with Byron. For Nottingham is very much in the foreground of the greatest of modern English novels — the town is almost a character in — *Sons and Lovers*. So many of the scenes in that unforgettable book come to mind : Paul and Mrs. Morel coming in from Bestwood (*i.e.* Eastwood) to look for a job for him. " The mother and son walked down Station Street, feeling the excitement of lovers having an adventure together. In Carrington Street they stopped to hang over the parapet and look at the barges below. ' It's just like Venice,' he said, seeing the sunshine on the water that lay between high factory walls." Somewhere about here was the surgical appliances business where Paul worked as a clerk. The strain of the interview over, Paul and his mother come down into the Market Place : " It was very sunny. Over the big desolate space of the market-place the blue sky shimmered, and the granite cobbles of the paving glistened. Shops down the Long Row were deep in obscurity, and the shadow was full of colour. Just where the horse trams trundled across the market was a row of fruit stalls, with fruit blazing in the sun — apples and piles of reddish

oranges, small greengage plums and bananas. There was a
warm scent of fruit as mother and son passed."

Later on, Paul, still a boy, has a couple of studies ex-
hibited in the gallery at the Castle and wins first prize with
one of them. Mrs. Morel goes up to see them, unknown to
him, gleaming with pride at her son's success; the collier
father is stunned at the thought of winning so much money
by a mere drawing. It is all very simple and touching. The
second half of the novel has Nottingham for its scene as
the first has the mining village of Eastwood. Clara, Paul's
second girl, lives in Nottingham; Paul takes up with her
there : she worked at lace-spinning at home when he first
met her and then came to work at the surgical appliances
factory where he was. There is a wonderful description of
the two of them going up to the Castle together in the dinner-
hour and of the town as they looked down upon it from the
rock, the pigeons preening themselves in their holes in the
sandstone, the trees below looking tiny in pools of their own
shadow, people scurrying about like so many tadpoles.

We see Clara and Paul riding in the tram through
Nottingham, down the Wilford Road, out past the rain-
sodden dahlias of Wilford churchyard; or Paul going to
Clara's home in the squalid Sneinton area — the latter half
of the book is full of the sense of the city. Then there is the
last meeting with Miriam in Nottingham, the people coming
out after evening service in St. Mary's, the organ still sounding within, the coloured windows glowing in the night, the
church like a great lantern suspended. And so to the last
scene of all, his mother though dead having the last word :
" she was the only thing that held him up himself, amid all
this. And she was gone, intermingled herself. He wanted
her to touch him, have him alongside with her. But no,
he would not give in. Turning sharply, he walked towards
the city's gold phosphorescence. His fists were shut, his
mouth set fast. He would not take that direction, to the
darkness, to follow her. He walked towards the faintly
humming, glowing town, quickly."

Nottingham was, in truth, a great figure in Lawrence's

life. As a boy he won a scholarship to the High School there and for three years or so travelled in and out by train from Eastwood. Then came the episode of the job as a clerk in the surgical appliances establishment — *Sons and Lovers* is almost wholly autobiographical. After that he went to the University College for two years — the most distinguished student, I suppose, that any provincial university has ever had. Actually he got little enough from it : the real passion of his life by then had developed and all the time he was at college he was writing *The White Peacock*, that lyrical and lovely translation of the life at Haggs Farm, Miriam's home. He made no significant friendship there — in a sense he always lacked a father and a friend. But that time at college altered the course of Lawrence's life. The only professor Lawrence admired was Weekley, whose favourite pupil he was. Here he met the woman who became celebrated as his wife : it seems to have been a case of marriage by capture.

Lawrence's sister, Ada, writes naïvely : " like another great English writer who came from Nottinghamshire, Lord Byron, he was reviled by his own people. He never came back to live among them. One day he will come home to them in his books and they will learn the truth about him and understand his life ; and, what is perhaps more important, they will learn a little truth about themselves." This is perhaps none the less true for being a little innocent. Before it is too late Nottingham ought to get the greatest of English sculptors, Henry Moore, to execute a statue of Lawrence, somewhere high up, perhaps from the Castle Rock as it appears in *Sons and Lovers*, brooding over the city. He has given it a new life, the undying life of art : it has its place now in our literature, through him. The sense of his presence, unnamed, unrecognised, almost unknown, hangs over the city as that of Joyce does Dublin, another exile impossible to exorcise. One almost sees it all now through his eyes — such is the power of genius to make its ineffaceable impression.

Lawrence's ancestry goes deep into the life of Nottingham.

His mother and his father, that discordant couple, were yet connected by their relations in the town. The coal-miner's aunt had married his wife's uncle; it was at their house that Lawrence's mother and father met, from that that it all flowed. The miner's parents were Nottingham people, his mother the daughter of Adam Parsons, once prominent in the stockings and silk industry in the town. Mrs. Lawrence's family also went back to good Nottingham bourgeois. Her father was a noted Nonconformist preacher and hymn-singer — rather a ranter, I fancy — who quarrelled with Jesse Boot as to who should run their chapel in Sneinton and with General Booth as to who should run the Salvation Army. (One observes this dogmatic quarrelsomeness in the grandson: D. H. left himself with hardly a friend, in the end.) But, further back, Mrs. Lawrence's grandfather, John Newton, another lace-maker, was a well-known hymn-writer, author of a hymn-book called *The Pilgrim*. There is no difficulty in seeing where the incantatory element in the great-grandson came from. It is also noticeable that several of these forbears had been flourishing people earlier in the century, until the decline of the lace-making trade. The sense of respectability, the struggle to maintain standards she felt slipping away, was ferocious in Mrs. Lawrence; there is nothing like 'coming down in the world' for sharpening it; class-consciousness was never more acute than in her famous son. Then, too, he was through and through a Nonconformist writer: a latter-day Bunyan on pilgrimage through the meaningless waste of the modern world. No-one has shown up its nothingness more savagely than he. It is touching to see that line of Nottingham lace-makers, hymn-singers and writers, colliery tailors, miners, flaring up in him — whose traits combine them all — and coming to an end in him.

Tonight, here in Nottingham, it is a rainy evening, cars squelching by outside and the familiar, comfortable bells of St. Mary's ringing a peal into the night as for so many centuries before. It seems a muffled peal, for some alderman, some civic ornament or dignitary, ringing on and on

P

interminably, penetrating the lanes and alleys, up darkened and forgotten streets that yet saw Charles and Newcastle, Colonel Hutchinson and his Lucy; the young Byron no more than a schoolboy slipping along the pavements with the wine of first publication in his head; the famous body borne through the streets; the gay, too vivid spirit of Bonington; dear John and Mary Howitt, kind friends to so many; and not so long ago the frail schoolboy, the miner's son from Eastwood, walking those streets with his mother, noting the warm southern colours of the fruit stalls in the Market Place, leaning over the parapet along the canal and thinking it like Venice, looking down upon the city from the Castle — the bells of St. Mary's ringing a muffled peal for all of them, while only one attentive heart, and that a stranger to the city, listens and understands.

(1950)

D. H. LAWRENCE AT EASTWOOD

IT is sometimes a mistake, if one wants to write about a subject, to know too much about it: one loses something of the sharpness, the tang, the excitement and the mystery. D. H. Lawrence meant something special to the men of my generation: he was an essential part in our awakening to maturity. We saw something of life through his eyes: his mode of experience intimately affected ours. He meant, naturally, even more to me. I could never regard him externally, as one does most writers. He was a part of me: he had entered into my veins at a very vulnerable moment, of adolescence changing into maturity. He was entwined in the fibres of my mind and heart, so closely that I remember a curious experience when he died. The day the news of his death came I went to walk alone on the coast of the bay at home in Cornwall: it was evening, and the image that consciousness of his passing took was that of a ship of death passing slowly along the darkening waters of the bay from west to east. It was only later that I learned that that was the image that had haunted his mind for weeks before his death, that the subject of the poem he left unfinished.

There was a very natural reason why he should speak specially to me: he was then the only writer of genius to come from my own class, the working people, and his books — especially his masterpiece, *Sons and Lovers* — were the only books that described the life of the people from the inside, with absolute fidelity and conviction, and at the same time transfused it with imagination and poetry, made a work of art of it. I was a predestined victim: my nerves vibrated in sympathy with his: the same sensitiveness, the touchiness, the irritability of the one skin too few, the confusion of emotion and intellect, the keen but easily discouraged response to life, the brittleness and toughness, the mixture of masculine and feminine: I was an unknown, unrecog-

nised, younger brother. How much he would have dis-
approved of me and the way I went : politics, the way of
the intellectual, pride of the intellect, historical research,
learning, burying the response of the senses to life under
many weary tomes, living in libraries and colleges he so
much despised, progressively withdrawn from life ; but
reaching, if by another avenue, the same disillusionment and
despair. (One could not arrive at a greater despair than
his.) And yet underneath the libraries, the works of history,
the layers of academicism, the buried life, something of
him goes on in my veins, the seed forgotten, its life not
extinguished. It is years since I read anything of his —
once I had read him almost all, absorbed him whole ; and
I had never yet visited the place where he was born and
grew up, that made him what he was — though I had always
meant to.

Here, at Nottingham, was my chance. At lunch-time
I did not know where I was going. My friends knew. I
thought I was going to the University. They said I was
going to Eastwood. After lunch we parted, they for Wollaton and Derby. Emerging into the great Market Place,
I felt lonely without them. My footsteps led me to the
Eastwood bus. When I returned late in the evening, transported, beside myself —

> Nor did the wizest wizard guess
> What should bechance at Lyonnesse,
> When I set out for Lyonnesse
> A hundred miles away —

I asked them where I had been. " To Eastwood, of course ",
they said.

I took my place humbly, apologetically, on the bus,
front row in the stalls, upstairs : excited to think that I was
following the road he knew so well, had so often come into
Nottingham and out along it. A kind young man took
charge of me — the Midlands courtesy, the Midlands nice-
ness, I noticed ; pointed out the sights to me. Some I
registered silently to myself, having already entered the
dream. Here was the cemetery that must have been so

familiar to the Lawrences — on the slope of the hill, the last lap into Nottingham : as on that merry walk of Lawrence's father with his pal Jerry into Nottingham, when after several drinks on the way he lay down and slept in the last field under an oak in view of the city, and came home drunk to put his wife out of doors in the last weeks before Lawrence was born. It is all wonderfully described in *Sons and Lovers* : the moonlit night, the scent of phloxes in the garden, the wife looking under the drawn blind to see her husband asleep on the kitchen table, tapping at the window to be let in.

We passed through Basford with the large house where Philip Bayley, author of *Festus*, a poem famous in its day, lived and wrote too much — for it is intolerably tedious, forty thousand lines of Victorian moralising. (No less popular in America, where thirty editions of it were pirated.) Thence past Nuttall Temple, the ruined shell of which surmounted the rise on the left. It was built in the mideighteenth century by Sir Charles Sedley — it is said, on the winnings of one race : a magnificent domed Palladian villa, like Chiswick House or Mereworth in Kent. It is mentioned somewhere by Lawrence in a description of the countryside. My companion told me that his father had helped to redecorate it in the years before the war. Now deliberately dynamited, a fragment of hollow-windowed wall on the horizon — like a Piper scene of war damage. But the Nuttall Temple petrol-filling station is all right, standing beside the dismantled entrance-gate, the forlorn pillars and the overgrown drive.

It is the end of a civilisation. Piper and Betjeman, Osbert Lancaster, Gerald Berners, Martyn Skinner, Jack Simmons — all my friends are right. In the heroic days of 1940–45 I used to put up a resistance and argue that there was a future. Now I know that they are right. There is no point in resisting any longer. It is the decay of a civilisation that I study — like Leland and Aubrey before me : the one " roving maggoty-headed " about the country, wishing that there were monasteries still for such as he to retire to ; the other ending up off his head, the spectacle of dissolution and destruction too much for him. Yes : it is a vanishing culture that I pursue, the débris that I lovingly cherish.

Descending from the bus, on the pavement I fell into the arms of luck. A passing fellow didn't know the house where Lawrence was born, but he could tell me the man who did, an old man of eighty-seven who had been his great friend and would tell me all about him. No, he himself had never seen Lawrence. No, Eastwood people usedn't to think much of him — until later years when he became famous, they began to take notice. He always understood that Lawrence resented Eastwood. He had been unhappy at school — no good at games, laughed at by the other boys, who thought him eff-eff-effo—what was the word ? Effeminate ? Yes, that's it. I explained that he would not have been a man of genius, able to create as he did, unless he had had a strong streak of feminine as well as masculine in him. He thought that was right. But Lawrence resented Eastwood, and the last time he visited it he said he hoped never to see it again.

The usual story, I registered, but said nothing. One knows the difficulties a neighbourhood will make over one of their own who stands out : no such trouble if it is the son of a squire or of a local bourgeois. Is it any wonder that Lawrence grew to hate it ? He said again and again that he would never come home to Eastwood. Nor did he. Switzerland, Germany, Italy, France, Australia, New Mexico — but never Eastwood. His father and mother, that ill-assorted couple — the drinking coal-miner who was such a beautiful dancer and his serious little wife with a soul above her surroundings — whose union yet produced a son whose genius was ripened by their jarring tension — lie in Eastwood Cemetery : not so their son. Yet how often, under alien skies, he revisited in mind the loved familiar places : the Breach, with its country look in spite of the proximity of the pit, the house in Walker Street with the ash-tree in which the wind moaned on winter nights and its broad view down the valley, and uphill to the trees behind which lay the farm where Miriam lived ; Strelley Mill and Nether-

mere and Beauvale, Hucknall where Byron lies buried.
Perhaps, in glimpses of the moon, the wraith — not of a
bearded famous man but of a grey-eyed schoolboy, eager of
step, lingers about those spots.

> He hears; no more remembered
> In fields where I was known,
> Here I lie down in London
> And turn to rest alone.
>
> There, by the starlit fences,
> The wanderer halts and hears
> My soul that lingers sighing
> About the glimmering weirs.

The first thing that struck me about Eastwood — and
what surprised me — was that, allowing for differences of
colour and accent, it might have been a china-clay village
at home in Cornwall. Not at all one's usual idea of a
mining town, as it might be South Wales or Yorkshire or
Tyneside. For one thing, it was clean, blowy, healthy.
There is still country round about, fields and holdings and
trees, and distant views towards Ilkeston and Ripley, places
mentioned in the novels, towards Moorgreen Reservoir —
the Nethermere of *The White Peacock*, towards Hucknall and
further afield, back to Nottingham. The lie of the land
reminded me of the china-clay district : windy ridges like
that along which Eastwood lies, in the valleys the pits.
There was the same rawness and rudeness about the place
— as it might be Bugle or St. Dennis — the rough-edged
angularity, the sharpness, the hideousness. Everything
recent and ugly and Philistine, the chapels in evidence : a
working-class and petty-bourgeois community. Nothing of
the grace of life : no taste, no culture, no relenting : nothing
whatever to stay the mind on or comfort the elect soul. How
he must have felt about it, once he had come to know something better — just as I used to feel about St. Austell and
the china-clay district !

Directed to the bungalow where Lawrence's old friend
now lived, I entered at once into the aura — there were

photographs of the lad he was, the one with the boyish hair and moustache, wide-apart eyes and an amused, enigmatic smile at the beholder, keeping himself in reserve, the with-drawal of youth, self-conscious yet friendly; next to it the image of the famous man, the bearded Christ with the infinitely sad eyes. So this was what he had come to — the suffering servant of Isaiah. His friend was away in Notting-ham for the afternoon but would return to his shop. Back through the main street, past the ' Wellington ' inn — no doubt patronised by the father, though the ' Ram ' was his usual haunt — past the little shops Lawrence would still recognise if he could come back : Hunter's Tea Stores must be the same and the Nottingham Trustee Savings Bank next door, and surely the shop with the lettering " Drapery — Millinery — Mantles " must be pre-1914, though not that of John Houghton of *The Lost Girl,* who had a passion for fine clothes and filled his windows with them, and was laughed at by the mining folk to whom he had to sell them at a loss in the end. In the window of the only bookshop there was a copy of *Forever Amber* and Daphne du Maurier's latest — but no D. H. Lawrence. How right, I reflected : it could not be more right! First to be disconsidered, and then forgotten.

At the shop the old friend's wife made out an itinerary for me to follow — again the Midlands kindness to the stranger — and all the afternoon I went over the ground alone. It was all the more poignant so. Only a step across the street was the house where Lawrence was born. Again, not exactly a miner's cottage : a small, mean house in a squalid street, with a little shop-window and gate-entrance at the side to a back-court, the row of outdoor privies against the wall at the end of the potato patches. Mrs. Lawrence in her early married years had tried to sell baby-clothes and ribbons and lace in the front room to help out, but had had no luck : off the main street, nobody came. It was from this house that she came with her baby, when the friendly shopkeeper first set eyes on him as she drew back the shawl : " I'm afraid I s'll never rear him ".

This is 8A Victoria Street: the whole neighbourhood gone downhill and really squalid now. The mean street runs steep down to the valley and the pit at the bottom, the sharp February wind blowing bitterly up, with occasional skiffs of rain from which I take shelter in a doorway opposite Searston's Groceries and Provisions, across from the large ugly Wesleyan Methodist chapel MDCCCLXVI. A few miners are coming uphill, black from their work. In the street behind me a loud-speaker van tours up and down: "What about the promises the Socialists made in 1945? The Conservative Party will *not* nationalise industry if they come in." An old miner's wife clops crippling up the hill to do her Saturday shopping at Searston's, trudges back wearily, hopelessly with her carrier, her old shoes worn over, her ankles swollen: Saturday afternoon and the end of life for her. My heart sinks for her — but what is the point? One can do nothing. A blowsy slut peeps out of her den, keeps me under observation the whole time I am in the street. Perhaps they take me for somebody to do with the Election. But all that is long over. They wonder at the well-dressed stranger who huddles about in doorways, sheltering from the showers, but who will not move away, is rooted to the spot — so strangely moved he does not know whether it is raindrops on his face or tears, for the thought of all that this huddled street gave birth to, the intensity, the passion, the mingled bitterness and sweetness of life. Thoughts come and go like the flickering lights of an aurora, as I once saw them in a snowstorm over Hensbarrow. How can language express these intense moments when the sense of life passes through one's mind with such poignancy, when one sees it all in a flash, in all its layers and dimensions simultaneously, as they say a drowning man sees it, all the pathos and manifold insatisfaction, yet touched by joy and love and incomprehensible consolations? Hardly thinking at all, I see the little family they were, making up the street for the Congregational chapel on Sundays, down the hill to the Breach where they next lived, the growing boy, the lyrical journeys to the farm and Miriam and her brothers, the obsessive love of mother and son excluding everyone else until she died, the brave face she put on life, the tragic division she inflicted on her son, the tension and the genius she gave him.

> I kiss you goodbye, my darling,
> Our ways are different now :
> You are a seed in the night-time,
> I am a man, to plough
> The difficult glebe of the future
> For seed to endow. . . .
>
> Is the last word now uttered ?
> Is the farewell said ?
> Spare me the strength to leave you
> Now you are dead.
> I must go, but my soul lies helpless
> Beside your bed.

The street has now an upper room, a Kingdom hall, of Jehovah's Witnesses. Lower down there is a clothes-drying ground : young Nottinghamshire lads cross it from time to time this Saturday afternoon, as it might be Bert Lawrence. But no Bert Lawrence will appear here again — ever.

At last I tear myself away to go on with my pilgrimage.

Back in the main street I retrace my steps past the Congregational chapel : very Early English and with a sharp little spire that looks as if it might prick you. Here it was that Mrs. Lawrence met Miriam's mother and the children first became acquainted — all described in *Sons and Lovers* and in the touching Personal Record that Miriam wrote after Lawrence died. The young minister used often to come down to the collier's house in the Breach to talk books and theology with the serious-minded wife, the best tea-things would be put out and the miner would be on his worst behaviour when he came home to find the minister there. Somewhere in a story of his, I remember, Lawrence recalled years after the text that was inscribed on the walls of the chapel — I forget what. And in an article he wrote shortly before he died he remembered the hymns he liked :

" Awake, my soul, and with the sun ". The Lawrence children used to sing in the choir :

> Dare to be a Daniel, dare to stand alone,

and

> Sound the battle-cry,
> See the foe is nigh,
> Raise the standard high
> For the Lord. . . .

Lawrence was certainly a Nonconformist writer, one of the greatest of them : he had no difficulty in daring to stand alone : it came naturally to him. *Ich kann nicht anders*. Impossible to over-estimate the Nonconformist element in his make-up : he was always sounding the battle-cry, raising the standard high, pedalling away at the harmonium of the Sunday school in which he taught. He thought of himself as a prophet : he was certainly a missionary, a local preacher, yes — and alas — a prophet too, a prophet of the destruction that would come on us. It fascinated me to think, as I went along (" What did Mr. Aneurin Bevan say in 1945 ? " The voice pursued me, an echo from my past. I'm sure I don't remember) — I wondered, my mind set on better things, what would have been the effect if the Lawrences had gone to the dead, deserted church at the other end of the town : a less harsh inflexion, a more graceful, a more tolerant culture, a greater sense of history and tradition, a kindlier, easier spirit ? There was the Sunday school they had all been brought up in, now an Employment Exchange. I longed to go into the little chapel : barred and bolted, the gate chained : I don't suppose anyone goes there now : there too an end of a way of life.

I go on my way along Dovecote Lane, suddenly noticing that it is the road to Hucknall and Byron's grave. In the playing-fields by the Greasley Miners' Welfare Centre, a dead-looking place, boys are playing football, white shorts and blue jerseys, green and black and red colouring the field. There is a gleam of sun. The wind is very fresh up here. In the distance the bells of Greasley church ring sweet in the sad February air. (Suddenly, a strange experience :

a man in a passing car scrutinises me : I thought I recognised the sloe-black, adder-black eyes : a false friend of
former days in Cornwall.) Hereabouts, in this parish, were
the meadows that Miriam's father and his sons used to mow,
and the young Lawrence would help. " We used to pack a
big basket of provisions to last all day," Miriam wrote, " so
that hay harvest had a picnic flavour. Father enjoyed
Lawrence's company quite as much as the rest of us. I
heard father say to mother : ' Work goes like fun when Bert's
there, it's no trouble at all to keep them going '. "

There is a lyrical description of it all in *The White Peacock*,
written when those days were but just over, the dew still
upon them. It is in the chapter called " A Poem of Friendship " ; a chapter in which one sees Lawrence's sense of
ecstasy in the life of Nature at its quietest and best. It is
dedicated to his love for Miriam's eldest brother — the
real, if transposed, subject of the book : in it he came as
close as he could to the subject of their coming together.
Afterwards, " we went together down to the fields, he to
mow the island of grass he had left standing the previous
evening, I to sharpen the machine knife, to mow out the
hedge-bottoms with the scythe, and to rake the swaths from
the way of the machine when the unmown grass was reduced
to a triangle. The cool, moist fragrance of the morning, the
intentional stillness of everything, of the tall, bluish trees,
of the wet, frank flowers, of the trustful moths folded and
unfolded in the fallen swaths, was a perfect medium of
sympathy. The horses moved with a still dignity, obeying
his commands. When they were harnessed, and the machine
oiled, still he was loth to mar the perfect morning, but stood
looking down the valley.

" ' I shan't mow these fields any more,' he said. . . .
This year the elder-flowers were widespread over the corner
bushes, and the pink roses fluttered high above the hedge.
There were the same flowers in the grass as we had known
many years ; we should not know them any more."

Now all about is asphalt and new roads, and bungalows
and houses for the too many people who inhabit England.

Having gone too far beyond the little Board School with its bell that called the young Bert to school, I returned on my track to Eastwood, going downhill to Lynncroft, where they lived last, and along Walker Street to which they moved up from the Breach. There in the bottoms was the house where their life was at its unhappiest : the four stark blocks of miners' houses Mrs. Lawrence so much hated. Yet there are still fragments of country within reach, on the doorstep : trees, a sounding stream, fields, a farm — and then the former colliery-manager's house in its grounds, I suppose " Highclose " of *The White Peacock*. House-proud, yoked to a man who would not pull with her, and whom she gradually excluded from the life of the family, the mother was proud of the house in Walker Street : a bay-window, three steps up to the front door.

" We loved living here ", the youngest sister wrote. " We had a wonderful view of Brinsley, Underwood, Moor-green and the High Park Woods in the distance. Immediately in front were the fields which stretched to the Breach — fields which made the best playground one could have. What fun we had round the ancient ash-tree which stood just opposite the house — although the moaning wind through its branches scared us as we lay in bed in the winter." D. H. himself has described it, more vividly, in *Sons and Lovers* : " They all loved the Scargill Street house for its openness, for the great scallop of the world it had in view. On summer evenings the women would stand, facing the west, watching the sunsets flare quickly out, till the Derby-shire hills ridged across the crimson far away, like the black crest of a newt." But the children were terrified of the moaning of the ash-tree at night. " The west wind, sweep-ing from Derbyshire, caught the houses with full force, and the tree shrieked again. Morel [*i.e.* the father] liked it. ' It's music,' he said. ' It sends me to sleep.' But Paul [*i.e.* D. H.] and Arthur and Annie hated it. To Paul it became almost a demoniacal noise. The winter of their first year in the new house their father was very bad." The moaning of the tree became a symbol of the discord within the house, the tension that imprinted itself upon the children, that left its stigmata ineffaceably upon one of them. One of his earliest poems is about it :

Outside the house the ash-tree hung its terrible whips,
And at night when the wind rose, the lash of the tree
Shrieked and slashed the wind, as a ship's
Weird rigging in a storm shrieks hideously.

Within the house two voices arose, a slender lash
Whistling she-delirious rage, and the dreadful sound
Of a male thong booming and bruising, until it had drowned
The other voice in a silence of blood, neath the noise of the ash.

No ash-tree now stands outside the house to disturb the peeping ghosts. All is as quiet as the grave.

It is indeed very quiet this Saturday afternoon. A couple of coal-miners are crossing the open space, their dogs rushing madly across where the children used to play. The view is much the same, the great tip that dominates the valley even larger; the wide view spreads upwards to where on the horizon are the trees behind which was Miriam's farm, and where lived the people of Nethermere. Life was not all misery at Walker Street : joy was inextinguishable in young hearts, and there is a delightful description in *Sons and Lovers* of the games in the street under the one lamp-post on winter evenings when it was not wet and the boys and girls came out to play.

From Walker Street the Lawrences moved just round the corner, going up one again, to Lynncroft. D. H. showed Miriam — they were now in the phase of adolescent friendship ripening into love — over the new house " with quiet pride. It had a little entrance-hall, with the stairs and the doors to the other rooms opening out from it. There was a cooking-range in the scullery as well as in the living-room, a china-closet in addition to the pantry, a cupboard under the side-window where the school-books were kept, and from the big window of the living-room was the view over the roofs of Eastwood to the square church tower standing high above. The garden was pleasant and adjoined a field.

This is the house that Lawrence describes in *Aaron's Rod*, where the husband returns surreptitiously at night."

It is also the house of Lawrence's martyrdom : the long-drawn-out agony of his mother's dying from cancer. Other people have experienced a like *supplice* ; but few people have loved with such intensity as this mother and son, have held on to life with a more terrible will-power until she had to be torn apart from him, or have had such capacity for suffering as this son born of it. It makes the most painful, the most unforgettable scene in our modern literature : once read one can never forget that, whatever else one forgets.

That house was also the house of Miriam's defeat and frustration, the working out of her own tragedy, the condemnation of her love for D. H. to nullity, breaking against the rock of his mother's will. She early sensed the tension within which he lived. " Perhaps it was the strong emotional tension between mother and son, and in a directly contrary sense, between husband and wife, and father and son, that made the strangely vibrating atmosphere." Or there were those gatherings on Sunday evenings after chapel. " There was the rustle and scent of Sunday clothes. . . . A general talk would go on, with Lawrence giving quick conversational change all round. . . . Mrs. Lawrence, in her black dress, would sit in the low rocking-chair like a little figure of Fate, coldly disapproving, while Lawrence fetched cakes and pastries out of the pantry, which he would press upon us who had a long walk home. Sometimes we went into the parlour, and A. would play the piano while we sang ' The heavens are telling ', ' O rest in the Lord ', ' Yes, the Lord is mindful of His own ', and the exquisite ' Hymn to Music ' Lawrence liked so much. It was exciting, but there was an undercurrent of hostility running strong beneath it all." How well one recognises that baleful atmosphere : it was the same in my own home, except that there weren't any friends who came in. " The father I rarely saw ", says Miriam. " He was always out in the evenings."

" He hates his father ", the mother once told her. " I know why he hates his father. It happened before he was born. One night he put me out of the house. He's bound to hate his father."

The result was this tragic division in Lawrence that made it impossible for him to respond to Miriam. Something was destroyed in him by this insatiable demand of his mother. Miriam's parents understood : " Bert belongs to his mother. She'll never give him up." Even after his mother was dead, it was " Don't imagine that because mother's dead you can claim me ". " I began to realise that whatever approach Lawrence made to me inevitably involved him in a sense of disloyalty to his mother." Hence the distortion he made in the presentation of Miriam in his great novel, in order that the mother might triumph. " As I sat and looked at the subtle distortion of what had been the deepest values of my life, the one gleam of light was the realisation that Lawrence had over-stated his case ; that some day his epic of maternal love and filial devotion would be viewed from another angle, that of his own final despair." It was Lawrence himself who taught Miriam to be a penetrating, watchful observer. " It was his power to transmute the common experiences into significance that I always felt to be Lawrence's greatest gift." And then — " With all his gifts, he was somehow cut off, unable to attain that complete participation in life that he craved for ".

But, of course, hence the genius : it comes from the fissure. The artist, the writer of genius, is half in life and half out of it — Henry James thought : if he were not drawn in he would not feel sufficiently acutely to write about it ; if he were not half outside he would not be able to see it and describe it. It is the acute discomfort, the maladjustment that creates the tension ; the desire to be within, enclosed like everyone else, secure and safe, that gives the nostalgia, the poignancy, the colouring — that looking-backward which is the infallible signature of the artist, whoever he is, Shakespeare or Scott or Hardy, Flaubert or Poussin or Duparc. No wonder Orpheus has always been the image, the symbol of the artist, the fated figure.

Back over the ground I trudge, a more dogged figure than Orpheus, more substantial than Persephone, to take Lawrence's place in the chair by his friend's fireside in the sitting-room behind the shop. All the afternoon I have waited for the friend to come back from Nottingham, at last with growing anxiety. The door opened and he came in: eighty-seven looking like sixty-seven, bearded, bright as a bird, untired at the end of a busy day. Extraordinary to think that here was the man whose life enclosed Lawrence's, lapped it round at either end: twenty years older than Lawrence, he is still alive twenty years after Lawrence died.

He had known Lawrence all his life, from the time he was two months old and he had asked Mrs. Lawrence across the way how the latest arrival was. But she was a foolish woman to think she could alter her husband and force him into her ways. She had never seen him dirty before her marriage: they met one Saturday night at a dance in Nottingham and fell violently in love with each other. He was a really *beautiful* dancer when young, known for miles around. (Lawrence one day to Miriam: "Father says one ought to be able to dance on a threepenny bit". "He seldom spoke of his father and we at once exclaimed: ' Why, does your father dance?' ' He used to, when he was a young man. He ran a dancing class at one time', he replied briefly. It seemed unbelievable; we had never thought of his father in that light.") When they were married, the first day he came home from the pit and insisted on eating his dinner — as miners do, tired with the day's work — without washing *appalled* her: she never got over it.

(Ada, Lawrence's youngest sister: " I wonder if there would have been quite so much misery in our childhood if mother had been just a little more tolerant. . . . As we grew older we shut him more and more out of our lives, and instinctively turned to mother, and he, realising this, became more and more distasteful in his habits. He was never really intolerable, and if, instead of wanting the impossible from him, we had tried to interest ourselves in the things for which he really cared, we should have been spared many

Q

unhappy and sordid scenes. . . . My brother's description of him in *Sons and Lovers*, when mother was dying, seems to me to be writing too deep for tears. He shows a lost man, bewildered by the realisation that she was going from him, and that somehow he had no part in anything." How relentlessly the wife made him pay for his failure to come up to her expectations of him! The irony of it is that his part in his son's genius goes unrecognised — and yet one sees that his was the artist's temperament, not hers; that the instinctual sense of life that made the creative strain came through him, the miner living his underground life of the senses, primitive and animal, shut out from the family, excluded, forgotten. Yet his was the dance, the ecstasy, the escape into dream. Some spark from his blood carried the germ from which the artist was born. D. H. had his father's cleverness with his hands, for ever making things, his dance-like rhythms of body. The poet was his father's son, the father unrecognised; the prophet, the uncompromising, relentless spirit of the mother.)

When Bert was in his teens (I had made a mistake and said David: he was never David here, always Bert) you would have thought he and his mother were more like a courting couple than mother and son. When she was dying I thought he would have gone off his head, clean off his head! He had written his first book, *The White Peacock*, and all Mrs. Lawrence was living for was to see Bert's book. He sent message after message, telegrams to the publishers for a copy to put into her hands. At last it came, and he rushed upstairs to place it in her hand. She was already unconscious. It was a great grief to him that he never could be sure whether she knew what it was that she was holding.

What Lawrence wanted all his life long was a man friend. (I remembered what he once said to Miriam: " If only you'd been a man, things might have been perfect," then added immediately, " but it wouldn't have been any good, because then you wouldn't have cared about me ". Miriam noticed his longing for the friendship of her elder brother — it is the inspiration of *The White Peacock*. The real emotion in the book is Cyril's love (suppressed, perhaps hardly realised) for George, the young farmer brother : whenever George is being described there is always passion behind the writing. Cyril is the pallid girlish type as his mother would have him. He only releases himself in disguise as Lettie — she leads George on, rouses his love and then does not satisfy it, leaving him to go to pieces in his own way. It is a sad piece of wishful *schadenfreude*. People understand these things better nowadays : no reason why Lawrence should have been so hopeless : but perhaps here too he was before his time. One realises why, in the novel, Cyril is about so much with Lettie, like a curious attendant shadow : he was not so much her brother as the same person, two extrapolations of Lawrence.)

But Lawrence never found the friend he needed. He himself, twenty years older, was the only man friend he had that stayed his friend all the time. Lawrence had had a false friend — he too. Of him Lawrence said — " He is my Judas Iscariot. And he will betray me. Not in my lifetime : he'd be afraid of what would come to him. But after I am dead, you will see."

I said, was it not partly or even largely his own fault that he never found the friend he needed ? One could not say such passionate things, quarrel violently and lacerate people's feelings, and then expect all to go on as it had been before. No friendship — no human relations could stand it. Curious that he never learned that, that he had not more self-control. I asked : " Did he never try to tell him when he was younger ? " " Oh dear, no. I never interfere with people. I let them go their own way." I said that lads growing up like D. H. as good as had no fathers, no-one to tell them or help them.

The thought struck me that if one has too intense a struggle in early days perhaps one needs unconsciously to perpetuate the struggle later on — one creates enmities, antagonisms. H. said that Lawrence had extreme antipathies. If he were sitting there where you are sitting — when the news went round that he was staying here, there'd

be a lot of women school-teachers who'd drop in in the hope
of seeing him — if someone came in he took a dislike to,
he'd sit there and not say a single word the whole evening.
And yet — he was a wonderful conversationalist. (Oh, the
usual story : how well one knows the symptoms.) Bert said
to me one day when I was putting out chairs for them to sit
down : " What are you putting out chairs for the bitches
for ? You know, Willie, you are making a great mistake.
When you get to Heaven for your good works, rather than
your faith, you'll be so busy putting out chairs for the bitches
that you'll fall backward — into Hell."

Clearly, the way Lawrence went, following his intuitions
and impulses absolutely, with no attempt at control, made
him pay a heavy price — an extreme loneliness and friend-
lessness in the end. It was the penalty for his abnegation,
his hatred of the rational, and the compensatory subtlety of
his intuitive senses, his response to the blood and the unconscious.

The last word has been said about him by Miriam, the
girl with whom he grew up here in his youth and whom he
left to make her own life while he travelled so far away in
space and in spirit. He always used to say that she would
write his epitaph. On H.'s last walk with Lawrence, a sad
one for him, he had said to him, " Why didn't you marry
Miriam ? " He burst out : " Mind your own bloody
business ! " And then, apologising, " I'm sorry. But she
wasn't the one for me." He continued in German — so
like this little circle : as a youth he would frequently come
out with French phrases to Miriam. I think I know the
psychological explanation : a sign of malaise. The upshot
of it was that she would have destroyed his genius; he
needed something to stimulate him. (In other words, too
much of a yes-woman. Like N., I registered from long ago.
No, Lawrence was right.) Miriam had married afterwards
and had had children. Mrs. H. : But she always loved
Bert. The last time she had been over to see them — she
died two years ago — they went up to Walker Street and
looked into the distance to the trees behind which was the

farm where they had lived. There was a pause between the two of them. The shrewd, practical, kind Mrs. H.'s eyes glistened as she remembered : " She was very sad ". He, after a pause : " Yes. She always loved him." The memory was too strong : they couldn't speak about it.

All the same, Mrs. H. realised, it was Lawrence who had made Miriam. And Miriam recognised it : " The realisation that our long, and in many ways wonderful, friendship had actually come to an end was a very deep blow, comparable to a kind of death. In the passing of Lawrence I saw also the extinction of my greater self. Life without him had a bleak aspect. I had grown up within his orbit, and now that he was gone I had to make a definite new beginning. For a long time in a quiet and deliberate way I wished I had done with life."

And no woman understood Lawrence as Miriam did. " Whatever my own lot it was easier to bear than his, for at least I had the positive value of love, and I was not frustrated as he was by inner division." She understood that at bottom " the whole question of sex had for him the fascination of horror, and that in the repudiation of any possibility of a sex relation between us he felt that he paid me a deep and subtle compliment ". I am sure that that is true. It all meant that " one could do nothing. He was like a man set apart. Only Lawrence might help himself. Anyone else was powerless." (How like Swift it all is!) And yet, there was his extraordinary capacity for joy — " No task seemed dull or monotonous to him. He brought such vitality to the doing that he transformed it into something creative. . . . There was his sensitiveness, too, his delicacy of spirit that, while it contributed vitally to his charm, made him more vulnerable, more susceptible to injury from the crudeness of life." Hers is the last word about him : " He was always to me a symbol of overflowing life. He seemed able to enter into other lives, and not only human lives. With wild things, flowers and birds, a rabbit in a snare, the speckled eggs in a hole in the ground, he was in primal sympathy — a living vibration passed between him and them, so that I always saw him, in the strictest sense of the word, immortal. . . . And with the clarification that time brings and its truer perspective, those of us whose youth was the richer for knowing him see again the dear familiar figure, and we remember how much of our joy came to us through the inspiration of Lawrence's gay and dauntless spirit."

I asked his old friend when did he realise that the boy he knew had genius and would be a famous writer. He said that he had always known it, from the time he grew up into young manhood. Miriam says that she realised it quite early — " I had so clearly the knowledge that he must inevitably move far beyond us, and felt that he knew it himself, and was trying to devise some means of not severing himself from us all ". There is a certain sadness in the way such a man passes out of the ken of his early friends. And yet — they had him at his youngest and best, when there was a charm upon life and horizons were illimitable.

Turning to say goodbye, I said to Lawrence's old friend that he had been a most fortunate man. He said simply, " I have been ". I said it was astonishing the way that a life like Lawrence's could light up a whole landscape, so that the place lived in him. It was obvious how these good kind people had been touched by the intensity of the dead man's personality, so that it *made* life for them — as Shelley's life was all in all for Trelawny and nothing that happened after had any significance.

But my last impression — so strong that the dream has gone on ever since — was of Eastwood, to which he would never come home : those raw streets and miners' terraces, the wind blowing gustily along the ridges and up Victoria Street from the Breach, the harsh corners and the sharp spire of the Congregational chapel pricking the sky from the places where he lived. Not palaces nor great houses nor castles nor monuments ever moved me so much as this small mining town with the February wind blowing through — and something else that made it so poignant and alive : the spirit of the dead boy who lived and suffered and was

often happy there and, leaving it, has touched every lane
and corner and view with the shadow of his genius — all
springing, like that first glance of Hardy's mother and father
in the church at Stinsford, from the mating of that unhappy
couple, the miner who was such a beautiful dancer and the
wife who felt herself superior to the life she lived with him
and yet gave birth to all this : both of them now sleeping
together in the cemetery under the hill from Eastwood
church.

ALUN LEWIS: A FOREWORD

I NEVER knew Alun Lewis: how I wish I had known him now! I regard it as all the greater an honour — in a world whose ' honours ' one does not set much store by — to be asked to write a Preface to these letters of his. And then there is the difficulty, the diffidence, the fear — the fear that I may not do justice to a man whom I so much admire, whose personality, as it comes through the writing he has left us, one cannot but love and be deeply moved by. But perhaps I may speak for all those who knew him only through his writings.

Since I came to know his work I have always regarded him as one of the two best poets to be produced by the war : both of them, alas, killed : such losses war brings to our State and literature. And yet one might say, with a sense of fatality, that each of them was chosen by the war : something in the genius of each of them responded to it, was elicited by it, so that they made something out of it by which they transcended the war and its accidents, even death. That was true of Sidney Keyes ; it was no less true of Alun Lewis. He seems to have been made aware of it, suddenly, in a flash, himself : in these Letters he says, " Thinking back on my own writing, it all seemed to mature of a sudden between the winter of 1939 and the following autumn. Can't make it out. Was it Gweno and the Army ? "

It was, of course, the conjunction of love and war : the stimulus, the excitement, the danger. The threat approaching ever nearer making infinitely desirable the beauty of life, of which, being a poet, he had so acute, so vibrant a sense. Of the price the poet pays for his extreme sensitivity there is a revealing passage in these Letters : " Yesterday and the night before I was enticed, seduced and destroyed by the long octopus arms and the hungry hard mouth of a shapeless poem that will never be written. . . . And I knew last night I couldn't *live* with the thoughts that encircled this particular poem, and I was afraid of being alone with them after I'd put the lamp out." Then, after the struggle, there comes the triumph, the victory of the man's indomitable spirit over the forces of the dark, expressed in lines that are among the most unforgettable of the war, that haunt the mind and will not, surely, be forgotten in our literature. Such lines as

> The gradual self-effacement of the dead
>
> But love survives the venom of the snake
>
> By day these men ask nothing, and obey
>
> But most men seek the place where they were born.

Or passages like

> If I should go away,
> Beloved, do not say
> " He has forgotten me ".
> For you abide,
> A singing rib within my dreaming side ;
> You always stay.

Or there are whole poems like " All day it has rained ", " To Edward Thomas ", " After Dunkirk ", " Mid-Winter ", " Corfe Castle ", " Westminster Abbey ", " Infantry ", " Song : On seeing dead bodies float off the Cape ". In short, he has left us a body of poetry that will last : I think of him as the Edward Thomas of this war, that poet of the last to whom he had a special devotion.

The paradox of his work is that it is both complete in itself and yet has promise of even greater things. I think these Letters show that. It is complete, a perfected art — in spite of the doubts that assailed him, as they assail all poets in the ardours and depressions of writing poetry ; the dissatisfactions he felt and sometimes expressed are so much evidence of the standards he set himself.

What is the peculiar value of his poetry ? What are its qualities, the source of its strength, the chances of its survival ?

Why do I rate it so high among all the poetry brought forth by the war? We must give reasons for our belief. Here a passage from the Letters helps us: " I always realise this when I'm trying to write a poem or a story — if I get too far away from the *thing*, the *thought* becomes flabby and invalid, and it weighs on me with a dead weight and all the creative vitality dies in me ". But exactly: that is what is so good and strong about his poetry: it is so concrete and visual, the general reflection rises naturally out of the observation, out of the particular springs the universal. So much of what his contemporaries write is so cerebral; it is not (as they think) their strength, but their weakness. For abstract poetry is the most difficult of all kinds of poetry to write, and there are few English poets to whose cast of mind it is natural: Donne certainly, Milton, Wordsworth and few others; in our time perhaps Yeats, but even in the later Eliot there are descents into prose — the constant danger that awaits an over-intellectualised poetry. And of course when abstract intellectual verse is written by so many — for it is the fashion — whose intellects are really rather second-rate, is it any wonder that whole stretches of contemporary writings of verse, which yet have a good deal of current *réclame*, are in truth arid desert with no life, no virtue, no sap in them?

Not so with Alun Lewis. I believe that his Welsh roots, the Celtic character of his genius, were a safeguard: that loving observation of detail, the sense of line and pattern and phrase, the attachment to the particular, yet clothed with an imagination sensuous in itself, the brightness of vision with which the object is seen. Those qualities appear in all Celtic art: they are in the instinct of the Celt. And Lewis was protected by his instinct: how wise he was to trust it, against the proddings and jabs of the critics, those persons who lay down the law about doing what they can't do themselves at all. Lewis notices in these Letters the " fussy interest " of the critics in him and his fortunes: " I react to these proddings by searching myself and concluding that everything is in the lap of the gods, and I will feel and do whatever I happen to feel and do — but I shall make no conscious effort to broaden, deepen, extend, alienate or resolve myself ".

Indeed he had something better than these useless recommendations from outside to guide him : the needle and the magnetic pole of instinct within him, and in addition, the fundamental seriousness towards life and art without which nothing great is ever achieved. He says, in announcing " a whale of a story in the air ", which he did not live to write — it was to have been on much the same theme as Forster's *Passage to India,* the effect of the Burma campaigns on the Anglo-Indian community — " this larger theme has a greater responsibility of judgment in it, and requires more time ". Time was the one thing he was not given ; he had everything else : genius, love, happiness, faith in man. He makes a revealing comment on the work of a distinguished contemporary : " I've been reading Graham Greene's *Brighton Rock* and I feel a sort of horror at the gusto with which so many modern writers portray the detailed disintegration and instability and bewilderment of modern humanity. I'd like to wait until I can get a stronger and more constructive purpose to guide my pen." How wise and true that was of him. He had so much more belief than the professional believers, more faith than the faithful, and, I cannot but think, more to offer in the end than they.

He had something rock-like in him to build on : " My longing is more and more for one thing only, integrity, and I discount the other qualities in people far too ruthlessly if they lack that fundamental sincerity and wholeness ". There he speaks for me. And again when he says : " It's the person who deludes himself who is the whited sepulchre that every great mind has pronounced the arch-miscreant of life. . . . I'm more careful about this integrity than about anything else, whether personal danger or advantage suffers." And then there is the special application of this rule of life to the vocation of the writer. A fellow soldier said charmingly that he thought Lewis thought the war existed for him to write books about it. Lewis comments : " I didn't deny it, though it's all wrong. I hadn't the strength to explain what is instinctive and categorical in me, the need to experience. The writing is only a proof of the sincerity of the experience, that's all." There he speaks for all true writers; he answers, with perfect simplicity, something that people never understand about them, the dedicated life that theirs must be.

But he achieved the most fruitful of all marriages for a writer, with a perfection that is given to few to achieve : the dedicated life with the natural capacity for, and an intense feeling for, the life of the common man. The war, that lost him to us, gave him much here, richly, generously : a quick, but full harvest. On every page of these Letters we see what a good and conscientious officer he was, willing to do his best at his trade of soldiering, and what an innate and loving sympathy he had for every quirk of human nature, every variety of human being. " I could give a hundred odd vignettes of my odd brethren from South Wales and all over, and I find more and more that we are all living through an identical experience in the same way — all of us cherishing the same simplicities, afraid to lose the same things, and willing to share the same tasks and the same anxieties. Will we get the same reward? No. Some of us will get good jobs, others disability pensions, others unemployment relief, others road labour, others nothing at all except darkness."

Of his own inner struggle, the struggle of any such man caught in such a fatality and so aware of it, these Letters provide, along with his poems and stories and the poems of Keyes, the most direct statement and the most moving evidence I know. " And although I'm more and more engrossed with the single poetic theme of Life and Death, for there doesn't seem to be any question more directly relevant than this one of what survives of all the beloved, I find myself quite unable to express at once the passion of Love, the coldness of Death (Death is cold) and the fire that beats against resignation, acceptance. Acceptance seems so spiritless, protest so vain. In between the two I live." In the realm of the imagination, in the symbolism of his story " They Came " — that epic story which is the finest I have read of the whole war — he had already made his submission, made his will one with his fate, made his account with eternity. In that story the soldier, after the death of his beloved, remembered how he had taken her hand in his and said, " In coming and in going you are mine ; now, and for a little while longer ; and then for ever ". And so remembering he said, " My life belongs to . the world : I will do what I can ".

We cannot but be thankful for what he wrote to speak for all that great company of men. Nothing that we can ever do is good enough for these men who were ready to lay down their lives, with all their gifts and powers, their sources of strength and promise of fulfilment — some of them men like him who gave up the rarest of human gifts, genius and vision.

The fruit of all this may be seen in his stories as in his poems ; indeed I take his volume, *The Last Inspection and other Stories*, to be the finest to come out of the war, certainly that I know. There are three masterpieces in that book : " They Came ", " The Wanderers ", " Private Jones ", besides much else that is authentic, convincing, true of the soldier's life, of the life of war-time. But it is not confined to that : " The Wanderers " is wholly outside of it and time, a portrait of gipsy life in caravan and country, realist and idyllic, passionate and sensuous, and always with that tenderness of his, seeing straight through to the other side of things. In its rich, dark poetry it is like a Courbet : a most interesting pointer to the future that was in him. His prose — one sees it in these Letters — has a Welsh luxuriance, a Celtic sensuousness : it would be hard to define that specifically, but I think it means a certain sensuousness of the imagination. (Keats had it ; but then Keats was Cornish.)

Lewis owed so much to his completely Welsh origin and environment. " When I come back I shall always tackle my writing through Welsh life and ways of thought ", he says touchingly. Yet these Letters show how the exotic experience of the war and travel in the East was broadening his field of vision and power of reflection. " The world is much larger than England, isn't it ? I'll never be just English or just Welsh again." There again his instinct spoke true : through the regional, through the life of his own people, to the universal. I believe that he had it in him to be a great novelist. He certainly had greatness in him : that moral quality — these Letters show it — such as Milton held it impossible for a great writer to be without. And he had the philosophical power and that fundamental sense of responsibility towards his art that makes the difference between a writer of talent and a potentially great one. I believe that he had it in him to write that great novel of Welsh life we all look for : a Welsh *Anna* perhaps. Certainly he had the gifts for it : a deep masculinity of nature along with a sensitive understanding and sympathy for the nature of women : a somewhat rare combination in contemporary literature. It gives us some measure of what we have lost in him.

I think I have shown how these Letters illumine his whole work, both poetry and prose alike. They have indeed a double interest, as a rare and fascinating revelation of the process of poetic and aesthetic creation, and as a portrait of a soldier's life. Not, it is true, of the soldier in action, but approaching action, drawing ever nearer and nearer, until the moment of action comes. But they have their own intrinsic interest too : these Letters will interest those who are interested in travel, those who are interested in India and in the war ; those too who care for Wales and for English letters, for the heroic struggle — all the more heroic for being, in the nature of our time, so utterly self-aware and without any illusions — of man's spirit.

What of the man ?

He speaks straight out to us from his pages, as clear and whole as if he were not dead. Though I never knew him, I can hear his accents. It is not a case of having the ' trick of style ' : true style is not a trick : it is simplicity and integrity, the translucent quality of the man himself. I see him in these Letters, as in his poems and stories, with his tart humour, the soldier's ' cynicism ' — in large part a defence-mechanism protecting an inner reserve — the concrete and careful observation, the loving observancy of the poet; his courage and fear, his acute nostalgic love of life, making it all the more difficult to give it up, his melancholy, reflective, brooding temperament, his stoicism and the conviction that what redeems all survives :

But love survives the venom of the snake.

We see him in these Letters occupied more and more as his term draws near with the question, What is it that survives ?

I never knew him, and yet after reading what he has left us, in his poems and stories, in these Letters especially, I feel I know all that was essential to him as a man, am in touch with his spirit, all there is of any of us that survives.

THE END

PRINTED BY R. & R. CLARK, LTD., EDINBURGH